David C. Fowler, MLS
Editor

E-Serials Collection Management
Transitions, Trends, and Technicalities

Pre-publication
REVIEWS,
COMMENTARIES,
EVALUATIONS . . .

"*E-Serials Collection Management* is an excellent portrayal of the migration from print to electronic resources, giving an accurate account of the behind-the-scenes activities associated with providing access to electronic resources. This book identifies the challenges and opportunities faced by both librarians and publishers.

As libraries and publishers transition from providing print-only access to materials to electronic access, issues regarding standardization of usage data, archival access, and the shift in the established rules arise daily. This book illustrates the constantly changing environment, explains the intricacies in managing e-serials, and offers solutions to key problems."

Sylvia Contreras, MLIS
Assistant Director, Health Sciences Libraries,
University of Wisconsin–Madison

"This book is a useful compilation that deals with many of the most significant e-collection management issues facing both academic librarians and serials vendors. Issues of particular interest are the increasing role of electronic resources in collection development, pricing models, the role of consortia in purchasing, accessibility issues such as IP versus password and dealing with missing data, and the importance of consistent and standardized usage statistics. *E-Serials Collection Management* successfully mixes case studies with analyses of recent and historical developments in both electronic resources and systems that manage them."

Christine Shupala, MLS, MBA
Associate Director,
Mary and Jeff Bell Library,
Texas A&M University–Corpus Christi

E-Serials Collection Management

Management
Transitions, Trends, and Technicalities

THE HAWORTH INFORMATION PRESS®
Serials Librarianship
Jim Cole and Wayne Jones
Senior Editors

E-Serials: Publishers, Libraries, Users, and Standards, Second Edition by Wayne Jones

Journals of the Century edited by Tony Stankus

E-Serials Collection Management: Transitions, Trends, and Technicalities by David C. Fowler

E-Serials Collection Management
Transitions, Trends, and Technicalities

David C. Fowler, MLS
Editor

The Haworth Information Press®
An Imprint of The Haworth Press, Inc.
New York • London • Oxford

Published by

The Haworth Information Press®, an imprint of The Haworth Press, Inc., 10 Alice Street, Binghamton, NY 13904-1580.

Cover design by Jennifer M. Gaska.

Library of Congress Cataloging-in-Publication Data

E-serials collection management : transitions, trends, and technicalities / David C. Fowler, editor.
    p. cm.
Includes bibliographical references and index.
ISBN 0-7890-1753-9 (alk. paper)—ISBN 0-7890-1754-7 (pbk. : alk. paper)
1. Libraries—Special collections—Electronic journals. 2. Libraries—Special collections—Electronic information resources. 3. Libraries and electronic publishing. I. Fowler, David C.
Z692.E43 E15 2003
025.17'4—dc21

2002151040

CONTENTS

ABOUT THE EDITOR

David C. Fowler, MLS, is Assistant Professor and Electronics Resources Coordinator for Acquisitions in the Technical Services Division of the Parks Library at Iowa State University in Ames. His professional experience began when he became the Serials Services Librarian at Texas A&M University in Corpus Christi. His work has been published in Collection Management and he is presently working on a series of articles on time and costs studies in a library acquisitions department. He holds an MLS degree from the State University of New York–University at Albany, and a BA in criminal justice from the University of Alaska–Anchorage.

CONTRIBUTORS

Carolyn Alderson is Consortia and Multi-Site Services Manager, Swets Blackwell Swan House, Wyndyke Furlong, Abingdon Business Park, Abingdon, United Kingdom (e-mail: calderson@uk. swetsblackwell.com).

Kevin Brewer is Electronic Services Librarian and Interim Head, Serials Department, Utah State University Libraries, Logan, Utah (e-mail: KevBre@ngw.lib.usu.edu).

Miriam Childs is Librarian, Law Library of Louisiana, New Orleans, Louisiana (e-mail: miriamchilds@hotmail.com).

Susan Clarke is Copyright Coordinator at Learning Services, Deakin University, Geelong Waterfront Campus, Geelong, Victoria, Australia (e-mail: susanc@deakin.edu.au).

Joanna Duy is Librarian in Chemistry and Physics Information Services Department at Concordia University Libraries, Montreal, Quebec, Canada (e-mail: Jduy@alcor.concordia.ca).

Paul Harwood is Managing Director of Swets Blackwell Limited, Swets Blackwell Swan House, Wyndyke Furlong, Abingdon Business Park, Abingdon, United Kingdom (e-mail: pharwood@uk. swetsblackwell.com).

LadyJane Hickey is Head of Cataloging, Newton Gresham Library, Sam Houston State University, Huntsville, Texas (e-mail: lib_ljh @shsu.edu).

Lee Ann Howlett is Associate University Librarian, Shimberg Health Services Library, University of South Florida, Tampa, Florida (e-mail: lhowlett@hsc.usf.edu).

Ebe Kartus is Metadata Librarian, Deakin University, Geelong Waterfront Campus, Geelong, Victoria, Australia (e-mail: kartus@ deakin.edu.au).

Janice Lange is Head of Technical Services, Newton Gresham Library, Sam Houston State University, Huntsville, Texas (e-mail: lib_jpl@shsu.edu).

Vivian Lewis is Business Librarian, Innis Library, McMaster University, Hamilton, Ontario, Canada (e-mail: lewisvm@mcmail.cis.mcmaster.ca).

Ed Loera is Electronic Resources Librarian, Newton Gresham Library, Sam Houston State University, Huntsville, Texas (e-mail: lib_ecl@shsu.edu).

Patricia A. Loghry is Head of the Serials Acquisition Department, Hesburgh Library, University of Notre Dame Libraries, Notre Dame, Indiana (e-mail: Patricia.A.Loghry.1@nd.edu).

Cheryl McCain is Acquisitions Librarian, University of Oklahoma Libraries, Norman, Oklahoma (e-mail: clmccain@ou.edu).

Gerry McKiernan is Science and Technology Librarian and Bibliographer, Iowa State University Library, Ames, Iowa (e-mail: gerrymck@iastate.edu).

Teri Oparanozie is Head of Acquisitions, Newton Gresham Library, Sam Houston State University, Huntsville, Texas (e-mail: lib_tlo @shsu.edu).

Sarah Robbins is Electronic Services Coordinator, University of Oklahoma Libraries, Norman, Oklahoma (e-mail: srobbins@ou.edu).

Betty Rozum is Associate Director for Technical Services, Utah State University Libraries, Logan, Utah (e-mail: BetRoz@ngw.lib.usu.edu).

Karen Rupp-Serrano is Head of Collection Development, University of Oklahoma Libraries, Norman, Oklahoma (e-mail: krs@ou.edu).

Barbara Schader is Head of Collection Development, Louise M. Darling Biomedical Library, University of California, Los Angeles, Los Angeles, California (e-mail: bschader@library.ucla.edu).

Flora Shrode is Reference Librarian and Interim Head, Reference Services Department, Utah State University Libraries, Logan, Utah (e-mail: FloShr@ngw.lib.usu.edu).

Matthew Smith is Senior Systems Analyst, University of Oklahoma Libraries, Norman, Oklahoma (e-mail: mesmith@ou.edu).

Wil Weston is Reference Librarian, Earl K. Long Library, University of New Orleans, Lakefront, New Orleans, Louisiana (e-mail: cweston@uno.edu).

Preface

This book in the Haworth Series in Serials and Continuing Resources looks at the increasingly important role of electronic serials in the overall library collection, both in the present and in the future. It is my belief that e-serials will continue to emerge as *the* key players in the library world, as the physical library gradually and inexorably gives way to the virtual library.

The subject matter covered in this book reflects many of the themes, problems, and questions raised by this newly ubiquitous medium, including e-journal publishing issues, collection development of online materials, access problems, e-journal statistical data, electronic troubleshooting, and accreditation issues regarding e-reserves and e-books, among others. These are subjects that are becoming concerns for all librarians, not just the electronic resources and information technology specialists, as e-journals insinuate themselves throughout the infrastructures of libraries and expand their reach globally.

Librarians all over the world are struggling with how to manage these products and their associated issues. In this book readers will see how library professionals like themselves deal with electronic journals and their transitions, trends, and technicalities.

List of Abbreviations

AASD	Academic Administrative Services Division
ADO	ActiveX Data Objects
ALA	American Library Association
AOL	America Online
API	application program interface
ARL	Association of Research Libraries
ASP	active server page
AVCC	Australian Vice-Chancellor's Committee
BOAI	Budapest Open Access Initiative
CAL	Copyright Agency Limited
CORC	Cooperative Online Research Cataloging
DEU	Digital Environmental Unit
DMCA	Digital Millennium Copyright Act of 1998
DOMS	digital object management system
DRM	digital rights management
DSL	digital subscriber line
EDI	electronic data interchange
ERIC	Educational Resources Information Center
FWP	free with print
GUI	graphical user interface
HTML	hypertext markup language
ICOLC	International Coalition of Library Consortia
IEE	Institution of Electrical Engineers
IEEE	Institute of Electrical and Electronics Engineers
IEL	IEEE-IEE Electronic Library
IIS	Internet information server
ILMS	Integrated Library Management System
ILS	integrated library system
IP	Internet Protocol
ISP	Internet service provider
ISSN	International Standard Serial Number
Jake	jointly administered knowledge environment
JISC	Joint Information Systems Committee

LANL	Los Alamos National Laboratory
LDAP	Lightweight Directory Access Protocol
MAP	Millennium Access Plus
MARC	machine-readable cataloging
MLA	Modern Language Association
OAI	Open Archives Initiative
OCCA	Online Communication Compliance System
OCCO	online communication compliance officer
OCLC	Ohio College Library Center
OCR	optical character recognition
OPAC	online public access catalog
OSI	Open Society Institute
PC	personal computer
POD	print on demand
RLG	Research Libraries Group
SPARC	Scholarly Publishing and Academic Resources
STM	scientific, technical, and medical
TLMS	Teaching/Learning Management System
TPP	third-party provider
UMI	University Microfilm Inc.
URL	uniform resource locator
XML	extensible markup language

Chapter 1

Current Trends in Electronic Journal Publishing: An Agent's Unique Insight into Pricing, Licensing, and Technological Aspects Based on Proximity to Publishers and Libraries

Paul Harwood
Carolyn Alderson

INTRODUCTION

Over the years, it has been difficult to identify a time when commercial publishers and librarians have been at one on any matter relating to journals. In 2002, it is quite clear that many are now in agreement on one thing in particular: electronic journals are a good thing, consequently the migration from print to electronic should take place as quickly as possible.

Ironically, the aspect of electronic journals that most unites publishers and librarians is also the one that has been the greatest source of conflict over the years: money. For publishers, although the investment in the technology necessary to deliver content electronically may be high, the savings on not having to manage and administer the print fulfillment process is even higher. For librarians, shelf space for printed volumes is expensive, and the staffing resources needed to maintain an extensive collection of printed journals are considerable. Electronic journals, with no printing to consider, ostensibly offer both parties a considerable cost-saving benefit.

With thanks to Caroline Mackay and John Tomlinson at Swets Blackwell, for help with providing National Electronic Site Licensing Initiative (NESLI) data.

1

However, nothing is that simple. The migration from print to electronic is not going to happen overnight, leaving publishers with the task and costs of delivering both formats for some years to come and leaving libraries with similar management issues and associated costs. Then of course, there is the small matter of just how much savings publishers will realize as a result of being able to cut out the print fulfillment costs and how much this will filter through to less expensive journals in electronic form for libraries.

The financial implication of the cautious migration from printed to electronic journals is just one area that the serials vendor—uniquely placed between publisher and librarian—observes. Inextricably linked to this are management challenges facing libraries, licensing issues, pricing models, and access routes. This chapter is devoted to a serials vendor's view of these activities and how they are changing the ways journals are purchased, sold, and accessed, as well as how they are encouraging and stimulating alternative publishing models and ventures.

MANAGEMENT CHALLENGES FACING LIBRARIES

Electronic journals have presented librarians with threats and opportunities in equal measure. The former revolves around the much wider issue of disintermediation and the idea that publishers have a much more direct route to the end user when delivering content directly to the desktop. The latter is all about cultivating new skills such as marketing and promotion, negotiation, and greater technical knowledge.

For large, research-based libraries, the challenges of successfully managing electronic journals are formidable. With standardization of pricing models for periodicals still some way off, maintaining accurate records of the arrangements held with each publisher is vital for financial management and audit purposes. Losing access to online content and the subsequent hoops that are required to be jumped through in trying to get it back is the stuff of many an e-mail list discussion.

In addition to managing both printed and electronic subscriptions, libraries frequently face the task of maintaining and updating the catalog and their own Web pages with the details of their electronic journals. This becomes a major task if the library opts for a publisher offer that includes all of their titles. Decisions also have to be made as to whether to use an aggregator service for much of the content, and there are implications here, too, for how that decision relates to the serials vendor used for the purchase of the bulk of the journals subscribed to, both print and electronic.

Some libraries find themselves with an embarrassment of riches in terms of content, which would be fine if they did not have to pay for it all. Such a situation can arise when the library still retains the printed copy of the journal in question, has access to the electronic version, and also happens to subscribe to an aggregated database of titles via an intermediary who has licensed the same content (or a slightly different version) from the publisher.

Another issue that many thought would disappear in the electronic environment is that of claiming for missing content. Content that is simply not there or content that exists in one service but not in another have been major issues for libraries. Librarians have to deal with irate end users, whose demands on librarians to explain missing electronic content that is expected from a "library-delivered" service are already significantly greater than when the print copy goes missing from the library. In addition, they also have to face the administrative burden of seeking refunds for missing content and checking the various services and delivery platforms to make sure that they are receiving what they have paid for.

Librarians have been working hard to ensure that they retain control of the process of managing electronic journals. Many have appointed specialists or developed new roles in this area. SFX (context-sensitive reference linking) software was the product of work undertaken by librarians with the aim of guiding users to the "appropriate copy" of the content they are seeking, and many libraries are now installing their own proxy servers, enabling users to access licensed content when away from the campus.

Electronic journals and the advent of e-mail and mailing lists have helped engender an even greater spirit of cooperation and support among librarians; this has quite often meant there is no hiding place for the errant publisher or aggregator! Perhaps the greatest sign of collaboration has been in the work of ICOLC, the International Coalition of Library Consortia (see <http://www.library.yale.edu/consortia/>). Not only does ICOLC provide a forum for members to compare experiences and to meet with publishers, it has also devised standards and recommendations in the area of usage statistics and pricing models, which it encourages publishers to endorse. In December 2001, ICOLC issued a declaration (see <http://www.library.yale.edu/consortia/2001currentpractices.htm>) in respect to pricing, making the following recommendations:

- An electronic version of a printed journal should be priced at no more than 80 percent of the print price
- Libraries should have the option of ordering the print separately from an electronic version
- A combined print and electronic subscription should cost no more than the printed subscription

ICOLC has also taken this opportunity to tackle a couple of other hot issues in this area:

- "Selective purchase," whereby publishers are encouraged to offer as many alternative pricing models and options as possible, not just the traditional individual title subscription or the "all-you-can-eat" variety
- A reminder to publishers that many libraries still wish to use the services of a vendor for the purchase and acquisition of serials

The relationship between the library and its vendors in the electronic world is undergoing continual change, and there appears to be a genuine divide in the library community between those who see a role for the agent in the future and those who do not. To a large extent, this will be decided more by changes in the publishing industry, by the development of business models for purchase, and by the sustainability of consortia, rather than by the whims or preferences of individuals.

A dramatically consolidated scientific, technical, and medical (STM) publishing industry, dominated by even fewer players than there are now, all offering multiyear, full-collection deals to regional and national consortia makes the prospects for vendors look quite limited. However, a different view is also emerging: a fragmented publishing world with a host of pricing models and packages, existing consortia dispersing as central funding disappears, the cooperative spirit evaporating in favor of self-interest, all suggesting that vendors will be part of the scene for as long as the commercial model exists in STM publishing.

It is not inconceivable that the library and the serials vendor could end up in competition in certain areas of this business. Both have expertise in the acquisition, management, and access of journals. Although for many years this arrangement has been totally complementary, as the pressure increases on both to prove and deliver their value-added services, we may see one, the other, or both attempt to encroach onto the territory of their traditional supply chain partner.

One thing is certain: the electronic title is coming to dominate the way librarians, agents, and publishers work. However, let us not forget that print still represents the majority of subscriptions managed by all of these players collectively. To illustrate this point, at the time of this writing (March 2002), only 22 percent of all subscriptions handled by Swets Blackwell globally were electronic subscriptions to individual titles or bundled content, or represented the electronic component of a print plus electronic subscription. However, it has been noted that a disproportionate amount of staff time in the customer service, publisher service, and support departments has been spent in processing electronic subscriptions/components and in dealing with associated issues; customers themselves have indicated that it takes six times as long to deal with administration of an electronic subscription compared to its print equivalent.

The Swets Blackwell database lists thousands of publishers, yet only 200 publishers accounted for approximately 93 percent of the 22 percent of subscriptions mentioned in the previous paragraph. Of these, only 100 publishers accounted for approximately 85 percent of all electronic subscriptions, and fifty publishers accounted for 75 percent of all electronic subscriptions (recorded as current on the Swets Blackwell database). These subscriptions covered electronic content that is either "free with print"(FWP) or paid for as a surcharge or separate Internet-only charge.

THE REQUIREMENT OF A LICENSE

As the digital environment has grown in complexity, and with it, the increasing trend toward the unbundling of electronic content from its equivalent print entity, serials vendors have seen a fairly dramatic shift in the traditional paradigm of library-agent-publisher, particularly in the academic and corporate research-based sectors. Many publishers have been approaching librarians directly, and vice versa, on the premise that the preferred arrangement involves more than the traditional role and services of a serials vendor, since site licenses and group purchasing are now involved. More recently, however, informal feedback from librarians directly to agents, and preliminary results from research commissioned by the Association of Subscription Agents relating to libraries purchasing and access requirements, undertaken by Loughborough University in the United Kingdom (see http://www.lboro.ac.uk/departments/dils/disresearch/purchaccess.html>) and reported at the 2002 annual conference of the Association of Subscription Agents, clearly suggests that library professionals would really prefer agents to be involved in this activity in the future.

Contracts between publishers and institutions for the provision of electronic content, therefore, have been on the increase. More commonly known as licenses, these documents come in a variety of forms and are essentially legal documents that outline the terms and conditions of the agreement between the two parties. They have historically been constructed to protect a publisher's own particular interests, in relation to copyright and authorized use, for example. A license usually becomes a requirement when electronic content is bought as a separate entity from its equivalent print title. However, there are no hard and fast rules, so a publisher's standard approach to licensing requirements varies depending on its own pricing and marketing strategies.

Library and information professionals, faced with the challenge of organizing electronic access across their organizations, soon realized that a publisher's own license often created difficulties of acceptance due to various factors, therefore, the logical route had to be a negotiated agreement to meet their own organization's particular requirements. The rise in consortia purchasing and multinational corporations requiring global access rights reflects this need. The license, therefore, became a source of critical scrutiny and protracted discussion before an agreement could be reached.

Over the past five years or so, several library-focused organizations have sought ways to protect the rights of institutions entering into electronic journal deals and have drawn attention to the inconsistencies and restrictive nature of many of the clauses in the licenses already available from the publishing fraternity. In doing so, these organizations and individuals have also provided a framework to enable publishers, both those who are willing to adapt their current licenses and others who are new to the e-licensing arena, to adopt an approach that is acceptable to the different groups within the library community. IFLA (International Federation of Library Associations and Institutions, see <http://www.ifla.org/>), the JISC and NESLI in the United Kingdom (Joint Information Systems Committee, see <http://www.jisc.ac.uk/>, and National Electronic Site License Initiative, see <http://www.nesli.ac.uk/>) and the PDR (Pharma Documentation Ring, see <http://www.p-d-r.com/>) are examples of organizations that have created licensing guidelines and adopted basic licensing principles. From such activity came the development of model licenses that aim to reflect the needs and strategic objectives of library communities in a local, national, or global context. The relevance of model licenses for both libraries and vendors has been explained by Croft (2001). The majority have been developed with academic organizations in mind, though others are available reflecting the requirements of different types of companies and organizations, such as the John Cox licenses (see <http://www.licensingmodels.com/>). These model licenses have proved particularly useful in consortium-based or multisite approaches to procuring electronic content from information providers and are available publicly so that all players in the information chain can gain access to them. In this respect, vendors, along with library staff worldwide, are in a position to advocate the use of such documents with the target publishers when they are in the position of acting on behalf of consortia and global corporations or mediating electronic deals. Primarily these licenses aim to standardize terms and conditions into categories such as key definitions, the agreement and the termination of agreement, permitted and prohibited uses, and publisher and licensee undertakings. Some of the main criteria to be negotiated involve issues such as legal jurisdiction, copyright and interlibrary loan, definition of "authorized users," remote access, perpetual archival access rights, quality and content issues, and remedy periods.

From the very early days of Web-based electronic journals, agents have had to build up their own knowledge banks of the publishers that use licenses for electronic provision, where these documents could be found, and how they must be processed. These, of course, are the publishers' standard licenses, forming the basis for comparisons with the model licenses in negotiations with publishers. Model licenses have become the building blocks upon which agreements are often reached, but much criticism has been directed at publishers for their unwillingness to accept these standardized legal documents in their entirety. However, not all publishers use licenses for electronic access; in a survey of publishers undertaken by Swets Blackwell in 2001, 55 percent of respondents indicated that subscribing institutions were not required to sign a license agreement to gain access to electronic content. Half of these same respondents did indicate that subscribers were expected to view the conditions of use at the publisher's Web site. With databases of information relating to both publishers and customers, agents are in a potentially omniscient position; as such, they can use their knowledge to provide licensing services for their customers, which can be described in various ways depending on the structure and organization of the service provided, from facilitator and mediator to broker and negotiator of licenses. Agents are also in a good position to help publishers who have not yet entered the electronic licensing arena to fully understand the needs of customers and the value of using a model license as the basis of an electronic deal.

Swets Blackwell has represented a growing number of library consortia and global corporations in different parts of the world and has been in the privileged position of appreciating the needs and requirements of differing library communities, as well as establishing a growing portfolio of publisher's special, consortium-based or multisite pricing offers and amended licensing terms and conditions. In 2001 and 2002, the company was instrumental in ensuring major agreements in Iceland, Belgium, and Sweden (see <http://www.swetsblackwell.com/> for relevant press releases). In the United Kingdom, Swets Blackwell, along with Manchester Computing (see <http://www.mimas.ac.uk/>) has spent over three years (since 1998) engaged as the managing agent for NESLI on behalf of the JISC, which in turn represents the needs and requirements of UK Further and Higher Education. NESLI incorporates several key strategic aims and objectives in publisher negotiations, one of which is the use of the NESLI model license. This license developed out of the Publisher's Association (PA)/JISC model license and is the precursor to many of the model licenses now available.

Using Swets Blackwell's experience as the managing agent of NESLI, the following examples give a brief overview of the main issues relating to the license.

In Table 1.1, data collected during 2002 in relation to NESLI agreements in place during March 2002 has been collated to show which publishers accepted the NESLI model license in full following negotiation and, if not accepted in full, how many amendments were incorporated before a final agreement was reached. In several cases, many amendments were minor in nature. The data has been sorted by acceptance of the license in full. The NESLI model license incorporates a clause concerning ongoing archival rights in perpetuity and, as can be seen in Table 1.1, this has proved the most contentious clause since its revision in late 2001 to provide *free* archival access. This clause, commonly referred to as Clause 2.2.2 is shown in Box 1.1.

One area of concern for the future in relation to Clause 2.2.2 of the NESLI model license, and other similar clauses in model licenses, is what happens to titles that are subsequently sold to another publisher? Under the terms of most model contracts, such titles remain part of the original deal and ongoing archival rights are an expected continuing right. However, Swets Blackwell, in its role as the managing agent for NESLI, has already observed and commented on several situations in which publishers have agreed to ongoing access clauses without considering and incorporating the necessary framework for ensuring that these aspects are addressed in future negotiations with other publishers, should titles change hands. It is gratifying to note, therefore, that this issue is being addressed by the Association of Learned and Professional Society Publishers (Nancy Gerry, Blackwell Publishers, personal communication, March 2002; see <http://www.alpsp.org/default.htm>).

NESLI members (individual libraries) are not restricted from direct negotiations with the same publishers that the managing agent is dealing with on their behalf, should they wish to do that for whatever reason. However, in that situation there are no guarantees that the autonomous library customer would benefit from the same licensing terms and conditions as agreed under NESLI, even if the price offered were comparable.

The Swets Blackwell 2001 publisher survey findings showed that 79 percent of respondents said they would consider using a model license at the request of a consortium or multisite organization. Not

TABLE 1.1. Which publishers accepted the NESLI model license in full?

Publisher	Accepted NESLI License in Full	Number of Amendments	Most Contentious Clause(s)			Country
			Archival Rights	Interlibrary Loan	Legal Jurisdiction	
Oxford University Press	No	>20		Yes		United Kingdom
Elsevier Science	No	14	Yes			Netherlands
Wiley	No	14	Yes			United States
American Chemical Society	No	11	Yes		Yes	United States
Springer-Verlag	No	5	Yes			Germany
Harcourt Health*	No	1	Yes			Netherlands
Internet Archaeology	No	1	Yes			United Kingdom
Kluwer Academic	Yes					Netherlands
Blackwell Publishing	Yes					United Kingdom
CABI Publishing	Yes					United Kingdom
Emerald (MCB University Press)	Yes					United Kingdom
Association of Computing Machinery	Yes					United States
CRC Press	Yes					United States
Johns Hopkins University Press	Yes					United States
Lawrence Erlbaum	Yes					United States
Mary Ann Leibert	Yes					United States

Source: NESLI Management Agent.
*Now part of Elsevier Science

BOX 1.1.
Most Contentious Clause of the NESLI Model License

Clause 2.2.2

After termination of this License, the Publisher will provide the Licensee and its Authorized and Walk-in Users with access to the full text of the Licensed Material which was published and paid for within the Subscription Period, either by continuing online access to the same material on the Publisher's server or by supplying an archival copy in an electronic medium mutually agreed between the parties which will be delivered to the Licensee or to a central archiving facility operated on behalf of the UK HE community without charge. Continuing archival access is subject to the terms and conditions of use of this License.

(*Source:* NESLI Managing Agent.)

---

surprisingly, this suggests that model licenses are likely to gain greatest acceptance by the publishing community only when organizations and library groups join forces to procure electronic content.

PRICING MODELS

Swets Blackwell's in-house data suggest that over half of all charged-for electronic titles in 2002 are represented by only five publishers: Elsevier Science (incorporating Academic Press and Harcourt Health Sciences titles), Blackwell Publishing, Kluwer Academic, Springer-Verlag, and Wiley. It is therefore not surprising that these publishers have dominated and influenced market perceptions—both of libraries and publishers—particularly in relation to what constitutes relevant economic models for consortia and multisite pricing, which is very often a form of the publisher's "collection" or "cross-access" model.

Just as most publishers' own licenses come in varying shapes and forms, so do publishers' pricing models. Publishers' standard prices usually depend on the format offered (print, print plus electronic, electronic only) and to some extent similar approaches to pricing can be identified. Print-plus-electronic subscriptions usually incur a surcharge; electronic-only subscription costs are more often lower than the equivalent print subscriptions, though they may be the same price as the print, and occasionally they may be priced higher than the same title in print. Increasingly publishers are also establishing consortia and multi-site pricing models, which may be adapted during negotiation with a particular consortium, global corporation, or multisite organization.

Since 1999, Swets Blackwell has surveyed publishers concerning special pricing for electronic journals. From the following responses received in the 2001 survey, it can be seen that the majority of publishers with electronic journals now offer consortia and multisite pricing models:

Publishers who have a consortia or multisite pricing policy	67 percent
Pricing based on number of sites	30 percent
Pricing based on historical print spend	20 percent
Combination of sites and print spend	50 percent

Results from the 2002 survey indicate that the figure increased only marginally.

The consortia and multisite pricing models adopted by publishers are various and wide ranging and, unlike model licenses, there has been no evidence to suggest that the library community has influenced publishers to standardize their approach to pricing the electronic content. Indeed, this would appear to be the area where many employees of publishers are able to adopt a creative and often complicated approach to maximizing their company's revenue stream. One of the main issues for publishers, which can also be considered their most challenging, is the requirement to price electronic content and also allow customers to continue with the paper copy, if that is the customer's preference, a necessity due to decreased budgets within the institution, or simply because there is no guiding policy on the matter. On the increase, however, is a willingness to price print subscriptions at a deeply discounted price (DDP) if an organization has chosen the electronic-only route yet still requires some print titles. The following list shows those publishers offering DDP in early 2002:

American Chemical Society
American Mathematical Society
Association of Computing Machinery
Cambridge University Press
Elsevier Science (E-Choice)
Emerald
IEEE (Institute of Electrical and Electronics Engineers)
Institute of Physics Publishing
Kluwer
Lippincott Williams & Wilkins
National Research Council of Canada
Project MUSE database publishers
Royal Society
Springer
Thieme
Wiley (Enhanced Access)

However, the conditions under which DDP is offered vary, so no generalization can be made that different consortia would receive the same terms from the same publisher.

Due to the complexity of pricing models, the various elements that comprise electronic deals, and the lack of any real standard in this area, it has proved almost impossible for librarians to compare and contrast offers from different publishers. The best that organizations can do is to try to assess the benefits of each offer in relation to their own particular needs and requirements. This is not to say that efforts are not afoot to change the situation. As mentioned previously, ICOLC has already made some suggestions on this matter.

The difficulties of the NESLI approach in the United Kingdom have been highlighted before (Ball and Wright, 2000; Bley, 2000), particularly in relation to negotiating acceptable agreements that suit all potential members of such a large consortium. Table 1.2 shows the range of publishers involved in the NESLI initiative in March 2002 and the main basis of the pricing offer for each publisher's collection of titles.

The most popular collection offers in terms of order instructions received by the managing agent were from Elsevier Science, Blackwell Publishing, and the Association of Computing Machinery (ACM). Blackwell Publishing offered electronic access to either a combined

TABLE 1.2. Main Basis of Pricing an Electronic Collection Offer to NESLI

Publisher	E-Only Offer	Main Basis of 2002 Pricing to NESLI	Print Cancellations Allowed?
Association of Computing Machinery	Yes	Fixed fee based on participation	Yes
American Chemical Society	Yes	Percentage surcharge on print expenditure	No
Blackwell Publishing	Yes	Banded fixed fee	Depends
CABI Publishing	No	Nonsubscribed print and electronic titles bought at a discount	No
CRC Press	Yes	Fixed fee	Yes
Elsevier Science	Yes	Banded percentage surcharge on print expenditure	Yes/No*
Emerald (MCB)	Yes	Fixed fee	Yes
Harcourt Health	Yes	Fixed fee	No
Kluwer Academic	Yes	Banded percentage surcharge on print expenditure	No
Springer	Yes	Banded percentage surcharge on print expenditure	No
Wiley	Yes	Percentage surcharge linked to print expenditure	Yes

Source: NESLI Management Agent, 2002.
*Print cancellations allowed with e-only offer

collection of nearly 600 titles, comprising social sciences and humanities titles and sciences and medicine titles, or two separate subject collections. Elsevier Science offered "cross access" to over 1,000 titles for a surcharge on print or electronic-only basis, and the ACM offered electronic-only access to a collection of over twenty subject-specific titles. All three publishers offered quite different pricing models.

The general conclusions in relation to these three popular and yet different offers must be that (1) many of the electronic titles were very important titles to the subscribing organizations, and/or (2) the price offered by the publisher was acceptable or affordable, and/or (3) the publisher added real value in the offer, and/or (4) the license terms were acceptable in consideration of the previous points. It can further be concluded that if a publisher can put together an offer that addresses all four aspects properly in relation to a particular purchasing group, it should be a win-win situation for all parties concerned. This may seem an obvious statement; however, the reason that many publishers' consortial offers may be unpopular could be due to both their inflexibility and inappropriateness to certain customer groupings, as well as because the offers do not differ much from the global standard consortium or multisite model already available. Moreover, agents, if not involved in representing their customers' interests in these discussions, will be pushed more and more into the role of "promoter of publisher's standard offer," with the predictable outcome that no parties will end up satisfied.

The debate about the pricing of electronic journals will continue, just as it has always dominated the relationship between publishers and libraries in the printed world. As publishers begin to digitize their back issues, life will become further complicated (and potentially expensive) by the different pricing and access models that may be adopted. Publishers may start looking at pricing strategies adopted by companies in other Internet-based industries, such as software, where pay-per-use versus licensing models are also being considered (Gurnani and Karlapalem, 2001).

ACCESS TECHNOLOGIES

One advantage of signing to collection or to the publishers' full-collection deals is that the publisher and the libraries concerned are usually able to monitor the usage of all titles available, over a period of one or two years. Publishers can use these figures to inform future, and hopefully more relevant, pricing models, and libraries can use the statistics to determine (along with other factors) which are key titles for the institution. Several publishers are already testing usage-based pricing models with their customers, and it is predicted that additional models based on usage will be forthcoming in 2003 and beyond. A move to pricing based on key usage at a particular institution is likely to have an effect on how libraries purchase subscription-based electronic content. Will a consortium-based approach be relevant in the future when key titles may vary significantly across organizations?

The ability to receive useful metrics and monitor usage statistics is closely related to the various access technologies available and what elements comprise the product or service offering provided. Unless every publisher adopts the same approach to providing metrics, the ability to interpret usage statistics to any extent is often impaired somewhat, since direct comparisons are meaningless. Several publishers have spent much time, effort, and resources in creating and developing their own online services; others outsource this task to experts in the field, such as Ingenta, HighWire, and Extenza, who then host the full-text content. Several serials vendors have developed gateway services, whereby customers are offered a single search engine, with links to full-text content that may be either at the agent's server, or available on a publisher's or host's site. Other providers, such as ProQuest and Ovid, have licensed full text from publishers and offer subject-specific collections of titles. It is very often the case, then, that customers have several options when it comes to choosing a route to full-text content, and in many cases organizations have several access points to the same content, residing in different locations.

There are several initiatives underway globally in relation to standardizing publishers', aggregators', and gateway services' usage statistics (see <http://www.library.yale.edu/consortia/2001webstats.htm/> for the work that ICOLC has done). This, of course, all depends on a willingness on the part of publishers to both participate in such activity and have the necessary resources to enable it to happen. Aggregators of content and gateway service providers are best placed to potentially make the most impact from such initiatives, due to the large amounts of content to which they provide access via their services. However, the situation is that in many cases customers want to continue using the publisher's own services, to benefit from the perceived additional value of the service, or because a change at this stage may prove too much of a drain on local library resources. In addition, such third-party services as Swets Blackwell's SwetsWise service (replacing SwetsnetNavigator) usually come at some cost, which cannot be ignored. It also raises the matter of omniscience again. When only a few providers, typically agents, can organize access to nearly all of an organization's required content and provide meaningful usage statistics and other benefits, such as a single search engine, is this likely to make both libraries and publishers feel somewhat uneasy? Although nobody is saying it, the past actions of both librarians and publishers suggest that this may be the case.

To illustrate this situation, another example from NESLI in the United Kingdom can be used. One of the aims of NESLI was to offer one access route/service to the publisher's content, using Athens authentication; how this was achieved has been described in detail by Bley and Macintyre (2000). From its inception, however, the concept of the "one access route" provided by the managing agent was criticized by both librarians and publishers, on the grounds that libraries now had no choice; therefore, alternative access routes were allowed, such as direct to the publisher's own service. Many libraries did decide to use the NESLI/Swetsnet route. The net result of allowing various access routes, however, is that NESLI usage statistics are not as robust as they otherwise would have been, to the detriment of both universities and publishers. Table 1.3 shows the top ten titles by usage for NESLI customers accessing NESLI publishers' titles via the NESLI Web site, for the period January to December 2001. It is likely that the data represent UK higher education institutions (HEI) usage generally. The results are interesting but could, of course, have been far more meaningful had more publishers participated in NESLI and more libraries used the single access route.

ALTERNATIVE PUBLISHING

Just as the development of electronic journals is allowing publishers to remove considerable cost from their business, both directly in terms

TABLE 1.3. Top Ten NESLI Titles by Usage via the NESLI Interface for the Period January to December 2001

Title	Publisher	Full Text Hits
Journal of Advanced Nursing	Blackwell Science Ltd.	41,062
Molecular Microbiology	Blackwell Science Ltd.	12,765
Plant Molecular Biology	Kluwer Academic Publishers Group	4,598
Journal of Business Ethics	Kluwer Academic Publishers Group	4,248
Critical Social Policy	SAGE Publications	3,940
Sociology of Health and Illness	Blackwell Publishers	3,881
Educational Management and Administration	SAGE Publications	3,839
British Journal of Social Work	Oxford University Press	3,663
Journal of Materials Science	Kluwer Academic Publishers Group	3,469
Howard Journal of Criminal Justice	Blackwell Publishers	3,366

Source: NESLI Managing Agent.

of the elimination of print fulfillment costs and indirectly in terms of bypassing middlemen such as the serials vendors, it has also opened the way for the potential killer application to their own business: alternative publishing models.

Paul Ginsparg's Physics Archive is the longest-standing and most-quoted example of how things can be without commercial publishers, although the Los Alamos repository seems to have developed a coexistence with the commercial world (Butler, 2001). Stevan Harnad, from the University of Southampton in England, is of late the most vocal critic of the current system and the strongest individual advocate for an alternative model (see <http://www.ecs.soton.ac.uk/~harnad/intpub.html>). An up-to-date overview of e-print archival activity in the fields of physics, mathematics, nonlinear science, and computer science can be found at the arXiv.org Web site (see <http://arxiv.org/>).

BioMed Central, PubMed Central, and E-BioSci can all be classed as alternative publishing models, although some are clearly closer to the commercial than to the noncommercial side, and all three systems will probably need further refinement of their business models if they are to operate successfully and challenge their commercial counterparts in any serious way.

Scholarly Publishing and Academic Resources (SPARC) (see <http://www.arl.org/sparc/home/>), an initiative drawn very much from the world of libraries, has probably made most progress in the past eighteen months, and the formation of a European chapter in early 2002 is clear proof of its determination to break the monopoly of certain publishers and key titles. Librarians are becoming increasingly active in trying to engage academics in these issues, and the idea of institutional servers hosting the output of research staff, searchable by way of the Open Archive protocol, is gathering momentum.

CONCLUSION

The world of STM publishing is undergoing a transformation as dramatic as anything currently being experienced in other industry sectors. Electronic journals and the associated changes in business models and supply-chain relationships are attempting to overturn a system and a way of working that has been in existence for over fifty years. At the moment, and for the foreseeable future, it will be very much a case of two steps forward and one step back as both publishers and librarians attempt to move the whole system without either party losing out significantly along the way.

This is a period of massive experimentation as publishers seek, at a minimum, to reduce their costs as a result of the gradual elimination of print and maintain existing income on the electronic version. For some of them, removing the serials vendor and the commission they pay to these vendors will be a bonus.

Just as the big publishers get bigger and the smaller publishers scramble for what is left of the library budget, so the challenge of alternative publishing models grows stronger as the library and information professional strives to convince the academic community that this situation is not sustainable. The very conservatism that has held the current model intact for so long will be the principal barrier in moving this community forward and away from the clutches of the commercial publisher.

For libraries and librarians, the electronic journal has created new opportunities. It has brought some glamour to a profession in desperate need of such a lift in the Internet age and given librarians the chance to develop new skills such as negotiation and marketing. Whether this is enough to keep the publisher from finding his way to the end user or ultimate budget holder, time will tell.

Serials vendors, such as the authors of this chapter, are privileged to have a unique insight into the supply chain by dint of their relationship with both publisher and library. The information they have about the activities and strategies of both should be enough to ensure their future survival, although simply knowing what the supplier and customer are doing is clearly not enough. Being able to act upon that information and deliver services to meet the needs of both is what is required. Historically, they have proved to be capable of rising to this challenge, although as we have seen throughout this chapter, what we are witnessing now is a complete break with what has gone before. We are entering uncharted waters.

REFERENCES

Ball, D. and S. Wright. 2000. Procuring electronic information: New business models in the context of the supply chain. *Library Consortium Management: An International Journal* 2(7): 145-158.

Bley, R. 2000. NESLI: A successful national consortium. *Library Consortium Management: An International Journal* 2(1): 18-28.

Bley, R. and R. Macintyre. 2000. NESLI—The National Electronic Site License Initiative. *VINE* 110: 34-37.

Butler, D. 2001. Los Alamos loses physics archive as preprint pioneer heads east. *Nature* 412: 3-4.

Croft, J. B. 2001. Model licenses and interlibrary loan/document delivery from electronic resources. *Interlending & Document Supply* 29(4): 165-168.

Gurnani, H. and K. Karlapalem. 2001. Optimal pricing strategies for Internet-based software dissemination. *Journal of the Operational Research Society* 52: 64-70.

Chapter 2

To Use or Not to Use:
The Benefits and Challenges
of Using a Subscription Agent
for Electronic Journals

Patricia A. Loghry

In his article "The Electronic Librarian Is a Verb/The Electronic Library Is Not a Sentence," Kenneth Arnold proposes that the librarian's role is that of one creating a syntax of digital knowledge. He goes on to state that "given the computer's capability to connect us to a seemingly unlimited array of subjects and objects in the digital language our challenge is to discover how to create that syntax most effectively. We [libraries] need a dynamic, constantly changing attention structure rather than a static fixed one."[1] If libraries are using electronic resources to create a "changing attention structure . . . with an unlimited array of subjects and objects,"[2] what is the role for the mediator in this process? More simply put, does it make sense for libraries to choose to eliminate subscription agents and subsequently to deal directly with only electronic resource vendors/publishers and other third-party providers? Are libraries able to work directly with these vendors/publishers and other third-party providers in order to be able to connect most effectively and efficiently with the vast array of objects available in the electronic world, or are there services that subscription agents can provide for electronic resources which others cannot? This chapter will explore both the advantages and the challenges of using subscription agents, vendors/publishers, and third-party providers.

Dr. Mohambir Sawhney's "Meet the Metamediary" discusses the deconstruction of the mediator and the reconstruction of what he

_21_

calls the metamediary. He examines the wealth of information available and states that the mediators who will survive are ultimately those who understand the products they market. These metamediaries will offer, from the customer perspective, a single point of contact for extended suppliers and for customers. They will also combine related activities in an "activity cluster" in order to alleviate the significant demands on customer time as customers aggregate information from a multiplicity of fragmented sources.[3] The three requirements of Sawhney's definition of an intermediary are the aggregated information itself, the bringing together of related activities (clustering), and the alleviation of significant time expended, all of which are examples of the benefits of employing a subscription agent. The newer third-party providers (services such as Jake, TDNet, and Serials Solutions) are becoming metamediaries as well. Katz and Gellatly state, "For a library with more than 100 periodical titles on order, it is generally a good idea to employ an agent. This is so, in the case of an agent whose service charge is from five to twenty percent."[4] If it is agreed that metamediaries will become increasingly important in the future, then this statement, although referring to paper subscriptions, will retain its validity in the electronic environment as well. Third-party services used by libraries may, for instance, provide holdings information to link library patrons to electronic resources contained in full-text databases, such as LexisNexis Academic Universe, and publisher packages, such as Elsevier's ScienceDirect. For the purposes of this chapter, the author is using Dora Chen Chiou-Sen's definition of a subscription agent as being an "intermediary sometimes called a vendor, jobber, dealer or agent."[5] So, the question remains, what are the competing benefits and challenges of using a subscription agent, using a third-party provider, and utilizing publishers/vendors directly?

THE BENEFITS OF USING A SUBSCRIPTION AGENT

Using a subscription agent can save the library resources, in terms of time and money, and can also simplify the acquisitions process. The agent's staff is able to place a very large number of library subscriptions with a wide variety of publishers and then collect the various charges into a single invoice for payment. A library's staff will usually deal with a single agent or, to use Sawhney's term, a metamediary. The library needs to be familiar with only the one agent's order process rather than with the individual requirements of hundreds of vendors/publishers. Once a subscription is established, should the library wish, the title can be easily added to the library's general invoice, eliminating the need for multiple invoices from multiple vendors/publishers each year. These invoices can be further customized to each library's special needs. Libraries may also request that the subscription agent provide a variable number of invoice copies and that the format information for each title be presented on them. Library staff can submit new orders with a library order number, fund code, and sometimes a subject area code as well. Much of this information is needed on the invoice for the library to be able to efficiently process payments. A possible problem here is that sometimes vendors/publishers have a standard invoice format and are not able to tailor them to an individual library's needs.

With the advent of electronic data interchange and computer-to-computer communication, libraries can have invoices and claims sent electronically. This provides a significant savings in staff resources, as performing data entry by hand for hundreds of individual publishers is quite costly and time consuming for the acquisitions staff. Invoices can be sent electronically with a predetermined number of line items per invoice. These line items can be matched to the library's order records, and price/term information is then loaded onto the individual orders. The acquisitions staff then verifies the line items, approves the payment, and forwards it to the business office for processing. The business office subsequently has to forward only a single check to a single location, rather than to send multiple checks to multiple locations. When requested, libraries and agents can also participate in a bank exchange program, rather than having to generate and use printed checks.

Subscription agents quite often tailor their services to the library's special requirements. For example, foreign language specialists at the subscription agent's office can handle foreign titles, and orders and claims for them will be handled by the agent's foreign representatives, with the results being returned to libraries in the language and format that they understand. Invoices with costs listed in foreign currencies are also converted into dollars, eliminating the need to convert amounts and pay invoices in those foreign currencies.

Subscription agents' operations are also configured to easily handle renewals. Agents keep up-to-date price information and can often provide advice on signing licensing contracts. One of the concerns with electronic subscriptions and their attendant licenses is being able to determine how to begin the renewal notification process in a timely manner. Many contracts have clauses that require a written notification of changes or cancellations from either party. These contracts need to be reevaluated to meet new or updated institutional needs before each renewal. Subject liaisons must look at pricing issues and product changes before the thirty- to ninety-day window, after which a written notice must be sent. Agents are also accustomed to providing renewal information to their clients, along with the inevitable price increases, in a timely manner.

Subscription agents regularly survey price increases. This historical information is maintained over multiple years and can be provided to the library, customized to the library's mix of titles. Knowledge about new changes in the marketplace, along with an explanation of the factors that contributed to the change, are helpful tools when dealing with internal budgets. Inflation information is critical. Agents have long provided inflation estimates to help libraries plan for ever-increasing costs of subscription. This information can be calculated using the library's mix of titles, include foreign and domestic pricing information, and contain data from multiple vendors/publishers to enable a more realistic evaluation of library expenditures.

In addition to inflation projections, subscription agents can often provide management reports to libraries. These reports can identify what products are provided to each subject discipline by the library. If the library has been with the vendor for a number of years, reports will also contain historical pricing trends. Agents have published paper-pricing trends for many years, and this information will be just as valuable for electronic journals (particularly as libraries use the pricing information to make collection development decisions that may negatively impact print titles). Many agents can offer discounts for early payment. Libraries, should they choose to do so, can deposit money with the vendor, receive interest on that deposit, and use the interest to offset some of their subscription costs.

Rush processing may be easier with the subscription agent. Finding the correct contact information for vendors/publishers can be extremely time consuming, a situation that is exacerbated when a library employs multiple vendors/publishers. Library staff are able to place all rush orders with a single location, and the agent can then deal with all of the individual vendors/publishers for the library.

Some agents provide a team of people to work with their clients. Having a single agent makes it easier for libraries to set up an effective working relationship with a team leader, who can pass library needs on to the other team members. Both sides then gain an understanding of the workflow problems of the other group. Team leaders also have access to internal agency experts; when libraries have problems unique to their situation, team leaders are able to easily contact in-house specialists to work with the library to solve the problem. In addition to the team leaders, many agents maintain regional offices with service or sales representatives, who visit their customers on a regular basis. Service agents are able to discuss the agent's overall performance and any problems that the library might be experiencing. These agents are also able to discuss specifics related to invoices, credits, refunds, or claims. The subscription agent may send agency people to help libraries automate functions such as electronic data interchange (EDI) invoicing, or electronic claims. Libraries should always be notified if a change in the agency's personnel impacts them.

If a service representative changes jobs or leaves the organization, a new one will be assigned, often before the other representative has left, so that both the libraries and the agent understand the changes in the chain of command, and so that both will still have contact options if they feel that problems are not being resolved. It is not unusual at all for library staff to discuss problems with their major agent on a weekly basis.

The subscription agent representative can talk about new services offered and discuss trends that might be developing based on common client concerns. With this broader perspective, he or she might be able to offer possible solutions.

One of the major benefits of using a subscription agent in the paper world was the agent's database of titles. These databases are huge and valuable warehouses of information. Over the past few years, as electronic journals have become more prolific, agents began collecting information on electronic journals in the same way they followed print titles. The database system creates a more convenient and efficient subscription process.

- The database shows whether the agent can obtain the subscription or if the library must "go direct."
- It provides bibliographic information, new title information, and information on title splits, mergers, and ceased titles.
- URLs are provided and updated in the database.
- Links to licensing information are available where possible, as are vendor/publisher contact names.
- There is pricing information for each purchase option—electronic, electronic/paper combination, or paper.
- Price options allow library staff to do price comparisons before purchase.
- New subscription start-up policies are provided with each title, as are any special vendor-publisher requirements.
- The library's current subscription information is available with the library's customer numbers, as customer numbers are often needed to activate new electronic journals or request assistance for access problems.
- Finally, because the library is a customer, new orders and claims can be placed from the database if the library wishes, thus decreasing the amount of time required to place a rush order.

The one-stop shopping idea for this information is very convenient for the customer, and the agent, thus, becomes the metamediary.

Subscription agents have begun to offer, as part of their suite of services, an electronic journals "virtual warehouse." This warehouse is provided when the agents have contracted with vendors/publishers to supply electronic journals. Multiple journals can become available through a single interface with a single search engine. Some vendors are also acquiring archive rights to back issues of many journals. Although there is an additional charge for use of the database, as well as a separate fee for the archive service, it again places the subscription agent in the role of metamediary for the library community. The database brings together in a single point of contact the related activities of current access, archives, and preservation. As more library contracts demand that vendors/publishers guarantee access to content through a third-party provider (TPP) should the e-journal or vendor publisher be sold, it seems that agents are more frequently positioning themselves to provide this service.

People from the subscription agency attend national meetings and join industry standards boards. They deal with many vendors/publishers and with many libraries. Agents can represent multiple client perspectives and can facilitate understanding between libraries and vendors/publishers. Because they represent multiple libraries and vendors/publishers, they are able to help lead in the formation of international standards to improve library/publisher business functions, which can aid in the development of new services based on new requests across their client base.

THE BENEFITS OF USING A VENDOR/PUBLISHER

Having looked at some of the benefits of using a subscription agent, we will now turn to some of the benefits of using a vendor/publisher.

Perhaps one of the biggest benefits to using a vendor/publisher is that there is no intermediary. If one uses Katz and Gellatly's 5- to 20-percent service charge criteria and the electronic subscription is as costly as some of the bundled packages are, then the service charges can add up to many thousands of dollars. In this era of small increases or budget freezes, libraries may need to eliminate some of their service charges by going directly to a publisher/vendor.

Some publishers/vendors will not work through a subscription agent, making it mandatory to order directly from them. When the library orders a title directly from a publisher/vendor, it receives a single invoice with the complete charge for the entire year on that invoice. Although this is not always the case, publishers' invoices will have the actual price. Because subscription agents create bulk renewal invoices and publisher pricing may not have been announced, libraries will receive a bulk renewal with an estimated cost based on the previous year, and an additional monthly billing or credit to adjust the estimated payment to the actual price.

Another benefit of working directly with the vendor/publisher is that a publisher can provide a more direct route to its journals. Electronic journals are highly visible to users, and some of the greatest benefits of e-journals are their ease of use from office or study and their around-the-clock availability, even when the library is closed. However, unlike their print counterparts, immediate problems arise when service interruptions occur. As a result, library systems staff need a direct line to a technical consultant when these service problems occur, as they need to be resolved quickly. Thus, the more direct the route to reach the e-journal provider, the easier the problems are to resolve. Not having to go through a TPP to access content can be a great help when access problems exist.

Vendors/publishers can also provide their back issues on the same server as they do their current content. Library patrons appreciate such a one-stop shop that is easy to use and will meet all of their research needs. Publishers are now contracting with linking services, and those links allow patrons to search for information, select the most relevant articles, and click on the link that takes them directly to the information source. The more linking services that can be connected to a particular journal, the easier it becomes for patrons to use the product.

As anyone who has negotiated a license agreement knows, there are hundreds of different permutations of vendor/publisher licenses. Individual contracts with vendors/publishers allow the library to address specific institutional needs, such as allowing the library to add other titles and negotiate multiyear contracts or contracts with a fixed inflation rate. Librarians can ask for an alerts service, which includes information on maintenance schedules and license changes. Information on problems can thus be sent directly to the library rather than notifying the agent, who would then notify the client.

Vendors/publishers can provide user statistics for individual electronic journals. As libraries continue to add e-journals to their collections, they will need to determine which titles are heavily used and which titles are not of interest to their patrons. The number of hits recorded for each journal title is very useful to know for collection development purposes. Collection development decisions will be made using that statistical information. If there are not enough hits on a particular subscribed journal, the librarian may try to trade it for another e-journal that may be more heavily used or may simply cancel it. These user statistics can also help to determine if there are enough access ports, so that if statistical reports show that patrons are being denied access, then the library may need to increase the number of concurrent users allowed for a title.

THE BENEFITS OF USING
A THIRD-PARTY PROVIDER

What are the benefits of using a third-party provider? A TPP service furnishes patron access to electronic titles in package deals or in full-text databases. These are titles not generally included in the library's online public-access catalog (OPAC) and are difficult to find. Full-text aggregators also tend to have titles frequently added or withdrawn from them. One of the most requested services is for library patrons to be able to access all of the library's electronic holdings through a single search engine, linking directly to the journal or article from their search screen. TPP services are helping to meet this patron need.

The library's holdings information is included and can be updated with the TPP each time the library adds or removes databases or e-journal packages. Third-party provider services monitor the publishers/vendors for title changes, splits, or mergers. When database aggregators add or remove new titles, the TPP changes its records and notifies the library in the next information exchange. This is a service that most libraries have been unable to provide to their patrons, due to the time and effort involved.

TPPs monitor changes in access points. When URL information changes, they change records to reflect the new URL. Most vendors/publishers have library update services, but they may or may not provide access change information to all of their clients.

THE CHALLENGES OF WORKING
WITH SUBSCRIPTION AGENTS

Having discussed the benefits of subscription agents, vendors/publishers, and third-party providers, let us now turn to some of the challenges encountered with each. Subscription agents often use an annual renewal system, with multiple additional billings as needed. As discussed previously, this can be a benefit for libraries, but it is also labor intensive for the staff. Although there are agents who offer a service that prevents additional billings, the charge is often based on the entire dollar figure of the annual renewal and not just on the titles that would require additional billing. The fee is also in addition to the regular service charge. The service charge can sometimes be calculated after this fee has been added to the total of the invoice. The United Kingdom's Association of Subscription Agents and Intermediaries recently issued a call for all publishers to do their "utmost to ensure the publication of their price lists by the end of July each year,"[6] saying that the delays do not give librarians enough time to make informed decisions about subscribing to an electronic journal. Late price announcements lead to late decision making, and that, in turn, leads to late renewals and late cancellations. In addition, subscription agents then bill libraries at the previous year's rate, causing incomplete payments, supplementary invoicing, and second payments. Thus, supplemental invoices are an administrative problem and costly to all parties.

One of the purposes of using a subscription agent is to consolidate as many titles as possible under one umbrella. As is the case with the annual renewal, there is a downside to using a subscription agent if the library has service concerns or if that agent is not financially stable. The challenge of changing subscription agents is difficult in the best of circumstances, and the electronic environment has only made it that much more complex.

The author's library recently sent out requests for information and pricing and later decided to change our subscription agent. Several lessons were learned during this process. The first of these lessons is to make sure that the library has a record of all of the vendors'/publishers' subscription numbers before the cancellation process begins. Early in the move, we began hearing that some vendors/publishers had received cancellation notices from our current agent, as the current agent had sent cancellation notices out before the new subscription orders were received by the vendors/publishers. Every title that needed a current subscription for electronic access became a problem for the library, including both FWP e-journals and titles for which we had contractual obligations to maintain subscriptions. Access went down frequently, and we needed to remind several vendors/publishers that we still had a paid subscription. Reinstatement of electronic access occurred only after we conveyed subscription numbers from our earlier vendor, as well as the subscription periods for which the library had paid.

The second lesson is to make sure that the collection development staff understands the transition process. Many of them received calls from the vendors/publishers, asking what had prompted our cancellation decision. Both collection development and serial acquisitions staff spent much time explaining that the library was in the process of changing subscription agents and was not canceling the titles. Serials acquisitions staff negotiated ninety-day grace periods with vendors/publishers, so that the library would be able to retain access, believing that the additional ninety days would give our new subscription agent enough time to make sure that the vendor/publisher had the new orders and to obtain new subscription numbers.

An unexpected problem was that many vendors/publishers felt that the library did not have contracts in place for all of the new electronic products that the new agent was requesting. With the new orders that were coming in, the vendors/publishers apparently believed that there should be new license agreements for them, and we had to provide the new subscription agent with a copy of our current contracts to fax to vendors/publishers whenever a new subscription was submitted.

Although some subscription agents do offer to negotiate contracts with vendors/publishers, this process remains a concern for libraries. Not enough of the stakeholders involved have agreed to use a standardized model license. Although standard licenses can be inflexible, and do not necessarily cover all of the individual needs of a particular institution, the sheer number of contracts that the library must negotiate frequently requires the use of an intermediary. Should the library designate an intermediary, there is a concern that the model license may not be updated to reflect the ever-changing face of technology, as well as changes in the law.

A second concern that needs to be resolved if the library chooses a contract intermediary is access problem solving. Who will do the problem solving, the agent or the library? One of the libraries' concerns is to restore access as quickly as possible, and it is unclear how a subscription agent could facilitate such rapid problem solving. Contracts must have specific wording that addresses access problems and the subsequent resolution of those problems. A final concern is that libraries may require usage statistics from the vendor/publisher. If libraries want to analyze usage statistics for collection development decisions, it is unclear how agents could provide meaningful statistics for anything that is not accessed through the agent's server.

THE CHALLENGES OF WORKING
WITH VENDORS/PUBLISHERS

A major concern when working with vendors/publishers to purchase electronic journals is the sheer number of publishers that the staff has to work with. They must search multiple Web sites for information, obtain multiple contracts, create multiple orders, receive multiple invoices, and generate multiple checks. With each of the vendor/publisher operations, library staff must determine who the correct contacts are and keep a record of them for future use. They must work with many people to resolve access problems in a variety of hardware and software environments. Contracts, correspondence, and invoices may not be in the customer's language, but vendors provide translated materials as part of their customer service. Other issues that may be encountered include invoices stated in foreign currency, or that may not have the special library fund information needed for correct payment, or that may not have billed for the number of copies the library requires, or that may not provide the correct vendor/publisher payee information. Unless many electronic journals are ordered from the same vendor/publisher, it is not cost effective to establish protocols for the electronic transfer of information.

Vendors/publishers are not as likely to use a team approach to managing library accounts in the manner subscription agents do. There may be a single, solitary contact, rather than a coordinating person who has specialists available to help resolve various issues. This is particularly true when dealing with license concerns. Some sales contacts are intermediaries between the libraries and the vendors'/publishers' corporate attorney and have little or no authority to change license phrasing. When access problems occur, the library systems staff needs other systems professionals to be able to query, without going through an intermediary. Personnel changes, business information, and changes in licensing policies may only be apparent when the access goes down and the library is unable to restore access in a timely manner. Some vendors/publishers have alert services and some do not. Without alerts, vendor/publisher system upgrades, changes in URLs, or changes in materials supplied become extremely difficult to manage. Sales personnel may visit libraries but may have to contact the home office before specific library problems can be resolved. The library may not understand or know the vendor/publisher chain of command, so it helps the library to know who to contact if concerns are not being handled by the library's own service representative.

Single libraries may not have as much influence with vendors/publishers as a subscription agent representing many does. Often the agent conveys to the vendor/publisher concerns held by multiple libraries. Conversely, individual libraries may have diminished leverage in license negotiations because their individual concerns are not addressed by vendors/publishers. Publisher/vendor sites may also change their licensing policies in their database. Often libraries unknowingly indicate acceptance of these changes when the next patron logs onto the site after the change has been posted. Price negotiations are also more effective if there is a group of libraries working together. Consortial groups have shown us that libraries have more power to effect changes in the license and pricing policies of a vendor/publisher collectively than would any single library acting alone.

Multiple vendors/publishers may mean that it is necessary to house multiple platforms, each with special needs that the library must support. Each group may have its own index, search engine, and controlled vocabulary. This creates training problems for public service staff and a larger learning curve for patrons.

There is no central warehouse for information on vendor/publisher staff or policies. Library personnel must hunt for each publisher's information. If the vendor has a Web site, it may not contain bibliographic information, such as title changes, splits, and mergers. The vendor Web site has been constructed to market its products, and rightfully so, but it does make it more difficult for libraries to obtain the information they need to order, license, pay for, and maintain subscriptions.

In the same way that there is no central warehouse for information, there is no single facility for creating management reports. Particularly useful are the historic pricing files. Libraries use them to determine inflation rates for their subscription mix and plan budgets levels for succeeding years. Nor do many vendors analyze and publish market trends. Libraries need to be aware of and plan for new market developments such as a value-added tax or new standard of billing that may affect their budgets or work flows.

THE CHALLENGES OF WORKING
WITH THIRD-PARTY PROVIDERS

Third-party providers are the most recent entry in the suite of electronic journal services and are still evolving, which means that they are the service type with the greatest number of challenges, including the time required for start up and ongoing maintenance. When initiating the service, the library must provide a file of e-journal packages, aggregator databases, and electronic holdings. If the library's FWP titles are also to be included, then the library must create, update, and maintain a file of the FWP information. Once the file has been sent to the TPP, the library may make adjustments to local records to indicate changes, and any adjustment must be sent to the TPP. Maintenance for this service will become an increasing concern as time passes.

Updates to the library's site can take as long as two to eight weeks. Some services offer biweekly updates, and others offer bimonthly updates to local information. This time lag can cause problems for public service personnel, as patrons may not be able to link to withdrawn titles that the service is listing as still available. In addition, new titles would not be added for several weeks, unless the library updates local records to reflect the change.

Third-party provider information is only updated in the TPP files. At the present time, there is not an alerting service for the library to indicate title changes, splits, mergers, or changes in URLs. This means that the local catalog information may be different from the TPP information. Third-party provider syntax information may also be more current than the URLs the library has acquired over time, necessitating local catalog changes to bring the library in line with TPP syntax.

CONCLUSION

After having discussed the advantages and concerns of subscription agents, vendors/publishers, and third-party providers, the question remains: Should libraries choose to use one group instead of another? Electronic journals operations need to have a metamediary. In the same way that libraries began using subscription agents to handle the large numbers of paper subscriptions, libraries will increasingly need assistance with the hundreds of electronic subscriptions and their linked objects. Current subscription agents bring many value-added services to the table, but they need to continue to develop services that will locate and manage linked images, charts, graphs, and data sets. Standard license agreements must be adopted, with a short schedule or appendix to deal with specific library requirements, so that agents can intermediate the library's e-journal materials in the same way they manage print subscriptions.

Publishers/vendors, third-party providers, and subscription agents should assist with the warehousing of electronic journals and with the preservation of links to their content. Libraries will need a central warehouse that contains updated information on all URLs. As more links become available, it will become impossible for libraries to query hundreds of publishers to maintain access. Libraries will still use subscription agents to locate information on electronic titles. Database maintenance would be a nightmare if there were no meta-mediary to assist library staff.

As has been the case in the past, it will be the subscription agent who will have to locate and deal with all of the small-press publications. Libraries will not be able to go direct for all of these titles, and scholarship cannot afford to lose access to these valuable small-press offerings.

The provision of bibliographic information and regular updates to that information will become increasingly important. Staying up to date with changes in titles and URLs will become critical as library users research more heavily within electronic products. Large vendors/publishers and subscription agents will need to develop themselves as metamediaries, each bringing more related services into a single arena. As this continues to occur, there will be increasing concerns about the lack of competition among intermediaries. Vendors/publishers, third-party providers, and subscription agents will need to step into the metamediary role, but it will be the subscription agent that will provide the wide range of services that libraries are used to receiving.

NOTES

1. Arnold, Kenneth. "The Electronic Librarian Is a Verb/ The Electronic Library Is Not a Sentence." Available at <http://www.press.umich.edu/jep/works/arnold.eleclib.html>.

2. Ibid.

3. Sawhney, Mohambir. "Meet the Metamediary." Available at <http:www.sili conindia.com/magazine>.

4. Katz, Bill and Gellatly, Peter. *Guide to Magazine and Serials Agents* (New York: Bowker, 1975), p. 3.

5. Chiou-Sen, Dora Chen. *Serials Management: A Practical Guide* (Chicago: American Library Association, 1995), p. 52.

6. Turner, Rollo. E-mail communication on late pricing, dated January 29, 2002.

SELECT BIBLIOGRAPHY

Books

Chiou-Sen, Dora Chen. *Serials Management, A Practical Guide.* Chicago: American Library Association, 1995.

Katz, Bill and Gellatly, Peter. *Guide to Magazine and Serials Agents.* New York: Bowker, 1975.

Tuule, Marcia and Cook, Jean G. *Advances in Serials Management.* Greenwich: JAI Press Ltd., 1986.

Articles

Arnold, Kenneth. "The Electronic Librarian Is a Verb/ The Electronic Library Is Not a Sentence." Available at <http://www.press.umich.edu/jep/works/arnold.eleclib.html>.

Edwards, Judith. "Electronic Journals: Problem or Panacea?" Available at <http://www.ariadne.ac.uk/issue10/journals>.

Harris, Lesley Ellen. "Are Model Licenses the Answer?" Available at <http://www.copyrightlaws.com>.

Kahin, Brian. "Institutional and Policy Issues in the Development of the Digital Library." Available at <http://www.press.umich.edu/jep/works/kahin.dl.html>.

Kidd, Tony. "Are Print Journals Dinosaurs?" Available at <http://www.ariadne.ac.uk/issue12/main>.

Knibbe, Andrew. "The Go Between: A Subscription Agent's Role in Electronic Publishing." *Journal of Electronic Publishing,* 4(4). Available at <http://www.press.umich.edu/jep>.

Sawhney, Mohambir. "Meet the Metamediary." Available at <http://www.silicon india.com/magazine>.

Sosteric, Mike. "Electronic First: The Upcoming Revolution in the Scholarly Communication System." *Journal of Electronic Publishing,* 7(2). Available at <http://www.press.umich.edu/jep>.

Chapter 3

Collection Development and Cataloging of Online Materials: What Libraries Are Doing Now

LadyJane Hickey
Janice Lange
Teri Oparanozie
Ed Loera

INTRODUCTION

The need for a survey of other libraries grew out of efforts in the Newton Gresham Library (NGL) technical services department to develop policies, procedures, and guidelines to manage online resources. Little pertinent information was found in the literature to address the question of current practices of libraries. Thus, the authors developed a questionnaire and conducted a telephone survey to find out what libraries are doing to collect, access, and catalog online materials. The term *online* was used specifically to narrow the focus to resources accessed via the World Wide Web rather than CD-ROM or computer disks used locally. That survey instrument, the libraries selected, the results obtained, and the authors' analysis are the focus of this chapter.

The survey instrument is designed to provide a snapshot of libraries' current practices for handling online resources. Topical questions are arranged in four categories on the survey instrument. Questions asked include the following: Are various categories of electronic resources (e-resources) treated differently in collection development policies? Which integrated library system (ILS) and software are used to provide access to these materials and also to validate the patron? How are URLs maintained and who is responsible for their maintenance? Does the library have guidelines on which e-resources will be cataloged? If cataloged, are they using the single-record or multiple-record approach?

Collection development decisions must be made first. Database providers must be selected. Electronic journal (e-journal) subscriptions need to be selected and managed along with other serial subscriptions. Many print journals have electronic counterparts that need to be managed. The print subscription and the online subscription may be from different vendors and run on different payment cycles. The online version may cover the entire run of the serial, or it may cover only from a certain date onward.

Should the various categories of e-resources be treated differently in the "decision to catalog" policy? Internet sites and online sources are a vast unlimited quantity of resources of varying quality. Obviously, any one library cannot collect, access, and catalog all of the resources available. Some selection is necessary. The selection takes place first in the decision to collect the online resource; then, another decision is made about the method(s) of access to the e-resource.

Should cataloged resources also be available on the library's home page? Should resources available on the library's home page also be added to the catalog? Because of the usual constraints of personnel, time, and money, choices and selection must occur. Although some online resources are stable, many others are not. Who will maintain the URL addresses? Should the URL be added to the print record? Should the e-resources have their own bibliographic record that can be removed when the item is no longer available? Each library has to make its own policy decisions for cataloging online resources.

METHODOLOGY

The Libraries

The authors selected ninety-two North American libraries, which included a random sample of eighty, plus twelve selected by location.

The sample included seventy libraries from colleges or universities with programs of four or more years (academic), nine from junior or community colleges with two-year programs (junior), and thirteen public libraries (public). Corporate, medical, association, and other special libraries were excluded. The main or largest library was selected if the institution consisted of several departmental or branch libraries. The libraries in the sample were from the following time zones: forty-three, eastern time; thirty-two, central time; and seventeen, mountain or pacific time. One library was located in Mexico, two were in Canada, and eighty-nine were in the United States. Each library was telephoned at least once. Responses were received from the two libraries in Canada but not from the library in Mexico. The number of completed questionnaires was seventy, which included fifty-five academic, six junior, and nine public libraries (i.e., a 76 percent response rate).

The 2001 *NASIG Membership Directory* and *OCLC/AMIGOS Collection Analysis CD: User Guide Supplement* for December 1997 were used to select eighty of the ninety-two libraries. Some members of the North American Serials Interest Group (NASIG) were known to be actively involved in collecting online resources. Two libraries per page were selected at random from the NASIG "Organization Index" for a total of forty libraries. In the *OCLC/AMIGOS Collection Analysis CD User Guide,* the database section, containing 2,646 libraries, was used. Every sixty-sixth library was selected, plus one from Mexico for a total of forty-one libraries. Eleven additional libraries were selected from the regional area.

Description of the Survey Instrument

The decision to use a telephone survey to gather the information was based on the speed of the response and the timeliness of the topic. The authors did a pretest of regional libraries and adjusted the survey instrument. The final version of the survey instrument contained both open-ended and closed questions. Section I: Your Library included six questions designed to collect demographic data about the participating libraries including the type of library, size, and ILS system used, so that this information could be aggregated and correlated with how libraries are handling their online resources. The four questions in Section II: Collection of Online Resources focused on the types of online resources to which libraries are providing access and their collection development policies. For the purposes of this survey, the term *online resources* referred to three categories of technology. The first category of resources was databases and their contents (including abstracts and indexes). The second category of resources was full-text electronic journals and documents (for example, ERIC documents or e-books). The third category was Web resources, which included Web sites and Web pages. In Section III: Online Resources (Access Software), four questions were used to explore some of the unique challenges involved in providing access to online resources such as the use of proxy servers, link checkers, and integrated title lists. Section IV: Cataloging had ten questions which dealt with the cataloging of e-journals, e-books, databases, and Web sites covering issues such as the criteria used for deciding which resources to catalog, whether to use a single- or multiple-record approach, how to handle holdings information and call numbers, whether to catalog databases as single entities or to catalog the titles within the database, and the pros and cons of using vendor records.

Collecting the Data

The telephone list of ninety-two libraries was divided among the four authors. The length of the calls ranged from ten to sixty minutes. Many of the respondents were willing to participate in the survey at the time of the initial phone call. Although the telephone survey was usually completed by one person, occasionally the interviewer spoke to more than one person because the respondent did not feel qualified to answer all of the questions in every part of the survey. In a few cases, the survey instrument was sent by e-mail or fax to respondents who requested it. Numerous follow-up calls were made.

Compiling the Data

The authors developed tables for compiling the data collected through the survey instrument. In most cases, the data in the tables is broken down into categories for academic, junior, and public libraries. Four derived questions were added to Section IV so that the data could be interpreted more easily. Although the results in the tables are recorded as "Yes" or "No," responders often qualified their answers (e.g., "No, not yet" or "Yes, we are doing that but only for certain types of e-resources"). Comments are taken into consideration in the Results and Analysis section of this chapter. The tables of aggregated data are available in the Appendix.

RESULTS AND ANALYSIS

Section I: Your Library

Ninety-two libraries were contacted, and seventy responded. The participating libraries include fifty-five academic (78 percent), six junior college (9 percent), and nine public (13 percent) [Appendix, Table I.1]. Thirty-four libraries serve as the only library location at their institution, and thirty libraries are part of a system with two to nine branches/libraries [Table I.2]. For the academic and junior colleges, twenty-five have enrollments up to 5,000 students, eighteen have from 5,001 to 15,000 students, and eighteen have from 15,001 to 50,000 students [Table I.3]. Thirty-four of the fifty-five academic libraries award doctorates [Table I.4]. For public libraries, five have a service area population count of up to 250,000 people, two libraries have a population of between 500,001 and 1,000,000, and two libraries serve between 1.5 million and 4 million people [Table I.5]. The surveyed libraries are using a total of fifteen different ILS systems, with one-third of the libraries using Innovative Interfaces (twenty-three libraries) [Table I.6].

Section II: Collection of Online Resources

The survey revealed that all seventy libraries provide access to databases, followed by e-books (sixty-six), e-journals (sixty-four), and Web sites (sixty-two) [Table II.1]. Only twenty-six of seventy libraries have developed specific policies for collecting online resources [Tables II.2, II.3]. Collection responsibilities for online resources are split between several positions: subject specialist (forty-three), committee (twenty-six), and "other" (twenty-seven). Often, more than one position is responsible for collecting online resources. The most frequently mentioned "others" are library administration (seven), collection development (seven), and librarians from each area (five) [Table II.4].

The data show that libraries are providing access to online resources and are slowly developing policies to meet those needs. Many positions are involved in the collection of these resources and this trend will continue to be a dynamic issue in the field.

Section III: Online Resources (Access Software)

Some form of identification and validation is needed to provide and restrict access to licensed database resources. Sixty-five of seventy libraries do use some method of validation. The answers to this question include both on-site and remote verification. The access points at which the validation occurs are at the library's Web page (fifty) and the URL in the OPAC (thirty-three) [Table III.1].

Links are required to attach the bibliographic record in the online catalog to the actual document. In the online environment, the address to the resource may change so that the link is no longer operational. To solve this problem, several link checker software systems are available. Libraries are evenly split in using link checker software: thirty-two libraries responded "yes," and thirty-five libraries answered "no." Some ILS systems have link checker software that is included or is an additional component to the system. Fourteen respondents have an integrated link checker in their ILS. Some libraries mentioned that using vendors such as Serials Solutions to maintain their serials list reduces the need to check URLs [Table III.2]. Nine ILS systems are used with a variety of link checker software packages [Table III.2b]. In many libraries the responsibility for maintaining the accuracy of the links is shared by several positions or departments. Those mentioned most frequently are cataloging (sixteen), electronic resources librarians (twelve), and systems (ten) [Table III.3].

Forty of the seventy libraries are using some type of integrated online list of e-journals. Thirty-two libraries are providing the list from their Web page and twenty-eight are including holdings with the titles. Twenty-one libraries are using a vendor to organize and provide the list. The vendors listed are Serials Solutions (seventeen), TDNet (two), and Periodical Locator (two) [Table III.4].

Section IV: Cataloging

None of the libraries subscribe to a service that provides and maintains a separate catalog for online resources. Fifty-six out of seventy libraries add bibliographic records for online resources to their online catalog [Table IV.2]. Only sixteen of the fifty-six libraries have a written policy or guideline on what their library will catalog [Table IV.2a]; however, a number of librarians commented that they are currently drafting one. The most frequently considered criteria when cataloging are paid subscriptions (fifty), library having a direct subscription (forty-five), government documents (forty-five), free access (forty-one), and in catalog already (thirty-nine) [Table IV.2b].

Fifty-one of seventy libraries catalog online journals [Table IV.2c]. Forty-four libraries provide links to the online version in the print bibliographic record [Table IV.3a] and only twenty-seven out of seventy libraries catalog the online version on a separate bibliographic record [Table IV.3b]. Fifty out of seventy libraries catalog their online-only journal subscriptions [Table IV.4a] and fifty-one libraries provide access to online journals from the library's database links [Table IV.4b]. Thirty-five libraries give all access points on one record when an online journal is available from several different database providers [Table IV.5a], while twelve libraries provide separate records for each access point [Table IV.5b]. Thirty-four include title coverage (holdings) information in the bibliographic records [Table IV.5c], while only thirteen respondents use a generic note instead of specific holdings [Table IV.5d]. None of these categories are mutually exclusive as numerous libraries do both.

Fifty-five participants catalog e-books [Table IV.6]. Seventeen include the link to the online version of the e-book in the print record [Table IV.6a]. Forty-six libraries use a separate bibliographic record to catalog the online version [Table IV.6b]. Forty-six libraries catalog databases and/or the e-journals included in them [Table IV.7]. Thirty-six provide a separate catalog record for the database as a single entity [Table IV.7a]. Thirty-four libraries catalog e-journal titles included in databases to which the library subscribes [Table IV.7b]. The following factors most frequently affect the decision to catalog the e-journals that are in a database: stability (twenty), full coverage (seven), and URL linking directly to the journal title (six) [Table IV.7c]. Forty-one participants acquire sets of catalog records for online resources from vendors [Table IV.7d]. The sets of records most frequently acquired are those from netLibrary (seventeen) [Table IV.7d.i]. "Not labor intensive," "Fast," and "Convenient" are among the many comments made for liking batch loading of bibliographic records. Paradoxically, "Labor intensive" and the need to edit the records for authority control, subject headings, URLs, and to meet local library standards/practice are mentioned as reasons for disliking these same records [Tables IV.7d.ii and iii].

Only twenty-nine out of seventy libraries catalog Web sites [Table IV.8]. Only three of those provide a separate record for each Web site linked from the library's home page [Table IV.8a]. Nineteen libraries issue "standard" call numbers to online resources [Table IV.9]. Only fourteen libraries participate in additional programs to catalog online materials such as CORC [Table IV.10].

Libraries are using the OPAC to bring e-resources to their patrons. However, the trend is to catalog selectively. E-books and e-journals are being cataloged more often than databases and Web pages. Comments from participants indicate that even within these categories, many factors are influencing decisions about what to catalog.

Web-based products make it easier for libraries in consortia to access the same resources and to enjoy lowered costs. Respondents from most of the surveyed libraries indicate access is provided for a wide array of e-resources, many through library consortia. Some of the junior and public libraries mention that consortia-based materials are the only e-resources available to their patrons. Access to e-resources is most often provided from the library's own Web page. Although all seventy libraries provide access to databases, only forty-six are cataloging any of them. A similar pattern exists for other materials (Table 3.1). Whereas the struggle used to be to acquire online resources, it is now to provide access through integrated serials lists and/or the OPAC.

TABLE 3.1. Access to and Cataloging of Online Resources

	Databases	E-journals	E-books	Web sites
Libraries interviewed	70	70	70	70
Access provided	70	64	66	62
Cataloging in OPAC	46	51	55	29

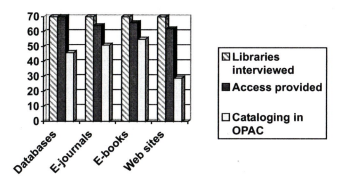

CONCLUSION

The authors are very appreciative of the many librarians who participated in the survey, especially those who offered comments and copies of policy, guidelines, and criteria. The librarians who catalog online resources made many comments about selection. Trend analysis looks at the overall picture to see where libraries are and where they are going.

Our profession is challenged as we develop new rules, new definitions, and new standards of service to manage e-resources and make them accessible to customers. The survey revealed that libraries do things differently. Some standards exist across the profession while others are adaptations within a particular type or size of library. Some libraries, such as NGL, are just beginning to grapple with these topics while other libraries are farther along the continuum.

Libraries are collecting online resources. They are selecting online resources that meet the mission statement and collection development policy statement already in place. Some libraries are enhancing the original statement to include online resources. Many libraries have additional people involved in the selection, approval, and authorizing processes needed to purchase leasing and licensing agreements to these large databases.

Libraries are managing online materials using the resources available to them. Most libraries are using a remote access system such as a proxy server. Many libraries turned to vendors to assist them. The vendors providing link-checking capabilities range from the libraries' familiar friends such as their ILS, to new software as listed in the tables. URL maintenance shows many respondents designating more than one person or department sharing responsibility as depicted in the tables. The vendors providing integrated lists of online journals are new to the market, and their very existence is one of the trends. Access is provided through the library's Web page; sometimes, a library will catalog the material. The answers to the cataloging questions reveal much more diversity than the other sections. The tables show that all categories of material are cataloged, but they do not all have the same priority. Decisions to catalog are based on other criteria, such as the value of a specific database (e.g., JSTOR or Project MUSE), or the needs of their patrons for specific subject matter. Both the single-record and the multiple-record approaches are used, often in the same library, based on the type of material, the availability of bibliographic records in batched sets, and the availability of existing records in the catalog.

One of the findings is that other libraries are grappling with these same issues and that the librarians wanted to talk about them. Often the response included comments about these multifaceted issues. The most consistent comment elicited was "selection," occurring at every stage from collecting to inclusion in integrated lists of journals to the decision to catalog. Participants frequently mention "staff time" in the response, usually explaining its relationship to the "selections" listed previously. These two comments are indicative of trends in the profession. Librarians are very resourceful, and the comments collected in the survey enlighten us to some of the many ways they are coping with the issues that accompany online resources.

APPENDIX

Tables

Section I: Your Library

TABLE I.1. Type of library

ACADEMIC	55
JUNIOR	6
PUBLIC	9
TOTAL	70

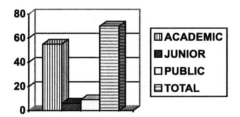

TABLE I.2. How many libraries/branches are a part of your institution?

NUMBER OF LIBRARIES/ BRANCHES	ACADEMIC	JUNIOR	PUBLIC	TOTAL
1	30	1	3	34
2	6	1		7
3	2	3	1	6
4	3			3
5	3			3
6	4			4
7	2	1		3
8	1		1	2
9	2			2
11	1		1	2
16			1	1
17	1			1
19			1	1
24			1	1
40	1			1

TABLE I.3. If academic, what is your enrollment?

	ACADEMIC	JUNIOR	TOTAL
Up to 2,500	11	2	13
2,501-5,000	12		12
5,001-7,500	4	2	6
7,501-10,000	2		2
10,001-15,000	9	1	10
15,001-20,000	5		5
20,001-25,000	3		3
25,001-30,000	5		5
30,001-35,000	1		1
35,001-40,000	2		2
40,001-45,000		1	1
45,001-50,000	1		1

TABLE I.4. Please indicate the highest degree granted

	ACADEMIC	JUNIOR
ASSOCIATE		6
BACHELOR	5	
MASTER	16	
DOCTOR	34	

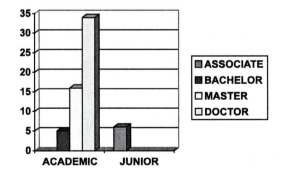

TABLE I.5. If public, what is the service area population count?

Up to 100,000	2
100,001-250,000	3
250,001-500,000	1
500,001-750,000	1
750,001-1,000,000	1
1,500,001-2,000,000	1
3,000,001-4,000,000	1

TABLE I.6. What ILS system do you use for:

	Cat	Acq	Serials	OPAC	OPAC web	OPAC telnet	Circ	A	J	P	Tot
ALEPH 500	2	2	2	2	2		2	2			2
CARL	1	1	1	1	1		1	1			1
DRA	7	6	3	5	5	2	7	5		2	7
Dynix	5	4	5	5	4	3	5	2		3	5
Follet	1			1	1		1		1		1
Geac	1	1	1	1	1		1			1	1
Horizon	7	6	7	7	7	2	7	4	1	2	7
III *	23	22	23	23	23	6	23	20	3		23
MPALS	1	1	1	1	1	1	1	1			1
Notis	7	6	6	7	7	3	7	6	1		7
SIRSI	4	3	3	4	4	1	4	4			4
TAOS	1			1	1		1	1			1
Virtua	1		1				1	1			1
Voyager	8	7	7	8	8		8	8			7
VTLS	1	1	1	2	2		1	1	1		2

* III – Innovative Interfaces includes Innopac and Millenium
Last 4 columns: A=Academic, J=Junior, P=Public, T=Total Libraries

Section II: Collection of Online Resources

TABLE II.1.What kind of online resources do you provide?

	ACADEMIC	JUNIOR	PUBLIC	TOTAL
Databases	55	6	9	70
E-journals	54	5	5	64
Online books/documents	53	6	7	66
Web sites or pages	47	6	9	62

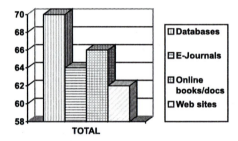

TABLE II.2. Has your library developed new collection development policies for online resources?

	YES	NO	DON'T KNOW
ACADEMIC	22	32	1
JUNIOR	1	5	
PUBLIC	3	5	1
TOTAL	26	42	2

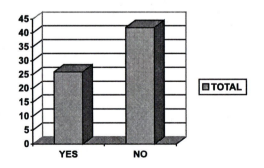

TABLE II.3. Does your library have separate criteria for collecting online and print resources?

	YES	NO	DON'T KNOW
ACADEMIC	21	31	3
JUNIOR		6	
PUBLIC	2	6	1
TOTAL	23	43	4

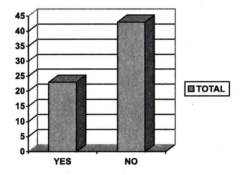

TABLE II.4. Whose responsibility is it to collect online resources?

	ACADEMIC	JUNIOR	PUBLIC	TOTAL
Librarian Subj. Specialists	37	1	5	43
Academic Dept. Faculty	22			22
Electronic Resources Coordinator/ Librarian	19	1	3	23
Committee	21	2	3	26
Other	26	1		27

	ONE RESPONSE	TWO RESPONSES	THREE RESPONSES	FOUR RESPONSES	FIVE RESPONSES
ACADEMIC	12	18	10	10	5
JUNIOR	5		1		
PUBLIC	2	6	1		
TOTAL	19	24	12	10	5

Breakdown of OTHER Category

LIBRARY ADMINISTRATION*	7
PUBLIC SERVICES LIBRARIANS	4
TECH. SERVS. LIBRARIANS	3
LIBRARY CONSORTIA	4
LIBRARIANS FROM EACH AREA	5
EACH LIBRARY IN THE SYSTEM	2
COLLECTION DEVELOPMENT	7

*Some of these administrators also have responsibilities in other areas such as Assistant Director/Head of Collection Development

Section III: Online Resource (Access Software)

TABLE III.1. Does your library use some method of validating users to access online resources (e.g., proxy server to provide access to remote users)?

	YES	NO
ACADEMIC	53	2
JUNIOR	5	1
PUBLIC	7	1
TOTAL	65	4

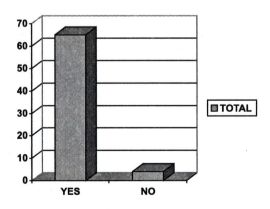

If yes:

TABLE III.1a. What method?

	ACADEMIC	JUNIOR	PUBLIC	TOTAL
IP ADDRESSES	20		1	21
PROXY SERVER	31	4	1	36
EZ PROXY	12			12
RPA SOFTWARE		1	2	3
REFERRER URL			1	1
VIRTUAL PRIVATE NETWORK	2			2
AUTOMATIC PROXY	1			1
ASA DIAL ACCESS LINE	1			1
ILS SYSTEM	4		1	5
LAN Gateway	1			1
OTHER	5		2	7

TABLE III.1b. At what point does this validation occur?

	ACADEMIC	JUNIOR	PUBLIC	TOTAL
LIBRARY'S WEB PAGE	43	4	3	50
URLs IN OPAC	30		3	33
HOME PAGE		1		1
VENDOR	1			1
DON'T KNOW	5		2	7

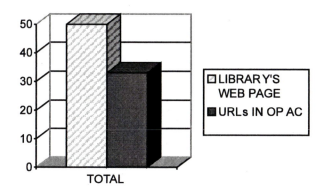

TABLE III.2. Do you have a link checker software program?

	YES	NO	DON'T KNOW
ACADEMIC	29	23	3
JUNIOR	1	5	
PUBLIC	2	7	
TOTAL	32	35	3

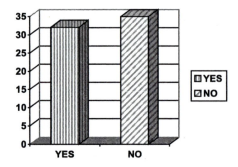

If yes:

TABLE III.2a. Which one?

	ACADEMIC	JUNIOR	PUBLIC	TOTAL
Home Site	1			1
Hot Bot	1			1
ILS system*	12	1	1	14
Link Bot	2	1		3
Link Lint	1			1
Link Scan	2			2
Watchfire	1			1
Other†	10		1	11

*Included here if respondent said its ILS system checks links (e.g., Dynix, III, Voyager)
†Includes responses such as "locally produced program," "handled at the consortia level," use of vendors such as Serials Solutions to provide updated URLs for the titles they handle which reduces the need to check URLs, and "don't know."

TABLE III.2b. ILS and Link Checker (Combines questions: Sec. I.6 and Sec III. 2)

	Link Bot	ILS* System	Home Site	Link Lint	Link Scan	Watch-fire	Other
ALEPH 500				1			
DRA							1
Dynix		1					
Geac							1
Horizon							4
III (Innovative)	1	11			1	1	5
Notis	1				1		
SIRSI	1		1				1
Virtua							
Voyager		1					3

Note: Table includes only correlated items.
*Link checker integrated into the ILS system

TABLE III.3. Who is responsible for maintaining the accuracy of the links? (See note following table.)

	ACADEMIC	JUNIOR	PUBLIC	TOTAL
NO ONE	2	3	3	8
ACQUISITIONS	6			6
CATALOGING	14		2	16
DIGITAL RESOURCES	1			1
DISTRICT LEVEL		1		1
DOCUMENTS LIBRARIAN	1			1
ELECTRONIC SERVS. LIBRARIAN	10	1	1	12
PUBLIC SERVS. WEB TEAM	4			4
REFERENCE	7		1	8
SELECTORS	3	1		4
SYSTEMS	10			10
TECH. SERVS.	4		1	5
DON'T KNOW	1			1

Note: (A) Many libraries have shared responsibility so more than one answer is valid. However, in aggregating the data, those people may be in the same category. Two items were counted when this occurred. (B) Libraries are very diverse in naming positions they use. Titles of positions were combined in the following list. The first name appears in the tables.

1. Electronic Services Librarian/Information Access Specialist/Serials and Electronic Resources Librarian
2. Systems/Web Master/LAN Department
3. Selectors/Bibliographers/Subject Specialist Librarians/Web Authors
4. Acquisitions/Serials Acquisitions/Acquisitions of Electronic Serials/Serials Management Librarian
5. Cataloging/Serials Cataloging/Bibliographic Control Unit

TABLE III.4. Realizing that most databases provide title lists of included e-journals, does your library provide an integrated online list of e-journals?

	YES	NO
ACADEMIC	38	15
JUNIOR	1	3
PUBLIC	1	8
TOTAL	40	26

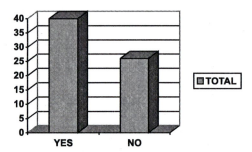

If yes:

TABLE III.4a. Where do you provide that list?

	ACADEMIC	JUNIOR	PUBLIC	TOTAL
OPAC	4	1	1	6
WEB PAGE	32			32

TABLE III.4b. What software do you use to produce the list?

	ACADEMIC	JUNIOR	PUBLIC	TOTAL
Filemaker Pro	1			1
Excel spreadsheet	1			1
Microsoft Access	1			1
Vendor supplies	12			12
Word processing	2			2
Derived from code in cataloged record	2			2
Don't know	18			18

TABLE III.4c. Do you include holdings with the titles?

	YES	NO
ACADEMIC	27	10
JUNIOR		1
PUBLIC	1	
TOTAL	28	11

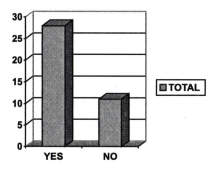

If yes:

TABLE III.4d. Do you use a vendor?

	YES	NO
ACADEMIC	20	17
JUNIOR		1
PUBLIC	1	
TOTAL	21	18

TABLE III.4e. Which vendor?

	ACADEMIC	JUNIOR	PUBLIC	TOTAL
PERIODICAL LOCATOR	2			2
SERIALS SOLUTIONS	16		1	17
TDNET	2			2

Section IV: Cataloging

TABLE IV.1. Do you subscribe to a service that provides and maintains a separate catalog for online resources (such as SIRSI's Library HQ)?

All answers were NO to this question, so no tables were developed.

TABLE IV.2. Do you add bibliographic records for online resources to your online catalog?

	YES	NO
ACADEMIC	49	6
JUNIOR	2	4
PUBLIC	5	4
TOTAL	56	14

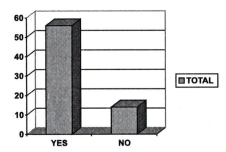

If yes:

TABLE IV.2a. Do you have a written policy or guidelines on what your library will catalog?

	YES	NO	DON'T KNOW
ACADEMIC	14	32	3
JUNIOR	1	3	1
PUBLIC	1	4	1
TOTAL	16	39	5

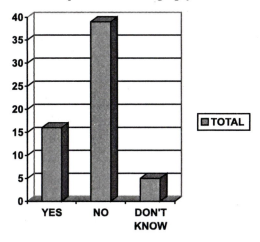

TABLE IV.2b. Which of the following criteria are things you consider when cataloging online resources?

	YES	NO
1. PAID SUBSCRIPTIONS	50	6
2. IN CATALOG ALREADY	39	14
3. RECORDS FROM VENDOR	24	22
4. LIB. HAS DIRECT SUBSCRIPTION	45	6
5. FREE ACCESS	41	8
6. GOV. DOCS.	45	8
7. CREATED LOCALLY	27	24
8. WEB SITES	33	19
9. LINKS TO TITLE	33	17
10. NEEDED FOR STATISTICAL PURPOSES	11	37
11. COVERED ALL CRITERIA	24	23

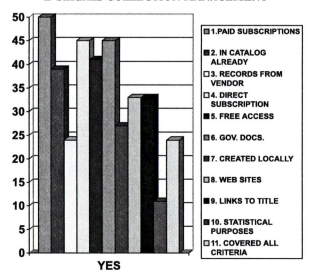

TABLE IV.2.c Do you catalog online journals? (Derived from answers to other questions, especially IV 2, 3, 4, and 5)

	YES	NO
ACADEMIC	46	6
JUNIOR	4	1
PUBLIC	1	6
TOTAL	51	13

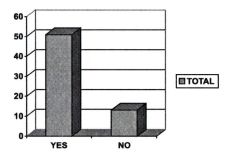

If yes:

TABLE IV.3a. Do you provide links to the online version in the print bibliographic record (i.e., MARC 856 field)?

	YES	NO
ACADEMIC	40	14
JUNIOR	2	2
PUBLIC	2	4
TOTAL	44	20

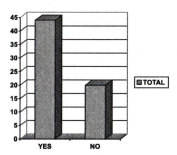

TABLE IV.3b. Do you catalog the online version on a separate bibliographic record?

	YES	NO
ACADEMIC	22	29
JUNIOR	3	1
PUBLIC	2	4
TOTAL	27	34

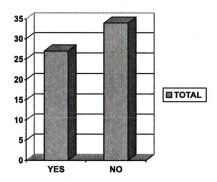

For online-only journal subscriptions (no print):

TABLE IV.4a. Do you catalog the online version?

	YES	NO
ACADEMIC	45	5
JUNIOR	2	2
PUBLIC	3	3
TOTAL	50	10

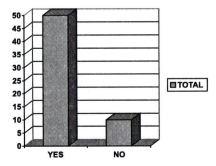

TABLE IV.4b. Do you provide access to the e-journal from the library's database links (i.e., library's Web page, specific database services, etc.)?

	YES	NO
ACADEMIC	47	7
JUNIOR	2	
PUBLIC	2	1
TOTAL	51	8

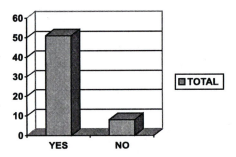

If you have access to an online journal through several different databases:

TABLE IV.5a. Do you give all the access points on one record?

	YES	NO	DON'T KNOW	NO ANSWER
ACADEMIC	34	11	1	4
JUNIOR		2		
PUBLIC	1	4		
TOTAL	35	17	1	4

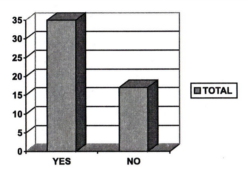

TABLE IV.5b. Do you provide a separate record for each access point?

	YES	NO	DON'T KNOW	NO ANSWER
ACADEMIC	11	33	3	3
JUNIOR	1	1		
PUBLIC		3		
TOTAL	12	37	3	3

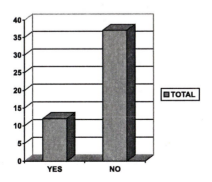

TABLE IV.5c. Do you include the title coverage (holdings) information?

	YES	NO	NO ANSWER
ACADEMIC	32	17	3
JUNIOR	1	1	
PUBLIC	1	2	
TOTAL	34	20	3

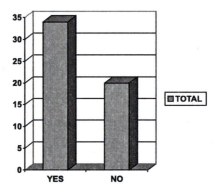

TABLE IV.5d. Do you include a generic note about coverage, which can be used on many different records such as a "coverage varies" note or "check database for holdings" note?

	YES	NO	NO ANSWER
ACADEMIC	12	33	3
JUNIOR	1	1	
PUBLIC		3	
TOTAL	13	37	

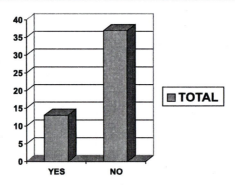

TABLE IV.6. Do you catalog e-books and/or e-documents? (Answer is derived from responses to other questions, especially IV 6a, 6b; IV 2, 2b; and II 1.)

	YES	NO
ACADEMIC	48	5
JUNIOR	2	3
PUBLIC	5	2
TOTAL	55	10

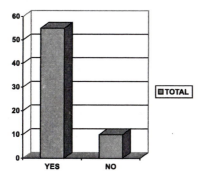

If yes:

TABLE IV.6a. Do you provide links to the online version in the print bibliographic record (i.e., MARC 856 field)?

	YES	NO
ACADEMIC	15	34
JUNIOR	1	2
PUBLIC	1	6
TOTAL	17	42

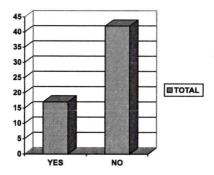

TABLE IV.6b. Do you catalog the online version on a separate bibliographic record?

	YES	NO
ACADEMIC	41	5
JUNIOR	2	1
PUBLIC	3	2
TOTAL	46	8

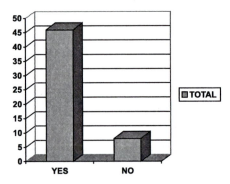

TABLE IV.7. Do you catalog databases and/or the e-journals included in them? (Answers derived from responses to other questions, especially IV 7a, 7b, and 7c.)

	YES	NO
ACADEMIC	43	9
JUNIOR	2	3
PUBLIC	1	6
TOTAL	46	18

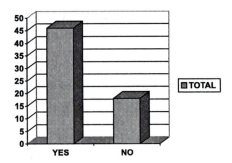

If yes:

TABLE IV.7a. Do you provide a separate catalog for the database as a single entity? (i.e., EBSCOhost, JSTOR, Academic Universe, etc.)

	YES	NO
ACADEMIC	34	18
JUNIOR	2	1
PUBLIC		5
TOTAL	36	24

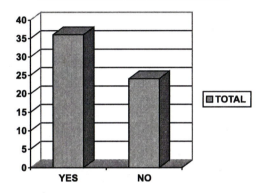

TABLE IV.7b. Do you provide catalog records for e-journal titles included in databases to which the library subscribes?

	YES	NO	DON'T KNOW
ACADEMIC	32	18	2
JUNIOR	2		
PUBLIC		1	
TOTAL	34	19	2

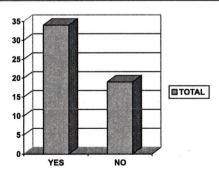

If yes:

TABLE IV.7c. Which of the following distinctions affect your decision to catalog the e-journals that are in a database? The database is stable/unstable; The titles provide full coverage/partial coverage; URLs to journal title/to the host database; Other.

	ACADEMIC	JUNIOR	PUBLIC
STABLE	19	1	
UNSTABLE	5		
FULL COVERAGE	7		
PARTIAL COVERAGE			
URL TO JOURNAL TITLE	6		
URL TO HOST DATABASE	2		

TABLE IV.7d. Do you acquire sets of catalog records for online resources from vendors such as Marcive, EBSCO, or OCLC?

	YES	NO
ACADEMIC	38	14
JUNIOR		4
PUBLIC	3	3
TOTAL	41	21

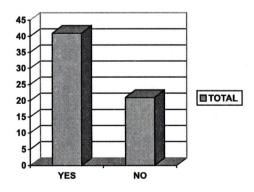

If yes:

TABLE IV.7d.i. Which ones?

	ACADEMIC	JUNIOR	PUBLIC	TOTAL
Books 24/7	2			2
Early English Books	1			1
EBSCO	7			7
LexisNexis	6			6
MARCIVE	11	1	1	13
netLibrary	15	1	1	17
OCLC	11	1	2	14
ProQuest	2			2

TABLE IV.7d.ii. What do you like about it?

	ACADEMIC	JUNIOR	PUBLIC	TOTAL
Ability for authority control	1			1
Accurate/higher standard of quality			1	1
Convenient	5		2	7
Easy	6			6
Fast	8			8
MARC format provided			1	1
Not labor intensive	7	1	1	9
Works with III system	1			1
Increases access for users	2		1	3
Can edit by batch	1			1
Cost productive	1			1

TABLE IV.7d.iii. What do you dislike about it?

	ACADEMIC	JUNIOR	PUBLIC	TOTAL
Cleanup of records required for authority control, subject headings, URLs, or to meet local library standards/practice	10			
Have to assign code to pull records out of OPAC if needed	1			
Have to depend upon systems staff to make loading a priority	1			
Have to know ILS system well to know how it will be affected	2			
Labor intensive	2			
Lack of control	2		1	3
More hits for patrons when searching the OPAC	2			
No local conventions	2		4	6
Problems with transfers	2			
Quality of records	1			
Too many differences in cataloging practices	1			
Updating required as title lists change	1			
Difficult to get adequate information for purchase	1			

TABLE IV.8. Do you catalog Web sites? (Answer derived from responses to other questions, especially II1, II4, IV2, IV2b8, IV8, IV8a.)

	YES	NO
ACADEMIC	25	29
JUNIOR	1	3
PUBLIC	3	4
TOTAL	29	36

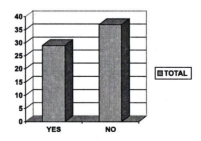

If yes:

TABLE IV.8a. Do you provide a separate catalog record for each Web site linked from the library's home page?

	YES	NO
ACADEMIC	2	37
JUNIOR	1	2
PUBLIC		6
TOTAL	3	45

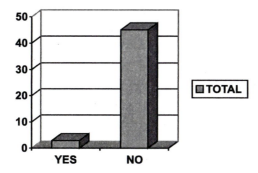

TABLE IV.9. Does your library issue "standard" call numbers to e-resources? (LC, Dewey, etc.)

	YES	NO
ACADEMIC	17	35
JUNIOR	1	4
PUBLIC	1	5
TOTAL	19	44

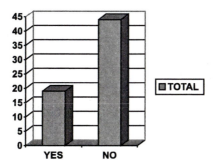

TABLE IV.10. Do you participate in any other program to catalog online materials?

	YES	NO
ACADEMIC	13	39
JUNIOR	1	3
PUBLIC		6
TOTAL	14	48

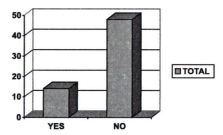

If yes:

TABLE IV.10a. What?

	ACADEMIC	JUNIOR	PUBLIC	TOTAL
BIOONE	1			1
CONSER	1			1
INTERCAT PROJECT WITH OCLC (became CORC)	1			1
OCLC CORC	3			3
OCLC	3			3
DIGITIZATION	2			2
RLIN	1			1
SHARED CATALOGING WITH OTHER LIBRARIES OR CONSORTIA	2	1		3

Survey

Collection Development and Cataloging of Online Resources:
What Libraries Are Doing Now

    I. Your Library
       1. Type of library
          a. Academic college or university

      b. Community/junior/two-year college
      c. Public library
   2. How many libraries/branches are part of your institution?
_____

   3. If academic, what is your enrollment? _____
   4. Please indicate the highest degree granted:
      a. Associate's
      b. Bachelor's degree
      c. Master's degree
      d. Doctor's degree
   5. If public, what is the service area population count? _____
   6. What ILS system do you use for
      a. Cataloging _____
      b. Acquisitions _____
      c. Serials _____
      d. OPAC _____
         Is your OPAC:
         a. Web version _____
         b. telnet version _____
      e. Circulation _____
II. Collection of Online Resources
    Definition of online resources: For the purposes of this survey, the term *online resources* refers to three categories of technology. The first category of resources is databases and their contents (including abstracts and indexes). The second category is full-text electronic journals and electronic documents (for example, ERIC documents or e-books). The third category is Web resources, which include Web sites and Web pages.
   1. What kind of online resources do you provide?

Type of Resource	Do You Provide Access?	
Databases	Y	N
E-journals	Y	N
Online documents	Y	N
(e.g., e-books, ERIC docs)	Y	N

Web sites or pages
   2. Has your library developed new collection development policies for online resources?   Y   N
   3. Does your library have separate criteria for collecting online and print resources?   Y   N
   4. Whose responsibility is it to collect online resources (circle all that apply):
      a. Librarian subject specialists
      b. Academic department faculty

    c. Electronic resources coordinator

    d. Committee

    e. Other (specify): _____

III. Online Resources

  1. Does your library use some method of validating users to access online resources (e.g., proxy server to provide access to remote users)? Y N

    If yes: What method? _____

    At what points does this validation occur?

    a. From library Web page

    b. From URLs in bibliographic records in the OPAC

    c. Other (explain): _____

  2. Do you have a link checker software program? Y N

    If yes: Which one? _____

  3. Who is responsible for maintaining the accuracy of the links?

    _____

  4. Realizing that most databases provide title lists of included e-journals, does your library provide an integrated online list of e-journals? Y N

    a. Where do you provide that list? _____

    b. What software do you use to produce the list? _____

    c. Do you include holdings with the titles? Y N

    d. Do you use a vendor? Y N

      (i.e., Serials Solutions, TDNet, Ask Jake [customized list])

    e. If yes, which vendor? _____

IV. Cataloging

  1. Do you subscribe to a service that provides and maintains a separate catalog for online resources (such as SIRSI's Library HQ)? Y N

    If yes:

    a. What service do you use? _____

    b. Are you satisfied with their service? Y N

    c. Is access restricted to selected groups of patrons? Y N

    d. If yes, who has access? _____

    e. Do you add bibliographic records for online resources to your online catalog? Y N

    f. If yes: Do you have a written policy or guidelines on what your library will catalog? Y N

    g. If yes: May we have a copy? Y N

    h. Which of the following criteria are things you consider when cataloging online resources?

       i. _____ Paid subscriptions (print, online, or both)

       ii. _____ Title is already in catalog in another format

       iii. _____ Bibliographic records are available from the vendor

    iv.   _____ Title is stable (i.e., library has a direct subscription)

    v.   _____ Free access (no ties to paid subscriptions)

    vi.   _____ Government documents

    vii.   _____ Created locally (online bibliographies, digital files, etc.)

    viii.   _____ Web sites

    ix.   _____ The link goes directly to the title

    x.   _____ For statistical purposes

    xi.   Have we covered all of your criteria? Y N

    xii.   If no, other criteria: _____

2. When you have a print and online version of the same journal title
   a. Do you provide links to the online version in the print bibliographic record (i.e., MARC 856 field)? Y N
   b. Do you catalog the online version on a separate bibliographic record? Y N

3. For online-only journal subscriptions (no print)
   a. Do you catalog the online version? Y N
   b. Do you provide access to the e-journal from the library's database links (i.e., library's Web page, specific database services, etc.)? Y N

4. If you have access to an online journal through several different databases
   a. Do you give all the access points on one record? Y N
   b. Do you provide a separate record for each access point? Y N
   c. Do you include the title coverage (holdings) information? Y N
   d. Do you include a generic note about coverage which can be used on many different records such as a "coverage varies" note or "check database for holdings" note? Y N

5. For e-books or e-documents
   a. Do you provide links to the online version in the print bibliographic record (i.e., MARC 856 field)? Y N
   b. Do you catalog the online version on a separate bibliographic record? Y N

6. For Databases
   a. Do you provide a separate catalog record for the database as a single entity? (i.e., EBSCOhost, JSTOR, Academic Universe, etc.) Y N
   b. Do you provide catalog records for e-journal titles included in databases to which the library subscribes? Y N
   c. Which of the following distinctions affect your decision to catalog the e-journals that are in a database?
      i.   The database is: stable/unstable?
      ii.   The titles provide: full coverage/partial coverage?

      iii. URLs: to journal title/to the host database?

      iv. Other: _____

  d. Do you acquire sets of catalog records for online resources from vendors such as Marcive, EBSCO, or OCLC? Y   N

     i. If yes, which ones?

     ii. What do you like about it?

    iii. What do you dislike about it?

7. For Web sites

  a. Do you provide a separate catalog record for each Web site linked from the library's home page? Y   N

8. Does your library issue "standard" call numbers to e-resources? (LC, Dewey, etc.) Y   N

9. Do you participate in any other program to catalog online materials? Y   N

Chapter 4

IP Ranges versus Passwords:
The Pros, the Cons,
and What's in Between

Lee Ann Howlett

In recent years, the avalanche of information available electronically has been both a blessing and a dilemma for librarians. Having so many resources, electronic and print, at our fingertips has forever changed the face of librarianship. However, accessing this information has become a rather tricky business. Even the most intrepid among us may begin to feel a bit like Dorothy in Oz, venturing along the yellow brick road—never knowing what may pop up next. Just when every possible set of "rules" for accessing e-journals has been learned, suddenly there comes another one—usually even more restrictive! Perhaps librarians have often wondered which class they missed in graduate school that might have qualified them to interpret the publisher's legalese and then enforce it after signing a license.

E-journals that require the use of passwords are nothing new. This was the usual method of access for most online resources after their Web sites were deemed ready for public use. Subsequently, the popularity of connecting via IP (Internet Protocol) address began to rise, particularly for e-journals that were grouped and sold together as part of an online database (often called aggregators). It was much easier to simply register the IP address(es) of one's computers at the time of online activation than to concern oneself with handling screen names and passwords for possibly several hundred titles. However, both of these methods—IP and password—present their own advantages and disadvantages, which are examined in this chapter.

PASSWORDS

E-journal access requiring passwords has always been better suited to individual subscribers than to libraries. One person can simply jot down this information for personal use and keep it close by the computer. Obviously, this is not a solution for librarians who must not only provide the information for authorized users but also keep this same information out of the hands of unauthorized users.

Small libraries (e.g., hospital libraries, which can have a fairly large user base) may just keep a "ready reference" list or file of screen names and passwords by the phone in circulation and/or reference. Identifying legitimate users of these databases should be the goal during any reference interview. When relaying passwords over the phone (a fairly common practice for those working the reference desk or in circulation on nights and weekends), there must be some way to ensure, as much as is humanly possible, that the person on the other end of the phone or e-mail is indeed an authorized user. Librarians in small libraries often know many of their patrons well enough so that it may not be necessary to request identification. However, new users do come along from time to time, so asking for a code or number from an ID card to check against a list of authorized users is certainly one way to accomplish this. It is true that there is no definitive way for librarians to prevent users from sharing passwords with friends who may or may not be authorized users. A few people who have no business gaining access may still manage to sneak a peek at restricted materials, but this would not be because libraries haven't taken proper precautions.

Medium- to large-size libraries, specifically ones in colleges and universities, often have online "sign-in" pages. The sign-in page may be located on the library's home page or may not appear until a user is attempting to access an e-journal from the public record in the library's online catalog. Utilizing the user name and personal password that patrons generally have for their school e-mail accounts, and/or a serial number from their ID cards, is probably the most popular method for this type of access. Patrons are then able to obtain access to e-journals that are available only through the password method.

Generally speaking, the fewer screens that users have to pass through, the better it is for them. A library sign-in program can also be created by someone within the library or the library's institution, in which any passwords are "scripted" into the URL. It helps to have either an information services/computer services librarian or a computer services department that can perform this function.

One method publishers can utilize to help prevent unauthorized access to an e-journal with a password account is to simply change the password regularly. This can be accomplished by the publisher or by the librarian in charge of administering electronic journals. If publishers insist on making the changes themselves, then they need to have a procedure in place to contact the librarian; an e-mail message will usually suffice. There have been instances of e-journals with passwords that are automatically set to expire after a certain amount of time and then, literally, prompt whoever logs in first to the e-journal's home page to make the change. Naturally, this is not the preferred method of change for a library—although some users would probably love it. For large libraries, this method would be a logistical nightmare. Records would have to be kept on each title requiring passwords, along with their expiration dates, and a librarian would have to be poised above the keyboard to ensure that he or she would be the first person to log in to make the change. Even a handful of these titles would be an anxiety-producing event, and dozens of these changes could turn into a marathon. If librarians, as the contact persons, are allowed to change the passwords when deemed necessary, they can always notify their patrons with a note in the online catalog on the journal's title record indicating that the password is changed (for example, on the first of each month). Although some patrons (and libraries) might not embrace the idea of changing passwords at first, they might find it more palatable when told that this is the only method currently available for remote online access.

Many of the e-journals that offer password identification are allowing this access due to the library's purchase of the same title in print. Because there is no extra charge for the online version, access to the online version is given as a courtesy. It has become common practice with many publishers either to include one-user access with the print subscription or to require that libraries purchase a site license to register all IP addresses for authorized users.

Most publishers will allow for the use of the same password and screen name for all of their titles that a library may own, but some publishers insist on different passwords and screen names for *each* title. This can be enough to cause otherwise reasonable librarians to reassess their career, even in a profession known for its often detailed and precise work methods. Juggling twenty different passwords for as many titles simply adds to the minutiae in which many librarians may feel they are already drowning. Thankfully, this practice is not the norm.

IP ACCESS

Access by IP address has its own set of advantages and problems. IP stands for "Internet Protocol," and every computer with online access has an IP number or address. Think of it as a zip code for the computer—unique to that particular machine. In the case of larger libraries or libraries within institutions, the IP addresses are often a set or sets of numbers that fall within borders or "ranges." Each IP address is actually a sequence of numbers in a set format, something like this: YYY.YYY.YY.YY.

For a brief explanation on how IPs work, a (very) simplified example would be a library that houses computers with IP addresses from 1 through 131. Each number signifies an address. The set of numbers that fall between these two numbers (1 and 131) are referred to as the range. Often institutions have more than just one range of IP addresses. This is particularly true for multicampus universities. Also, in some cases, the IP addresses are not static or fixed. Static IP addresses are just that—they do not move from computer to computer. In most libraries, computers are part of a network—they are all linked into one system. In this case, they may have "floating" IP addresses. Whenever one of the networked machines is used, the system pulls an available IP address from the library's range of addresses for that particular session. This is usually not a problem unless a publisher restricts access to a specific number of computers and requests the IP addresses for those individual machines. It is not possible to simply extract, for example, three IP addresses in order to access a particular e-journal when there is no way of knowing which computers will be connecting from those particular addresses at any given time.

No discussion of IP addresses can be addressed without mention of the dreaded, and basically useless, example of single IP address access. Some libraries don't even bother to activate online access to a title that can be viewed from just one IP address. Even when it is possible to designate a computer in the library for this purpose, it is usually not practical to do so. Not only can there be no access outside the physical library building, but other problems also arise, such as, "How do we let patrons know that *this* computer is the only one on which they can view title X?" Of course, signs can always be placed around the computer/workstation, but then the location must also be noted on the public viewing record of the library's online catalog. A direct link for the title added to the record will be useless unless the patron is working from the computer with the designated IP. This may be less of a problem for small libraries with only two or three computers for patron use. However, when larger libraries are involved, limited or fixed IP access is almost an impossibility.

Publishers do have it within their power to limit unauthorized access without resorting to the use of the "one IP only" rule. They can simply restrict the number of simultaneous users (and many of them, in fact, do). Whether access is by password or IP address, if only one, two, three, etc., users at any one time are allowed to view the e-journal, the Web site won't be likely to be bombarded by unauthorized persons. Also, by changing the password periodically (whether by librarians or the publisher), it is less likely that the password will end up being posted on a student's Web page.

Proxy IP

Adding another dimension to the IP method is the use of "proxy" IP addresses. The proxy system is used frequently by university and college libraries around the world. Generally, students, faculty, and staff are encouraged to set up access to the library's resources using the institution's server as their Internet service provider (ISP). This way, whenever they log in to their university account from home, the server recognizes the IP address and allows access just as though they were connecting from a computer on campus. However, with the popularity of commercial services such as America Online (AOL) and/or high-speed access with services such as cable modems or DSLs, many users do not want to have to wait for the often slower access offered by the school's server. This is where proxy IP addresses enter the picture. A proxy IP address is simply one more number (or range of numbers) on the institution's server that a patron's computer must connect through in order to gain online access to restricted resources.

Proxy access allows the system to recognize the user's computer when it connects. Patrons may use their own ISP if they access the institution's resources through the proxy IP. Libraries generally provide information regarding proxy use for authorized users on their home pages. Setting up access by proxy is usually a fairly simple matter of changing a few settings in the Web browser (or when accessing the proxy server, to be prompted for an ID number). Besides the actual instructions, libraries can post an offer of assistance by phone during regular business hours and on their Web page to guide proxy users. Proxy software programs are also available for purchase by institutions that make it even easier for people to set up their computers and get connected.

However, for the librarian, the proxy IP is one more address that must be submitted on the e-journal Web site when activating online subscriptions. Also, some publishers will not allow access by proxy even though they will accept all of the library's other IP addresses or ranges for "physical" addresses. The major reason for this is the possibility that unauthorized users, who have gained the information for setting up the proxy address illicitly (perhaps from a borrowed or stolen ID card), could tap into resources that they are not legally entitled to use. Unlike passwords, which can be changed, this could actually be a more serious problem for publishers attempting to keep as many paid subscribers as possible. Of course, without proxy access, a frustrated cry of "I can't get into this journal from home!" is sure to be heard from users. Unfortunately, this is when librarians may be able only to commiserate with their patrons, saying to them, "Yes, I agree—it's unfair" and "I would change the rule if I could." Finally, when all else fails, one can always blame the publisher for the access problems.

Publisher License Restrictions

In addition, there are the always "interesting" and varied stipulations in the licensing agreements of e-journals allowing access by IP address. It is not unusual for a publisher to require that an e-journal be viewed by patrons in only *one* city. There are, of course, variations on this theme—one geographic location only, one campus location only, etc. The designated city is generally the one where the library with the print subscription is located. This is a common problem for libraries in institutions that have multisite libraries and share one online catalog. A note on the public record for the journal stating that electronic access is restricted to users in that city due to "publisher's licensing restrictions" is one way to handle this. Of course, the librarian will still hear complaints from patrons who may use the library in the specified city but commute from a town nearby. In state/city/county institutions, this situation is usually followed by patrons exhorting that, "I'm a taxpayer! I helped pay for this! Why can't I see it?" or "I'm a student/faculty member/staff member here! All of the materials owned by this library should be open to me!"

Explaining that the library must purchase a site license in order for all of the libraries in the system to access the material online may mollify some patrons. Often the reason for this is budgetary constraints, as purchasing site licenses can frequently be very expensive. Once this is explained to most people in terms of dollar amounts, they are usually more understanding. They may even be motivated to write their legislators, city council members, the governor, etc., to ask for more funding for the library. Having another advocate in the librarians' corner never hurts!

IP AND PASSWORD!

Whether publishers use password or IP access is one issue; however, it can really become interesting when they decide to use a combination of both methods. A number of popular weekly journals that were available via IP address through packaged databases decided to place an "embargo" on their most recent issues.[1] Because of this, patrons were only able to view the full text contents of these titles for issues that were anywhere from six to eight weeks old. To view the current issues, librarians had to register each title from the e-journal's home page and assign a password for access. This method allowed patrons to see the most current issues. So there was password access for the most recent issues and IP access for all issues six to eight weeks old or older. Once the fields and notes for both types of access are added to the journal record, all librarians can do is hope that people will actually read all of this information—no matter how brief it may be. There seems to be an opinion among some publishers that since these popular weeklies are frequently read for their current content, IP access may be allowing some nonpaying customers access to the more highly desired articles. People may be more likely to cancel their personal subscriptions and less likely to make an impulse purchase from the news rack at the grocery store or the local newsstand when they can read that cover story directly from their computers. Although this may be true, it certainly doesn't make librarians' lives any easier.

It is also not unusual to encounter a license which specifies that online use is limited to the IP addresses assigned to computers physically *in* the buildings of the section of the campus where the library resides. This means no online access for authorized users whose offices may be in a building on the other side of the campus. This also can create some very unhappy patrons, and rightly so. Of all of the conditions that have been put forth in license agreements, this can be one of the most frustrating. Once again, people find themselves tied physically to the library, defeating the aims of libraries that are attempting to establish a virtual collection.

PASSWORD ADVANTAGES

Even though IP access is the preferred route, there are some advantages in the use of passwords over IP addresses. Authorized users who find themselves logging in from a remote site such as a conference or meeting may still access the e-journal. As long as they are able to officially log in to their institution's library through some type of in-house method (e.g., their e-mail account information), they can view the password for the e-journal they wish to access (or the password can be scripted into the URL). When access is through IP only, the library's server will not recognize the foreign IP address and will simply deny entry. Proxy access *may not* be a viable alternative here, either, since it involves changing browser settings. When computers are set up for a group of varied users, such as conference attendees, modifying the browser might be frowned upon. Password access does allow the user to view the desired material even if the computer settings have been locked in to prevent changes.

Password access is also a widely used method for people who may be members of an association that publishes a journal which has online access. Since many faculty members of colleges and universities belong to various organizations, they often have personal online accounts to the publication and/or services offered on a particular site. The same can be said of libraries that have an associate membership of some kind with the organization that distributes the journal. Password access is usually part of the membership, and the rules for use are generally the same as for an individual member. Occasionally, an association may give the choice of password or one IP address access. For an individual user, registering the IP address of an office or home computer may be fine. However, the single IP address method simply doesn't work for libraries. Site registration that either assigns or allows the user to select a password is still the best way to ensure ease of use and, of course, mobility. The use of passwords is far preferable to the limitations imposed by a static IP address.

It should be noted that there are also libraries with networked computers that, for various reasons, are not able to use the IP method. In their case, passwords may be the only feasible method to gain access to their e-journals. However, there are many publishers and aggregators that will accept *only* IP access. This creates a very difficult situation for libraries that are willing and able to pay for online subscriptions but are then faced with a brick wall when publishers will not budge regarding their "IP-only" rule. This is definitely an example of an area in which publishers could be more flexible in dealing with various types of libraries. Although most academic libraries prefer IP access only, if, for example, an institution's network does not allow exclusive IP addresses for its various sites, then librarians cannot provide a range or ranges restricted to their particular site. This is mostly a problem for multicampus institutions, particularly those located in different cities. The institution's network may not have separate pools of IP addresses for each campus. If a publisher's site license is restricted to one site or one city only (as many are), the librarian may not be able to provide a range of IPs restricted to a single site. When a multisite university's network consists of one range of floating IP addresses covering all sites, the library may be unable to meet the terms of a publisher's license agreement. In a case such as this, password access may be the only alternative, so cooperation from publishers would be a necessity. Considering the percentage of a library's budget that is spent on print and e-journals (specifically academic libraries) and the effort that most librarians make to safeguard online access to authorized users only, a little leeway would be much appreciated.

ACCESS THROUGH AGGREGATORS

By now, it is rather obvious that there are few standards or established rules regarding the licensing restrictions of e-journals, although attempts have been made at writing boilerplate license models. Since publishers own the content, they are able, to a large degree, to make the rules. Publishing is a business and, for the majority of publishers, the bottom line is profit. Standards that one publisher may agree to, another publisher (particularly some of the smaller ones) might object to for financial reasons. For example, it is easier to sympathize with the smaller publishers who may not have the economic resources needed to set up an IP-based Web site or to guarantee archiving for their e-journals. However, some regulation in this area is desperately needed by the library community. This is probably one of the biggest advantages of purchasing aggregators. If the aggregator is actually a publisher deciding to offer some or all of their e-journals as a package, then the same license agreement applies to each and every title. The same can be said of aggregators that are established strictly for the purpose of acting as a portal to a group of e-journals. Often the aggregator is not produced by the original publisher but by a middleman vendor instead, and the e-journals that are a part of the database are from various other sources. In this case, the license agreement for the aggregator would apply to all of the e-journal titles they offer. Since the e-journals are from different publishers, this does offer the librarian some sense of order in setting up the titles in the library catalog without having to read the license agreement of each and every participating publisher.

Dealing with aggregators or other package deals from publishers does have an impact on the librarian's ability to carefully cultivate and develop the library's collection. E-journal packages often contain a fair amount of chaff along with the wheat, and ideally a library doesn't want to pay for material that may be out of a particular institution's scope and that never would have been selected under ordinary circumstances. There is no doubt, however, that the ability to set up access to hundreds of titles with one license agreement is a time-saver. Since these databases are almost always IP based, with the librarian permitted to establish connections to as many IP addresses as necessary, there are fewer problems with user access as well.

LIBRARIANS MAKE A DIFFERENCE

Despite the complications that abound in dealing with e-journals, librarians do have a voice and they *can* make a difference—sometimes it's just a matter of how loud they yell and how many of them are willing to storm the publishers with lit torches and pitchforks. A situation occurred recently in which a prominent (and very popular) weekly medical e-journal was going to switch from password access to IP access.[2] Normally this news would have been met with a joyous reaction from most librarians; however, the society that published the e-journal in question decided to require libraries to supply anywhere from one to five static IP addresses and, further, these IP addresses would have had to be from computers physically *within* the library. Of course, this raised a plethora of problems and questions for librarians. In larger libraries, such as the medium-sized medical school library in which the author works, floating IP addresses are utilized. There are very few static addresses in the entire library, and they are usually reserved for specific staff machines used for maintenance purposes. Even if it were possible to assign static IP addresses to specific computers, this method would eliminate the basic reason that most patrons want electronic access. Patrons want to be able to browse/read/print the material from their home and/or office. Otherwise, this means a trip to the library, which, of course, negates the biggest advantage of electronic journals over print. Without remote access, most people don't care *how* many computers allow them to view the e-journal in the library.

After an outcry from librarians all over the country, this publisher decided that libraries could have a choice of using the five static IP addresses or continuing with the password method. (This wasn't ideal but was certainly better than a single IP.) The original reason for this particular publisher's desire to limit access is understandable. Apparently, some libraries were actually posting the password on their Web sites or on the title record in their online catalogs, so security was very lax, and users were passing it along to other users through e-mail, word of mouth, etc. The traffic that this generated on the e-journal's Web site demonstrated to the publisher that it might be experiencing a financial loss in this situation. After all, some of these users may have been potential paying customers if they had been unable to access the material so easily at no cost. Although loss of revenue is certainly a legitimate concern for publishers, they must find ways to work together with librarians to ensure full access for authorized users. Otherwise, problems with viewing the online title might be so great as to raise questions regarding whether it is really worth the time and effort involved when the print journal *is* sitting on a shelf in the library.

Ideally, online access is fast, convenient, and inexpensive for the user. The e-journal issues are almost always there when needed (although, in this imperfect world, some access interruptions are bound to occur). Users can make their own copies from their printers, which for them also means no more digging in pockets for change or having to purchase a debit card for photocopy purposes. The hours, rules, and regulations of the library and the distance to it are moot points. If patrons want to perform research and reading activities at three o'clock in the morning while eating a pizza, stark naked, then that is their prerogative. (There *are* some things the librarians would rather not know.)

FUTURE OF PASSWORD AND IP ACCESS

Will IP access ever completely replace password access? Probably not in the near future. Smaller publishers, along with associations that produce journals, usually do not have the personnel or computer equipment to handle direct access to their material. They may be outsourcing the work of setting up home pages for e-journal access, along with the updating of the site, addition of new issues, and maintaining the site while dealing with everyday glitches. Archiving is another issue that must be handled reliably. It is certainly easier at this time for these publishers to use the password method for access. This may also be why some of the journals offering password access to their online version do so in conjunction with a print subscription. Often they don't offer an online-only subscription because they can't guarantee archival access.

If a library cancels a print subscription in favor of the online version, which is increasingly desired now by both libraries and publishers, they need to be assured that five years into the future, if they should decide to cancel this same title, they would have online archival access to the five years that they purchased. (Remember, in this situation, those five years *would not* also be available in the library in print form.) Libraries must be assured they will receive guaranteed archival ownership/access along with reliable online service in order to build a successful virtual collection. This is the ultimate goal of both libraries and publishers. Libraries would save the cost of binding and the staff time necessary to check in, process, and shelve journal issues, and publishers would certainly save on printing and mailing costs.

IP access for all titles is the ideal method for the majority of librarians dealing with e-journals. The subscriptions are easier to set up, maintain, and troubleshoot. The use of passwords will continue to lag behind as a distant second choice, only superior to the dreaded static-IP method. However, as long as individual publishers continue to determine which type of access they wish to employ, librarians must continue to deal with the various rules, stipulations, license agreements, etc., that often seem to rain down upon them. Librarians must also continue to make their voices heard if they expect to bring about any changes in the choices (or lack thereof) that they have now. Because there are so few, if any, rules governing e-journals, efforts must be made on both sides, libraries and publishers, in order to deliver the information to its intended audience in a smooth and timely fashion.

Publishers need to offer more options for access in order to assist libraries in situations where their methods to connect to e-journals are limited. If librarians cannot obtain standardized guidelines, they would at least like to have more options. This is the only real advantage to the current situation of everyone making their own set of rules. It should not be that difficult to assist librarians in tailoring access to e-journals to fit the needs, limitations, and/or restrictions of their libraries. IP access is the overwhelming favorite, but, whether by IP or password, librarians still have to deliver the goods!

NOTES

1. Bell, Steven J. "The New Digital Divide: Dissecting Aggregator Exclusivity Deals." *D-Lib Magazine,* July/August 2001. Available at <http://www.dlib.org/dlib/july01/bell/07bell.html>.

2. Welch, Eileen. "Important Notice to NEJM Institutional Subscription Administrators." Online posting. NEJMINST-L@LISTSERV. August 23, 2001. *The New England Journal of Medicine.* Available at <http://library.med.cornell.edu/Library/HTML/notification.html>.

Chapter 5

Consortia and Electronic Journals: An Overview

Miriam Childs
Wil Weston

The decade of the 1990s turned out to be a period of extreme upheaval and transition for academic libraries, which underwent budget crises that prevented the direct acquisition of expensive digital products. These were commercially available products that often featured full-text electronic versions of scholarly journals. The only way that libraries could afford to offer these resources to their users was through cooperative efforts in the form of consortia. Libraries across the globe now consider membership in a consortium to be a way of life because of the proven benefits to users and the improvements in service to users and libraries.[1]

It can be said that the most important development in recent times for academic libraries has been "the move from organizational self-sufficiency to a collaborative survival mode as personified by the growth of library consortia."[2] Consortia are basically a means for libraries to reduce costs and to publicly demonstrate efforts to increase services to users, as well as to the broader community.[3] The Internet, the World Wide Web, and other distributed information systems have enabled resource sharing among libraries in ways that were not possible in the past.[4] This "rapid emergence and development of electronic information technologies" makes it possible to imagine "different ways of organizing collections and services that libraries have traditionally provided."[5] Through consortia, libraries have been able to effect many positive changes in their environment, but there are also some negative aspects that bear examination.

THE IMPETUS TO COOPERATE

What do consortia offer that makes joining or forming them so desirable? Cost reduction, more specifically the "unit cost of providing core services," is a primary benefit gained from consortial membership.[6] The continual erosion or stagnation of library funding coupled with an exponential increase in material and information costs have given libraries a strong interest in reducing their operating costs.[7] Resource sharing, a common consortial activity, is one way that libraries attempt to reduce expenditures. Sharing resources, especially electronic resources, has become a necessity due to libraries' decreasing ability to develop "independent collections of excellence."[8] As libraries in consortia have discovered, the group has "a combined set of resources that is greater than the resources of a single member."[9] Because of high material costs, especially for periodical subscriptions, libraries are interested in getting more bang for the buck out of their budgetary expenditures. Membership in a consortium allows a group of libraries to "pool their financial resources to leverage greater control over their marketplaces."[10]

A second benefit for libraries that join consortia is the ability to improve the quality of services offered to their patrons by enhancing collections and by increasing access to information.[11] There is a general feeling within the profession that no one library can be large enough to house all of the needed resources anymore.[12] Years of decreasing materials budgets have left institutions without all of the information resources they need. Faced with such a hurdle, libraries are perceiving a need to enhance their in-house collections, and so "must increase the delivery of information if they are to succeed."[13] Consortia use the ability of the group to purchase costly information products, enabling member libraries to increase patron access to information by enhancing and increasing resources that would otherwise be unavailable to their users.

Historically, libraries have joined or formed consortia because of geographic proximity, in order to create and share union catalogs, for reciprocal borrowing privileges between member libraries, and sometimes for cooperative collection development programs.[14,15] As libraries were introduced to various technologies, such as expensive audiovisual equipment and computers, they joined groups to help make sense of how to incorporate these resources into library operations.[16] The historical development of consortia in the United States will be examined in greater depth in the following section.

HISTORY OF COOPERATION AND CONSORTIA

Libraries cooperated with one another long before the practice was documented. The concept of the word "'consortium' as 'association or partnership' has long been a tenet of librarianship, generally encompassed in the terms 'cooperation,' 'coordination,' and 'collaboration.'"[17] Documentary evidence of interlibrary cooperation in the United States dates from the beginning of professional librarianship in America.[18] The then newly formed American Library Association created a Committee on Cooperation in Indexing and Cataloguing College Libraries in 1876, and during the following decade, the *ALA Bulletin* regularly featured its reports.[19] Articles on the subject of cooperation were published as far back as 1879.[20] By the 1890s, "major national programs of academic library cooperation" had begun in earnest.[21] These programs involved shared cataloging or interlibrary loan initiatives. The ALA, for example, started publishing "analytic cards as part of a shared indexing/cataloging program" in 1898.[22] Library of Congress subject headings appeared in the early 1900s as the first nationwide subject classification system, and the Library of Congress also "began to provide cataloging for participating libraries" during this period.[23] By the turn of the twentieth century, interlibrary lending "emerged as a focal point of library cooperation."[24]

Cooperative efforts continued to grow during the pre–World War II years. The 1930s witnessed some of the first instances of cooperative practices that in later decades became commonplace. Union card catalog production greatly increased in libraries across the nation.[25] Other cooperative efforts involved collection development, cataloging, and the first regional consortial arrangements. The Oregon State Board of Higher Education in 1932 unified the state's academic libraries under its control, appointing one director over the entire system. The board also "established programs for reciprocal borrowing and central ordering."[26] The Program for Cooperative Cataloging appeared in 1932, growing to include almost 400 American and Canadian libraries in less than ten years.[27] The earliest academic consortia, such as the Cooperating Libraries of Upper New York (CLUNY) and the Atlanta University Center corporation, formed in the first half of the 1930s.[28]

The post–World War II era, with the expansion of higher education and the explosion of scientific research, provided fertile ground for new ways of cooperation to emerge. The cooperative efforts that developed during this somewhat heady time became more formal, extensive, and expensive than previous efforts. The Universal Serial and Book Exchange (USBE), the Center for Research Libraries (CRL), the Farmington Plan for "cooperative foreign acquisitions," and the Latin American Cooperative Acquisitions Program (LACAP) were postwar programs that demonstrated this new scope.[29] However, the coming onset of the information age, which arguably had its roots in postwar America, would soon begin to monumentally affect libraries across the country.

By the 1960s, the Department of Defense and industry giants such as IBM were utilizing supercomputers and networks (ARPANet) for research and data management.[30] The first efforts toward library automation began in this decade, as libraries realized the effectiveness of using computers to manage data.[31] Computers soon were put to use in libraries as tools for bibliographic processing and database searching.[32] Libraries began to seek advice from one another about these new tools and formed or joined existing consortia to share their automation expertise.[33] The reasons for joining consortia in the previous decades continued to remain relevant, and the number of consortia in the country rapidly increased throughout the 1960s and into the 1970s. This virtually nonstop growth "illustrates that the consortium was an attractive solution to many institutions addressing a number of longstanding (as well as new) processes and problems."[34] It is not surprising then, that the term *consortium* began to appear in library and education literature during this era.[35]

In 1970, the United States Office of Education commissioned a landmark study of academic consortia. The study was conducted in response to a lack of available information about library consortia, in recognition of the increasing significance of consortia to everyday library operations. Out of the study came two reference sources, *The Directory of Academic Library Consortia* and Ruth J. Patrick's *Guidelines for Library Cooperation: Development of Academic Library Consortia.*[36]

Consortia in the 1970s adopted a network model, utilizing the computer networks that had multiplied in the previous decade.[37] The development of online, networked union catalogs frequently served as the catalyst for the formation of consortia in this period.[38] Early networks were usually geographically based, served multiple states and types of libraries, and brokered bibliographic services for their member libraries.[39]

The most important factor that influenced library cooperation in the 1970s was the development of "megaconsortia," also known as bibliographic utilities, such as the Ohio College Library Center (OCLC), the Research Libraries Group (RLG), and the Washington Library Network (WLN).[40] Megaconsortia were really "outgrowths of those activities for which library consortia had been formed up through the early 1970s," and they featured cataloging and inter-library loan components.[41] As libraries began implementing locally integrated systems, participation in one of these utilities became "'mission critical'—not just from catalog card production and inter-library loan activities, but increasingly as the source for machine-readable records to be loaded into local systems."[42] With this intense focus on internal changes, interest in cooperating and sharing with other libraries decreased somewhat.[43]

During the 1980s, the decline in adequate library funding caused libraries to think twice about involving themselves and their re-sources in consortia. Bibliographic utilities provided services that had been partially fulfilled in the past by cooperating with other li-braries. This circling of the wagons, however, was fairly short-lived, as in the late 1980s and early 1990s there was a resurgence of cooper-ative efforts due to the "confluence of several technological, fiscal, organizational, political," and other factors.[44] The pace of consortial activity quickened when libraries "were forced to confront an un-precedented array of challenges, including rising user demands, an escalating number of publications, hyperinflation in the prices of many scholarly journals, and rapid technological change."[45] The 1990s proved to be a pivotal decade in the development of consortia, with the "proliferation of network-based electronic resources," in-cluding indexing and abstracting databases and full-text electronic journals.[46]

The newer consortia exploited the "advances in information tech-nology" and "developed as strategic partnerships," with different purposes from the networks of the past.[47] The main aspect of contemporary consortia that make them different from their predecessors is the rapid growth of the World Wide Web and the development of Web-based information resources that are not only expensive but also very desirable. These new alliances often base themselves on "identifying and addressing common needs arising from development[s] in information technology."[48] Due to more sophistication in networking, modern consortia have begun to "meet specialized needs of specific types of libraries" and are sometimes geographically limited to one state or may be located in multiple states with a focused membership and community of interest.[49]

Cooperative efforts now focus on providing electronic resources (especially journals) to users, sharing resources through virtual union catalogs, and providing document delivery services.[50] Contemporary consortia have been quite effective at acting as agents "on behalf of member libraries to seek a reduced group purchase price for information . . . that is lower than that which any one institution could achieve alone."[51] As stated, these efforts lead to collection enhancement, improved patron service, and greater user access to information.

However, consortia are not merely "buying clubs." They have the potential to affect the "future as to how information will be created, marketed, and purchased by libraries."[52] With their collective power, contemporary consortia seek to "have an effect upon the national and international agendas concerning issues such as pricing policies and copyright laws" and certainly to "bring pressure to bear upon information providers (particularly commercial publishers) to reduce the rate of rise in the cost of information, and to bring down the cost of information."[53]

DESCRIPTION OF A CONSORTIUM:
OhioLINK

OhioLINK fully demonstrates the benefits of membership in a modern consortium. OhioLINK is a shared, statewide network that includes more than seventy public and private higher education institutions.[54] Funded by the Ohio State Board of Regents, it provides for its member libraries a central catalog, "individual library-based systems using the same hardware and software, a library-to-library delivery system, and centrally supported databases and full-text resources."[55]

The central catalog allows patrons to initiate loans of resources from other libraries. Member libraries may also take advantage of "opportunities for strategic alliances," such as digital library and cooperative lending services.[56]

Originally an effort to control new library construction by setting up a regional storage facility, OhioLINK formed in the late 1980s "under the aegis of the Ohio Board of Regents as a way to foster interlibrary cooperation."[57] Then, the concept grew to include the sharing of materials through a central library system, with a centralized union catalog on a common vendor platform as the first consortial product.[58] Users could initiate loans of materials from member libraries through this platform.[59]

A governing board runs OhioLINK, along with a council that includes the member library directors and four subcommittees that report to the council. As a cooperative organization, its agenda is set mainly by library directors, other chief academic officers, and staff.[60] The four library-based committees develop policies and practices that the governing board reviews.[61]

In addition to the centralized catalog and interlibrary loan services, OhioLINK provides electronic resources to its members. The consortium is renowned for its ability to leverage its collective weight "for the purpose of providing as many electronic resources as possible at the lowest negotiable price."[62] The group discounts that OhioLINK receives from vendors mean that expensive databases can be purchased at a "cost far lower than if each institution has to buy them separately."[63] Ultimately, the state saves valuable operating dollars and, in the process, a resource is created that is "greater than the sum of its parts."[64] Tom Sanville, the director of OhioLINK, avers that the "objective is not saving money per se but making our expenditures more cost effective while raising the standards for information accessibility."[65] Member institutions are not required to pay for the centrally funded resources, but they may contribute to a "war chest" that is used to purchase other resources.[66] This commitment to increasing access to information raises the level of service at each member library, which is able to provide through the consortia what would not be possible otherwise.[67]

Currently, OhioLINK provides access to more than ninety research databases, over 2,500 electronic journals, and a digital media center. Its Electronic Journal Center (EJC) contains the complete electronic journal collections of Elsevier Science's ScienceDirect OnSite, Academic Press, Project MUSE, Kluwer Academic, Springer-Verlag, and the American Physical Society. This resource has been successful beyond expectations, with "over 450,000 articles down-loaded" within the first seventeen months alone. More than half of the articles were from journals not originally held by the requesting insti-tution.[68] This high usage demonstrates that "students and faculty are employing previously unavailable electronic citations and full-text at unprecedented levels."[69]

SUPPORT FOR CONSORTIA

Support for consortia can come in several forms, the most obvious being financial support. However, a less obvious source of support is organizations, such as the International Coalition of Library Consor-tia (ICOLC). The ICOLC is an informal group with members from all over the world. Twice a year, meetings of the ICOLC provide oppor-tunities for consortia and vendors to discuss different ways of acquir-ing materials. More important, ICOLC provides the opportunity for all members to hear one another's concerns. For the ever-evolving re-lationship of consortia and vendors, the opportunity for support and understanding exists.

The position of the ICOLC is clearly stated in their "Statement on Electronic Information": "Publishers today increasingly act globally to provide electronic information, and it is incumbent upon libraries to act globally to express their market positions on the pricing and other terms and conditions related to the purchase of that informa-tion."[70] The prevalence of electronic resources has grown dramati-cally over the last few years. They have replaced the printed index and the printed journal in many instances. The ICOLC's mission and guidelines will hopefully make this transition a smooth one for both vendors and library consortia alike.

So, where does the money come from that is used to support con-sortia? Often it depends on the type of consortia, and these can vary wildly. This wide range runs "on a continuum from highly decentral-ized organizations to highly centralized ones."[71] Every consortia is established according to its own values, objectives, and political real-ities. The type of funding for each consortium depends on its own agenda, how it was created, and how it is managed. The following types of consortia lend an overall understanding of the comparative differences; however, these generalizations obviously cannot apply in all cases.[72]

The first type is the *loose federation,* which is the most common form of membership and is usually governed by member libraries or by a sponsor with a group chaired by a member.[73] There is typically no consortial funding source; thus, there is little risk or investment, but it may yield some minimal benefit.

The second type is the *multitype/multistate network,* which has a separate governing board elected by its members. The multitype is formally incorporated and has a dedicated staff employed by the network. Its funding is received through membership fees and/or through charges for services provided.[74] For instance, Southeastern Library Network (SOLINET), a regional membership network, provides centralized accounting, billing, and consulting services for licensing activities in its region.

The third form, the *tightly knit federation,* has a highly select membership; for example, it may be limited only to research libraries or to statewide libraries. The federation also has a dedicated staff, like the multitype, that coordinates the program. The funding for this type of consortia comes from the participating institutions but is sometimes supplemented by foundation or grant funding. The programs are typically flexible, but vendors often limit discounts.

The final general type is the *centrally funded statewide consortium* which is restricted to state colleges and universities within a particular state. The consortium reports to a state agency but may have its own governing board.[75] The consortium receives state funding which is usually enhanced by participating institutions, and some external funding. A dedicated staff is available to further the consortium's agenda, but the administration may dictate the agenda and policies.

Obtaining support and funding for consortia can be a daunting task. Overcoming political and historical problems, lack of sponsorship, and external support in the face of dramatic changes occurring in higher education, academic libraries, and scholarly publishing can prove to be a difficult endeavor, to say the least. Yet it is for these reasons that consortia often are a viable option and a way to guarantee future success. "Where does the money come from?" is a valid question; ultimately, it will depend upon the institutions, the state, and the consortia to answer it, given their own agenda and individual requirements.

CONSORTIA: WHAT WORKS

Historically, the reason for forming a consortium is to combine institutional buying power in order to receive better prices. This concept of consortia as just a "buying club," as Sharon Bostick phrases it, has evolved, and consortia are becoming an increasingly important part of the library culture, particularly because the costs of library collections and services have soared.[76] Thus, buying power does remain one of the foremost reasons for establishing a consortium.

In regard to cost, this is usually a win-win situation for both the consortia and the publisher. By offering publishers the opportunity to sell to a large organized group, businesses can save on marketing and administrative costs. The publishers are also able to include more specialized titles by packaging them with higher-demand journals.[77] This means that individual libraries, in turn, not only get a lower price for journals but may also gain access to previously unaffordable titles.

A large part of the consortium's buying power is derived from its ability to negotiate license agreements. This negotiating power is especially important in regard to electronic journals. It is not only the access to these journals that the consortia manages but also the support services that the consortia negotiates. Consortia need

> easy-to-mount Web-based publications. And consortia need publishers and vendors who can give them lots of help. Consortia want to refer staff at member libraries to readily available technical and reference help. They want title lists of the contents of each database and discussion lists through which librarians can keep current on the changes. . . . They want support for distance education students. Consortial offerings must meet the needs of varied libraries.[78]

For a consortium, cost and discount may be the starting criterion but are often not the determining factor in the negotiating process.

Another positive aspect of consortial agreements for electronic journals is increased access. Better access means greater use and better circulation of information, which in an academic setting is crucial. The ability of the library user to research and read remotely from a home computer, office, or laboratory is an extremely effective service that meets the challenges of academia's newfound technological speed and demand of efficiency. In addition, this greatly empowers the growing nontraditional student population in our universities, who usually are holding full-time jobs and are more likely to be distance-education students.

It is this ease of access to resources through technology that the consortia can, if properly empowered, best mediate. The rapidly changing landscape of technology, and particularly the nature of information itself, makes the formation of library consortia more attractive. Electronic journals, a large part of this evolving structure of information, demand new, large-scale solutions that consortial policy and licensing may be able to ameliorate.

The intellectual property rights issue lies behind many of these problems, including journal pricing, database pricing, bundling of print and electronic versions, access, and licensing. Perhaps the most far-reaching impact is the disenfranchisement of scholarly authors and the users of their research. Through broader access by libraries, consortia may alleviate some of these vigorously contended issues and prompt research institutions to take responsibility for hosting and archiving published research in perpetuity. This, in turn, may encourage research institutions to recognize the Web as a valid medium for scholarly publication. Consortia are in a position to exploit these possible changes by establishing a workable model for online publication, ensuring a solid infrastructure, and protecting document delivery. Having said all of this, in general most librarians agree that the advantages of electronic journals outweigh their disadvantages; however, the decision to purchase journals under the umbrella of a consortium should be made on a case-by-case basis.

CONSORTIA: E-JOURNAL PROBLEMS

The positive aspects of membership in consortia, including access to digital information, resource sharing, shared virtual catalogs, and automation, are all tangible benefits.[79] However, Sanville warns that membership in a consortium has "prerequisite underpinnings, which, if not met, will lead to limited benefits if not outright dissatisfaction."[80] Some of the difficulties stem from the consensus-building process for making decisions about resources and policies. The greater the number of participating libraries, the greater the chance that there will be conflicting priorities and agendas.[81] The shared agenda that a consortium develops should be "sensitive and responsive to a wide variety of perceived needs."[82] All parties must be in agreement, with a "consistent, collective commitment" each year, or the economy of the group license could be endangered.[83] Necessary group commitments require individual libraries to give up a certain portion of their budgets for the common good. Though institutions recognize the value of cooperation, the autonomy of the individual library can be hard to overcome.[84]

Since a portion of a library's budget is set aside for consortial expenditures, libraries often find that there are fewer "discretionary funds to spend at the local level."[85] To cover the costs of consortial resources, monograph funds may need to be reallocated and/or periodical titles canceled.[86] Local resources that are deemed to be of greater value than resources provided through consortia may have to be eliminated when there is less money in the budget for local spending.[87] In this situation, selectors have less control over how funds are spent at their institution, thereby diminishing their influence in shaping the local collection.[88] The effect in libraries with smaller budgets is proportionally multiplied.[89]

Cleveland State University, an OhioLINK member, is a case in point. The success of purchasing electronic resources for the consortia, using public funds and funds from the central consortium office, led to the possibility of purchasing more resources. The consortium looked for other ways to fund these acquisitions. When the Electronic Journal Collection was purchased, OhioLINK decided to charge back costs to member libraries, based on what each library held in paper subscriptions. This formula was fixed in time with no opportunity to change it based on future cancellations. The university found that each year this fixed amount dedicated to electronic journals increased, going from 1 percent in fiscal year (FY) 1997 to 17 percent in FY 2000. The projected impact for FY 2001 was 23 percent, but only if no new electronic resources were purchased at the consortial level.[90]

All libraries have some sort of perceived historical social and cultural values that inform local selection decisions, and many historically selected periodicals have a basis in this "cultural capital."[91] Some licenses for electronic journal products limit the cancellation of print versions, so titles that are not digitized by vendors become vulnerable.[92] If these titles are of historical value to the institution, then providing access to "titles of unknown worth" that a library may neither need nor want is accomplished at the cost of canceling those with perceived value.[93] Since it seems that in this manner, journal retention decisions could be "taken out of the hands of individual librarians and their institutions," librarians should be vigilant to hold on to the "power to select journal literature at the journal title level."[94]

Digital collections, being overwhelmingly commercial in nature, consist mainly of "representative and core materials."[95] These collections tend not to include journal titles that are important in a field, but instead feature titles that are not widely held or known.[96] With fewer local funds with which to purchase a balanced variety of materials, consortial collection development activities centering on providing electronic journal collections can lead to a form of homogeneity in making selections.[97]

The practice of journal bundling, when a publisher offers a consortium access to all of its titles for an incremental price over current subscriptions, groups the strongest journals from the publisher with the weakest, the "essential with the non-essential."[98] Bundling doesn't have much added value for a library that already has developed a strong collection. When libraries agree to accept a bundled journal package, publishers have little incentive to maintain the quality of their selections. The relative sales of less important but still expensive titles decrease the funds available for more prudent selections.[99]

Within databases purchased by consortia, there is not necessarily any consistency in the depth, breadth, or extent of full-text coverage that the titles provide. Fullness of coverage changes, depending upon the provider.[100] Aggregators often drop and add titles, seemingly at random, in their databases, resulting in partial title runs; some publishers will only provide to the aggregator "significant articles, not the full journal."[101] In addition, aggregators have different types of products that vary in coverage and searchability. Users, and sometimes purchasers, may not understand that all full-text databases are not created equal. For example, content aggregators such as EBSCO, Information Access Company (IAC), and UMI provide materials through archival coverage and a large amount of full text, whereas

OCLC's Electronic Collections Online (ECO) and Blackwell's Electronic Journal Navigator (EJN) are an alternative to document delivery for specific publishers and/or titles, with much more limited archival coverage.[102]

Users have the general belief that electronic journals are, or at least should be, accessible from anywhere at anytime. Librarians, in the desire to accommodate users as much as possible, want to believe in the concept of universal accessibility of information, yet authentication and access technologies have not caught up to this vision. Electronic journals are accessed via passwords, IP filtering, or through credential verification. Password protection allows authenticated users to access electronic journals from any location. When publishers offer libraries passwords for user access, the burden of authentication is shifted to the vendor, but libraries have to determine how to distribute the passwords to users. These distribution methods tend to require patrons to go through multiple steps to acquire the passwords, which may lead to some frustration on the part of the user. In addition, some publishers restrict passwords by allowing only librarians to have them.[103]

When publishers allow libraries to register an IP address range, the library, as opposed to the publisher, is responsible for determining how to authenticate off-campus users. One authentication method is IP address filtering, which would allow access only to users whose IP addresses match the range that was registered by the library. However, this method is not effective on campuses that utilize dynamic IP ranges, which do not remain constant. Off-campus access is often accomplished using a proxy server, which masks remote users with a registered IP address to allow access to the desired resource. If the proxy server is down, however, access is severed for all off-campus users. Proxy servers don't necessarily do a good job of recognizing specific subnets and IP addresses that publishers may require, and there are some publishers that explicitly do not allow access to their electronic journals through proxy servers.[104]

Credential-based authentication provides the user with a certificate that verifies the user's identity within a community. The user, once verified, is then passed either to the server housing the resources or to the proxy server. Credential-based authentication is tied to a specific workstation, so it is not an option for patrons attempting access from publicly shared computers. This method is increasingly being used in libraries, but it requires complex infrastructures and can be technically overwhelming to manage for smaller institutions.[105]

THE FUTURE OF CONSORTIAL ARRANGEMENTS

It is difficult to make predictions about the future of consortia and consortial arrangements concerning electronic journals, but then, peering into the future is always a difficult task. Change is happening at a faster rate than libraries or library suppliers are accustomed, though none question the benefits of this advancing technology, which brings a wealth of information to an ever-widening audience.[106] One issue that perhaps clouds the future vision of electronic journal publication is the wide variety of roles all those involved can play.

Libraries are consumers of electronic publications, but they can also be the creators of content, publishers, and mirror sites for publishers and publisher partners. Vendors can be publishers, aggregators, or both. Libraries are becoming publishers, publishers are becoming jobbers, and so on.[107] Thus, forecasting can be difficult, but despite this confusion there are a few certainties.

Vendors will offer more desirable products; this is an economic necessity for any company. In addition, it is likely that agreements will become more customizable between consortia and vendors. As the Web grows and the ability to control what access is turned "on" or "off" develops, the individual library may get more say in what it does and does not want.

The future also points to expansion and to long-term use of consortium-based licensing. "There is no better tool on the horizon to accomplish many of the objectives we have and the changes we need to see."[108] OhioLINK is an example of this, where funding, decision-making mechanisms, operation, and administration have all been packaged and developed to deliver maximum benefit at a reasonable cost.[109] In addition, new models such as the Journal Access Core Collection (JACC) for California State University (CSU) system are likely to become prevalent. Although the consortial licensing activities focus on providing access to electronic journals in high demand, the JACC enables CSU libraries to address the demand for print journal collections in a cooperative acquisitions project.[110]

It is a little less certain whether there will be more competition among vendors, aggregators, and publishers. As quickly as publishers are created, they are also being bought and sold. It would seem that as technology becomes increasingly widespread, and as new journals are established, that new competitors would appear. Yet this hasn't always been the case, particularly in the past few years. Equally uncertain is the development of policies for intellectual property management, emphasizing the broad and easy distribution of material. The ICOLC states that

> licenses should permit the "fair use" of all information for non-commercial, educational, instructional, and scientific purposes by authorized users, including unlimited viewing, downloading and printing, in agreement with the provisions in current copyright practices as applicable in the country of origin. Providers should allow e-information to be used to generate copies for non-commercial interlibrary loans between two academic libraries in support of their teaching, learning and research missions."[111]

Nevertheless, it largely boils down to being anyone's guess as to whether either of these issues will be addressed with any immediacy. Consortia still have great roles to play, but if their focus remains clear and they concentrate their efforts on improving the information infrastructure, improving information access, and helping librarians serve users, then they will ultimately meet with success.

CONCLUSION

There is a potential for consortia to continue developing into an essential tool for the library. The economics of current publishing and library funding of journals, both in print and electronic, encourage this potential by making materials and services available that no single institution could manage by itself. Further research and study into new consortial models will have to be done, because there are many different types of consortia, and there will be the need to develop new pricing models, revenue sources, and licensing practices for electronic journals. The consortia is an old tool, yet it may still have far-reaching implications for libraries and publishers; how the two parties forge their relationship will directly impact their existence and how they will operate together in the future.

NOTES

1. Bostick, Sharon L. "The History and Development of Academic Library Consortia in the United States: An Overview." *The Journal of Academic Librarianship* 27(March 2001): 129.

2. Allen, Barbara McFadden and Arnold Hirshon. "Hanging Together to Avoid Hanging Separately: Opportunities for Academic Libraries and Consortia." *Information Technology and Libraries* 17(March 1998): 36.

3. Dannelly, Gay N. "'Uneasy Lies the Head': Selecting Resources in a Consortial Setting." *Journal of Library Administration* 28(1999): 58.

4. Allen and Hirshon, "Hanging Together," 37.

5. Alexander, Adrian W. "'Toward the Perfection of Work': Library Consortia in the Digital Age." *Journal of Library Administration* 28(1999): 10.

6. Allen and Hirshon, "Hanging Together," 36-37.

7. Ibid., 36.

8. Ibid., 37.

9. Alexander, "Perfection of Work," 6.

10. Peters, Thomas A. "Agile Innovation Clubs." *The Journal of Academic Librarianship* 27(March 2001): 149.

11. Alexander, "Perfection of Work," 5; Sanville, Thomas J. "A License to Deal." *Library Journal* 124(February 15, 1999): 122.

12. Oder, Norman. "Consortia Hit Critical Mass." *Library Journal* 125(February 1, 2000): 148.

13. Sanville, "License," 122.

14. Woodsworth, Anne. *Library Cooperation and Networks: A Basic Reader* (New York: Neal-Schuman Publishers, 1991): 21.

15. Thornton, Glenda Ann. "Impact of Electronic Resources on Collection Development, the Roles of Librarians, and Library Consortia." *Library Trends* 48 (Spring 2000): 848.

16. Ibid., 843.

17. Kopp, James J. "Library Consortia and Information Technology: The Past, the Present, the Promise." *Information Technology and Libraries* 17(March 1998): 7.

18. Alexander, "Perfection of Work," 2.

19. Ibid.

20. Kopp, "Library Consortia," 8.

21. Alexander, "Perfection of Work," 2.

22. Ibid.

23. Bostick, "History and Development," 128.

24. Alexander, "Perfection of Work," 2.

25. Ibid., 3.

26. Ibid., 4.

27. Ibid., 3-4.

28. Ibid., 4.

29. Ibid.

30. Thornton, "Impact of Electronic Resources," 843.

31. Kopp, "Library Consortia," 8 ; Thornton, "Impact of Electronic Resources," 845.

32. Thornton, "Impact of Electronic Resources," 843.

33. Kopp, "Library Consortia," 8.

34. Ibid., 10.

35. Ibid., 7.

36. Ibid., 8; Delanoy, Diana D. and Carlos A., Caudra. *The Directory of Academic Library Consortia.* (Santa Monica, CA: System Development Corp., 1972); Patrick, Ruth J. *Guidelines for Library Cooperation: Development of Academic Library Consortia* (Santa Monica, CA: System Development Corp., 1972).

37. Allen and Hirshon, "Hanging Together," 37.

38. Peters, "Innovation Clubs," 149.

39. Allen and Hirshon, "Hanging Together," 37.

40. Kopp, "Library Consortia," 10.

41. Ibid., 10-11.

42. Ibid., 11.

43. Ibid.

44. Ibid.

45. Peters, "Innovation Clubs," 149.

46. Alexander, "Perfection of Work," 2.

47. Allen and Hirshon, "Hanging Together," 37.

48. Kopp, "Library Consortia," 11.

49. Ibid.; Allen and Hirshon, "Hanging Together," 37.

50. Thornton, "Impact of Electronic Resources," 850.

51. Allen and Hirshon, "Hanging Together," 37.

52. Peters, "Innovation Clubs," 150.

53. Allen and Hirshon, "Hanging Together," 37.

54. Thornton, "Impact of Electronic Resources," 851.

55. Dannelly, "Selecting Resources," 60.

56. Hirshon, Arnold. "Library Strategic Alliances and the Digital Library in the 1990s: The OhioLINK Experience." *The Journal of Academic Librarianship* 21 (September 1995): 384.

57. Ibid.

58. Thornton, "Impact of Electronic Resources," 851.

59. Allen and Hirshon, "Hanging Together," 39.

60. Hirshon, "Strategic Alliances," 384.

61. Dannelly, "Selecting Resources," 60.

62. Thornton, "Impact of Electronic Resources," 851.

63. Hirshon, "Strategic Alliances," 385.

64. Ibid.

65. Sanville, "License,"123.

66. Thornton, "Impact of Electronic Resources," 851.

67. Hirshon, "Strategic Alliances," 385.

68. Thornton, "Impact of Electronic Resources," 851.

69. Sanville, "License," 122.

70. ICOLC Statement of Current Perspective and Preferred Practices for the Selection and Purchase of Electronic Information. Accessed on December 5, 2001 <http://www.library.yale.edu/consortia/statement.html>.

71. Hirshon, Arnold. "Jam Tomorrow, Jam Yesterday, but Never Jam Today: Some Modest Proposals for Venturing Through the Looking-Glass of Scholarly

Communication." Paper prepared for NASIG (Ann Arbor, June 1997) and IATUL (Trondheim, Norway, June 1997). Accessed on February 1, 2002, at <http://educate.lib.chalmers.se/IATUL/proceedcontents/fullpaper/hirspap.html>.

72. Ibid.
73. Ibid.
74. Ibid.
75. Ibid.
76. Bostick, "History and Development," 129.
77. Landesman, Margaret and Johann van Reemen. "Consortia vs. Reform: Creating Convergence." *The Journal of Electronic Publishing* 6(December 2000). Accessed January 18, 2001, at <http://www.press.umich.edu/jep/06-02/landesman.html>.
78. Ibid.
79. Bostick, "History and Development," 129.
80. Sanville, "License," 122.
81. Thornton, "Impact of Electronic Resources," 850.
82. Dannelly, "Selecting Resources," 59.
83. Sanville, "License," 124.
84. Ibid.
85. Thornton, "Impact of Electronic Resources," 854.
86. Nabe, Jonathan. "E-Journal Bundling and Its Impact on Academic Libraries: Some Early Results." *Issues in Science and Technology Librarianship* (Spring 2001). Available online at <http://www.library.ucsb.edu/istl/01-spring/ article3.html>.
87. Thornton, "Impact of Electronic Resources," 851.
88. Ibid., 850, 854.
89. Dannelly, "Selecting Resources," 66.
90. Thornton, "Impact of Electronic Resources," 853.
91. Peters, "Innovation Clubs," 149.
92. Nabe, "E-journal Bundling."
93. Nabe, "E-journal Bundling"; Peters, Thomas A. "What's the Big Deal?" *The Journal of Academic Librarianship* 27(July 2001): 302.
94. Ibid.
95. Dannelly, "Selecting Resources," 63.
96. Ibid.
97. Dannelly, "Selecting Resources," 61; Peters, "Big Deal," 303.
98. Goodman, David. "Where's the Fiscal Sense?" *Library Journal* 125(June 15, 2000): 48; Peters, "Big Deal," 302.
99. Goodman, "Fiscal Sense," 50.
100. Brennan, Patricia B.M.; Burkhardt, Joanna, McMullen, Susan, and Wallace, Marla. "What Does Electronic Full Text Mean? A Comparison of Database Vendors and What They Deliver." *Reference Services Review* 27(1999): 126.
101. Meyer, Richard W. "Consortial Access Versus Ownership" in the Scholarly Communication and Technology Conference, organized by the Andrew W. Mellon Foundation. Available online at <http://www.arl.org/scomm/scat/meyer.html>.
102. Majka, David R. "The Seven Deadly Sins of Digitization." *Online* 23 (March/April 1999). Available online at <http://www.onlinemag.net/OL1999/majka3.html>.
103. Krieb, Dennis. "You Can't Get There from Here: Issues in Remote Access Electronic Journals for a Health Sciences Library." *Issues in Science and Technol-*

ogy Librarianship (Spring 1999). Available online at <http://www.library.ucsb. edu/istl/99-spring/article3.html>.

104. Ibid.

105. Ibid.

106. SPEC Kit 223: "Electronic Scholarly Publication." *Transforming Libraries* 3(June 1997). Available online at <http://www.arl.org/spec/223fly.html>.

107. Ibid.

108. Sanville,"License,"123

109. Ibid.

110. Healy, Leigh Watson. "California State University Initiates an Electronic Core Journals Collection" *Educom Review* 34 111 (May/June 1999): 46.

111. ICOLC Statement.

Chapter 6

Usage Data: Issues and Challenges for Electronic Resource Collection Management

Joanna Duy

INTRODUCTION

Management of serials collections has been one of the most challenging issues facing academic libraries in the past decade, due to the high inflation rate of journal prices. Librarians typically use a number of factors in making serials collections decisions. These may include cost, indexing, relevance to the institution's research priorities, and input from faculty. In addition, citation data, such as provided by ISI's *Journal Citation Reports* or *Local Journal Utilization Reports,* have been used in academic libraries as an indication of which journals might be candidates for cancellation.[1] However, citation data does not necessarily reflect current awareness use by undergraduates or other groups of individuals who may not be publishing or use for instructional and clinical purposes.[2] Even with shelving studies, it is difficult if not impossible to determine to what extent print sources are being used. Indeed, the difficulty of making serials collections decisions is compounded by libraries' general lack of accurate data regarding the use of journals; traditional methods of studying the use of print collections are unable to capture every kind of journal use.[3]

With the advent of information delivery via the World Wide Web has come the potential for vendors and libraries to collect data regarding the usage of full-text journals and databases or any information resource offered over the Web. This is because each communication between a Web server and a Web browser is stored in a Web server log. So a library or vendor Web server log will have hundreds or thousands of entries every hour, as people make requests for information from that site. By sorting and manipulating their Web server logs, using commercial software or locally produced programs, libraries and vendors can obtain useful information about Web resource use.

Although usage data is still new and unstandardized, it may in the future be useful for libraries in three important ways. First, in a reporting capacity, such information can help libraries accurately indicate how their virtual collections are being used and justify the increasing amounts of money being spent on electronic resources.[4] Second, usage data can give libraries insight into how patrons are using their Web-based resources and what products they are using most; these data, combined with data about the libraries' overall Web site usage, may be useful in terms of restructuring the Web site, deciding which instructional courses to offer, or determining which electronic products to highlight. Third, usage data may help librarians make collections decisions for their electronic products. Because libraries often don't buy electronic content outright, but instead purchase access to a product, the question of whether to renew an electronic product is key; libraries should be able to incorporate usage data into their renewal decisions and possibly even their decision-making process for new products.

This third potential function has not been widely explored in the literature, particularly in relation to electronic journals. Because of the unstandardized and incomparable nature of usage statistics, the varied types of electronic products, and the difficulty of determining value in relation to use, it is indeed a difficult issue for libraries. Still, it is worthwhile to begin thinking of how useful usage statistics might be in terms of making renewal decisions for electronic resources, including electronic journals.

This chapter provides an overview of the attempts to standardize usage data and some initiatives to study usage data, primarily in academic libraries. In addition, important use measures are outlined, and there is discussion of useful measures for e-journals and other types of electronic products, as well as some of the pitfalls of usage data. There is also an overview of methods for collecting, organizing, and disseminating usage data within an academic library. It should be noted that the following discussion will encompass not only electronic journals but *all* electronic products—at this point, unfortunately, few authors/researchers who publish on e-usage data clearly distinguish among formats. In addition, given the blurring distinctions between products, it would be difficult to discuss issues pertaining only to traditional electronic journals. However, an effort will be made to focus on the electronic journal as a full issue, browsable entity.

GUIDELINES, STANDARDS, AND INITIATIVES RELATING TO USAGE DATA

Why should we be concerned with standardizing usage data from vendors? Currently, different vendors can report the same usage measure (for example, "number of searches"), but each vendor may actually count the number of searches differently. For example, the number of searches reported by one vendor could indicate the number of times the whole product was queried, but for another vendor the search could be counted for each specific database within its package. So, if a user performed a search across ten different databases, one vendor might report one search and another would report ten; thus, the same amount and type of use is being reported in different ways by different vendors. The way in which log-ins or sessions are counted is also unstandardized. Usually, a "session" begins being tracked when a user with an IP address not currently in use within that product arrives at the site and ends when that IP address leaves the site or when no activity has been registered for that IP address for a certain amount of time. However, this "time-out" value (the number of minutes during which an IP address is inactive before the vendor counts the person as having left the site) is unstandardized—for some vendors the value is seven minutes, for others it may be thirty minutes.[5] This time-out value can affect the number of sessions/log-ins— and the length of session, if reported—for a vendor. These standardization issues are further compounded by the fact that few vendors give detailed definitions or reports of how each measure is counted.

Because each vendor may collect and define its use measures differently but use the same terminology—session, search, full-text download, etc.—it is nearly impossible for librarians to accurately compare data among vendors, but this is precisely what librarians want to be able to do for collections purposes and to compare the use of all of their products. Hence, standardization efforts are needed to bring vendors and libraries together in agreement on definitions for the measures being collected. In addition, there needs to be more standardization of the ways in which usage data is reported, formatted, and made accessible.

Efforts to standardize the collection and presentation of usage statistics for licensed Web resources began in the late 1990s. One of the earliest attempts to develop guidelines was undertaken by the JSTOR Web Statistics Task Force, a group of volunteers who helped define a core set of measures and guidelines for measuring the use of Web resources.[6] The specific charge of the task force was to identify units of measurement, explore the capability of vendors and systems for Web-based products to record and measure use, and devise analytical models and reports formats for evaluating and applying use measurements.[7] The task force established early guidelines for providers of bibliographic and full-text resources on what usage data should be reported. Indeed, JSTOR has remained a leader in terms of the quality of usage data reports provided to libraries.

Another group that has been a key player in the development of guidelines for the collection and reporting of usage data is the International Coalition of Library Consortia (ICOLC). This group began meeting in 1996 and is an informal, self-organized group consisting of library consortia from around the world. The coalition serves primarily higher education institutions by facilitating "discussion among consortia on issues of common interest."[8] In November 1998, ICOLC released its *Guidelines for Statistical Measures of Usage of Web-Based Indexed, Abstracted, and Full Text Resources*—which drew heavily upon the guidelines developed by the JSTOR Web Statistics Task Force. The ICOLC document (which was revised slightly in December 2001) outlines required elements that providers should report in their usage data, as well as how various measures should be broken down. In addition, it contains guidelines on privacy and user confidentiality issues, institutional and consortial confidentiality, provision of comparative statistics, and how reports should be made available. The ICOLC measures appear to have become the de facto standard against which vendors compare their usage data. However, although numerous vendors claim to provide usage reports that are in compliance with the ICOLC guidelines, many vendors' reports actually do not conform to the guidelines.[9] Again, this is an area in which standardization is badly needed, as there is currently no organization in place to verify that these vendors' claims of conforming to the ICOLC guidelines are actually true.

In October 1999, the Association of Research Libraries (ARL) Statistics and Measurement Committee and the ARL Research Library and Management Committee started the ARL New Measures Initiative. One of the five projects that comprise the initiative is the E-Metrics (Measures for Electronic Resources) study, designed to explore the various kinds of data that can be gathered to effectively report the usage and value of electronic resources. From May 2000 to December 2001, the E-Metrics project was under contract with the Information Use and Management Policy Institute at Florida State University and was funded by a group of twenty-four ARL member libraries. This part of the project consisted of three phases: Phase I described how the participating libraries currently collect and use statistics and measures for networked services (which include databases, electronic journals and books, as well as the library's Web site and online services) and described the key issues involved in the production of effective statistics and measures. In Phase II, statistics and performance measures were developed, analyzed, field-tested by libraries participating in the project, and recommended for use. In Phase III, the researchers created tools (for example, training modules) to help libraries institutionalize statistics and performance measures. In addition, a data collection manual was produced. Other goals for the ongoing E-Metrics project include engaging in discussions with database vendors to work on standardized measures of database usage and developing a proposal for external funding to maintain the development and refinement of networked statistics and performance measures.[10]

The E-Metrics Phase II report and the data collection manual are highly recommended reading for anyone involved in gathering or using usage data. Although the ARL project's scope is broader than just measuring usage of electronic resources, the discussion of the various measures for electronic resource usage data is insightful and provides an in-depth look at certain measures and the accompanying collection and standardization challenges.

Another key document that outlines the complexities and challenges of collecting and analyzing usage data—from the perspectives of both libraries and publishers—is the Council on Library and Information Resources' (CLIR) *White Paper on Electronic Journal Usage*

Statistics, authored by Judy Luther. It focuses on usage statistics for electronic journals, but the broader issues raised by Luther are applicable to the usage data of almost all Web-based resources. Luther emphasizes that publishers and librarians need to work together to standardize the way in which usage measures are collected and reported, as well as the context in which they are reported.[11] She discusses the complexities of making collections decisions based on current usage data, which is often quoted out of context and is not comparable. In her paper, Luther encourages librarians and publishers to work together to develop a standard methodology for collecting *and* analyzing data.

In terms of standards work, the National Information Standards Organization (NISO) *Library Statistics Standard* (ANSI/NISO Z39.7-1995) was first released in 1968 and then revised in 1983 and 1995, with agreement to review the standard in five years to include measurement of electronic resources and performance measures. The NISO Forum on Performance Measures and Statistics for Libraries was held in February 2001, and the NISO Standards Committee AY was tasked to revise ANSI/NISO Z39.7-1995 with regard to new measures for electronic resources, including measuring electronic network performance, vendor and publisher-based use statistics, and reporting methods. The committee will revise the base standard and recommendations and is planning to release both for comment no later than July 1, 2002.[12]

In addition to these American-based initiatives, there have also been many international organizations working on the standardization of usage statistics. For example, the European Commission's EQUINOX Project ran from November 1998 to November 2000, and was funded under the commission's Telematics for Libraries Programme. EQUINOX had two main objectives: first, to further develop existing international agreement on performance measures for libraries by expanding these to include performance measures for the electronic library environment; second, to develop and test an integrated quality management and performance measurement tool for library managers. In its final report, EQUINOX proposed fourteen performance indicators complementing ISO 11620—the *1998 Information and Documentation: Library Performance Indicators.* These performance measures go beyond straight usage measures of electronic resources and instead try to measure the impact of electronic services on libraries and library users.

The Publishing and Library Solutions Committee (PALS) Working Group on Online Vendor Usage Statistics was established in the United Kingdom and has been tasked with developing a common code of practice to enable publishers and vendors to record online usage statistics and deliver them in a consistent way to libraries. The aim of the group is to provide guidance on (among other things) definitions of data elements, output report formats, and method of delivery of the reports. This group's representation from both libraries and the publishing industry make it a potentially important player in terms of standardization efforts.

A new and exciting international initiative, Project COUNTER (Counting Online Usage of NeTworked Electronic Resources), holds the promise of building on previous initiatives and the work of other international groups. COUNTER was initially conceived of by the PALS group, in the United Kingdom, but was formally launched with an international steering group in March 2002. The group quickly gained support from a number of organizations, including ARL, NISO, and publishers' groups, among many others. The international scope of the group is encouraging, as is the fact they have received so much support from a variety of organizations.

The goal of COUNTER is "to serve librarians, publishers, and intermediaries by facilitating the recording and exchange of online usage statistics."[13] This includes the important objective of allowing librarians to be able to compare usage statistics from different vendors. To this end, COUNTER released a Code of Practice in December 2002, which consists of a general summary of COUNTER, as well as a well-developed list of definitions for terms relating to electronic resources and their use. In addition, the Code specifies the content, format, and delivery specifications that vendors must meet if their reports are to be deemed "COUNTER-compliant." Generally, the types of reports required by COUNTER do not deviate widely from the recommendations that we've already seen from groups such as ICOLC and ARL. Perhaps the most interesting aspect of COUNTER (and the thing that may make it most successful), however, is the claim that as of 2004, vendors will have to submit usage reports for auditing by an approved third party (specifications and a list of approved auditors are expected to be released sometime during 2003).[14] COUNTER encourages implementation of their Code by offering librarians a standard clause that can be incorporated into their electronic resource license agreements, indicating that vendors must provide COUNTER-compliant usage data. In addition, by creating a list of "COUNTER-compliant" vendors, COUNTER hopes to encourage compliance with their Code.[15] Indeed, their intention to have third-party auditing, and a decision about whether or not a vendor is compliant with guidelines, is something that has been missing from previous initiatives, and although it will likely be difficult to implement, it is very much needed.

COUNTER claims that the Code will be a work in progress (this first Code is "Release 1"). The first release focuses on electronic journals and databases, and further releases may have more specifics regarding the measured use of e-books and other kinds of content, as well as providing guidelines for the provision of more granular reports.[16]

Early signs indicate that librarians are encouraged by the work of COUNTER,[17] and that the group is making an effort to ensure that the library community's needs are being met by this project—another important attribute. This promises to be an exciting initiative that will hopefully succeed in developing widely adopted standards and—perhaps most important—holding vendors more accountable for the quality of their reports.

COMMUNICATION BETWEEN LIBRARIES AND VENDORS

It is important that librarians who are making use of the data provided by vendors offer feedback about the quality of the vendors' usage reports, and in that way contribute to the ongoing dialogue about the improvement and standardization of usage statistics. This can be easily done via e-mail or phone call to the vendor representative or technical help team, and many vendors respond well to constructive criticism and suggestions for improving their reports. In some cases, librarians may share their specific comments regarding usage data from a certain vendor on an electronic mailing list, and encourage their colleagues to contact the vendor if they share the same concerns. This is an important and proactive way for librarians to share their thoughts, ideas, and concerns with vendors about what is important in usage reports. Indeed, the reports and measures of many vendors are in a relative state of flux, and new features, measures, or changes in format can occur in the course of a year, often in an attempt to address specific requests or concerns from librarians.

CAN LIBRARIES COLLECT THEIR OWN USAGE DATA?

Standardization efforts will likely continue for a number of years, and it may be some time before libraries are able to obtain vendor data that is comparable and an accurate reflection of usage. In the meantime, many vendors are making their usage data available to libraries, and some libraries collect their own usage data. How can libraries collect their own data, and what are the benefits of locally collected data?

Using their library's Web server logs, librarians can gather information about how users navigate the library Web site; they can also, with some extra effort, keep track of how many people tried to access a particular electronic resource (Marshall Breeding gives an excellent overview of homegrown methods for counting e-resource use in his "Strategies for Measuring and Implementing E-Use"[18]). For example, the URL of each resource can include a script that counts the attempted visits to that resource using a resource-specific, library-designated tag that will appear in the Web log. Web log analysis software or locally written programs can then go through the log and group together all of the attempted visits for each product, based on the tags. In addition, some integrated library systems have a similar data-gathering process and produce regular reports on how many times users tried to access a particular resource.

Unfortunately, however, once a user leaves the library's site and travels to a particular information resource over the Web, the library can no longer track that user in its logs. Hence, libraries must rely on vendors to provide the most in-depth data on exactly how their products are being used. In addition, although the tracking of usage for large databases or journal packages is fairly easy to implement, obtaining title-level electronic journal usage information can be much more time consuming. Nonetheless, it is a good idea for libraries to try to collect some basic data on their Web resource usage, as the library may own products for which vendors do not provide usage data. In addition, sometimes vendors can send a library the wrong usage report, or their servers could have been malfunctioning and they may not have a complete report for a certain time period. Also, almost all vendors collect data in different ways, or they may not provide details on how they are collecting data, so it is difficult to confidently compare usage data from one vendor to the next. Finally, it is a good idea for libraries to count their own usage if only to verify that the numbers provided by vendors are correct, especially if the level of use drives up the cost of the product.[19] For these reasons, librarians should consider working with their systems department to develop a "homegrown," consistent approach to collecting basic usage data on electronic resources, in addition to keeping track of vendor-provided data. Library-gathered data may not give in-depth information about how patrons are using the library's Web resources, but it can at least give the library an approximation of the number of users trying to access a resource.

In addition to library-gathered statistics, some consortia may also collect their own usage data, by counting users as they enter the consortial "gateway" on their way to the Web product. Indeed, if a library purchases or receives certain Web-based products through a consortium, then the consortium-gathered data may be all the usage statistics that the library will get, but sometimes that will be less data than what the library could obtain if it purchased a product directly from the publisher or vendor.[20]

KEY USE MEASURES FOR VENDOR STATISTICS

Efforts have been made by both ICOLC and the ARL E-Metrics project to identify the most meaningful measures of Web resource usage. The December 2001 revision of the ICOLC Guidelines outlines several key measures that the coalition recommends be provided for every Web-based information resource. In the Phase II report of the ARL E-Metrics project, the authors present a number of recommended measures for "Use of Networked Resources and Services." A comparison of the two can be found in Box 6.1, which indicates the overlap between the two sets of recommended measures. It should be noted that this is a broad overview of the key measures recommended by both groups—in addition to these measures, ICOLC and ARL provide further discussion on how, when, and in what format the measures should be reported.

BOX 6.1.
Comparison of ICOLC and ARL E-Metrics

ICOLC Guidelines

ARL E-Metrics Measures*

Number of sessions (log-ins)

Number of log-ins (sessions)

Notes/Definition: ICOLC recognizes that the definition, collection and reporting of this measure are subject to interpretation. In the "stateless" web environment, statistics gathered as "sessions" can provide only a rough indication of the number of actual sessions conducted, thus limiting the overall meaningfulness of this indicator.

Notes/Definition: Number of user-initiated sessions in licensed electronic resources. A session or log-in is one cycle of user activities that typically starts when a user connects to a database and ends with explicit termination of activities (by leaving the database through log-out or exit) or implicit termination (time-out due to user inactivity). This measure will produce a count of how often specific databases are used and complement traditional physical attendance counts.

Number of queries (searches)

Number of queries (searches)

Notes/Definition: ICOLC notes that this measure must be categorized as appropriate for the vendor's information. A search is intended to represent a unique intellectual inquiry. Typically a search is recorded each time a search form is sent/submitted to the server. Subsequent activities to review or browse among the records retrieved or the process of isolating the correct single item desired do not represent additional searches, unless the parameter(s) defining the retrieval set is modified through resubmission of the search form, a combination of previous search sets, or some other similar technique. Immediately repeated duplicate searches, double clicks, or other evidence indicating unintended user behavior should not be counted.

Notes/Definition: Number of user-initiated queries (searches) in licensed electronic resources. A search is intended to represent a unique intellectual inquiry. Typically, a search is recorded each time a search request is sent/submitted to the server.

(continued)

(continued)

Number of full content units examined, downloaded, or otherwise provided to the user

Notes/Definition: ICOLC provides examples of what should be provided, according to the type of information resource. For journal articles, the number of full content units examined should be by journal title with ISSN and title listed; for e-books, by book title with ISBN and title listed; for reference materials, by content unit appropriate to resource (e.g., dictionary definition); for nontextual resources, by file type as appropriate to resource (e.g., image, audio, video, etc.). ICOLC also lists here number of turnaways, peak simultaneous users, and any other indicator relevant to the pricing model applied to the library or consortium.

Items requested in electronic databases

Notes/Definition: Number of items requested in all of the library's licensed electronic resources. These resources may include journal articles, e-books, reference materials, and nontextual resources that are provided to the library's users through licensing and contractual agreements. The user requests may include viewing, downloading, e-mailing, and printing to the extent the activity and printing to the extent the activity can be recorded and controlled by the server rather than browser. It is noted that this statistic provides a circulation count for electronic contents in a way analogous to the traditional circulation of books.

Number of menu selections

Notes/Definitions: Categorized as appropriate for the vendor's system. If display of data can be accomplished by browsing (the use of menus), this measure must be provided (e.g., an electronic journal site provides alphabetic and subject-based menu options in addition to a search form). The number of searches and the number of alphabetic and subject menu selections should be tracked.

Source: Data elements from International Coalition of Library Consortia (2001), Statistical measures of usage of web-based information resources (December 2001 revision of original November 1998 guidelines), available at <http://www.library.yale.edu/consortia/ 2001webstats. htm>; Wonsik "Jeff" Shim, Charles R. McClure, Bruce T. Fraser, John Carlo Bertot, Arif Dagli, and Emily H. Leahy (2001), Measures and statistics for research library networked services: Procedures and Issues: ARL e-metrics phase II report (Washington, DC: Association of Research Libraries), available at <http:// www.arl.org/ stats/newmeas/emetrics/phasetwo.pdf>.
*Only measures dealing with usage of electronic databases are outlined here (U2, U3, U4 in Shim et al., 2001).

As can be seen, both ARL and ICOLC make similar recommendations in terms of measures to be reported and how they are defined. Indeed, ARL notes that their recommended measures related to electronic networked resources drew heavily on the ICOLC guidelines.[21] Note that ICOLC includes a measure (number of menu selections) that is not included in the E-Metrics measures list.

Which of the measures outlined by these two groups are most useful for librarians interested in knowing how their electronic journals are being used? This is a difficult question to answer. Print journals are fairly uniform in their presentation and setup, but electronic journals can be accessed in many different ways. Contents from a journal may be included as part of a large aggregated full-text database, or journals may come as part of a large, searchable package of electronic journals from one publisher or provider. Alternatively, libraries may purchase a single electronic journal from a small or specialized publisher or society. Most libraries have a combination of all these products. Given this variation in resource type, it is important, when evaluating electronic journals for collections purposes, to keep in mind the broader "electronic setting" in which the journal is being accessed and used. For example, undergraduate students may access a journal's contents most frequently via a full-text aggregator database. However, given that libraries rarely have input into the kinds of titles that are selected for inclusion in these databases (and given that usage statistics for these products rarely include information on a title-by-title level), the discussion here will focus mainly on the types of electronic products that most closely mirror print journals—those products which provide browsable, full-issue electronic journals—this can include large and small electronic journal packages or individual subscriptions.

The vendors of large packages of electronic journals often provide some kind of usage data, although such data may be more difficult to obtain from smaller publishers or societies. For those providers who do offer data, the reports can be quite lengthy, depending on how many titles are included in the package; because of this, many providers give the option of obtaining the data in comma delimited format, or in some other format that allows the easy transfer of data into a spreadsheet for analysis. The type of data offered by electronic journal package providers can vary greatly. Some provide detailed information on the use of each title in the package, as well as an overall summary for use of the package as a whole; some provide only one or the other. Measures provided may include number of sessions, searches, table of contents accessed, abstracts viewed, full-text articles viewed (often broken down by html or pdf format), and pages printed (although this can be difficult to track). The session or log-in measure may be the least useful for determination of electronic journal usage. In addition, one could say that for making serials collections decisions the number of searches is not very important, but it does provide insight into how the product is being used. Perhaps the most useful current means of measuring electronic journal usage is the "number of full content units examined, downloaded, or otherwise provided to the user" (ICOLC) or "items requested in electronic databases" (E-Metrics) measures, which are often reported as full-text articles viewed. Indeed, Shim and colleagues point out that

> this statistic provides a circulation count for electronic contents in a way analogous to the traditional circulation of books. Given the fact that libraries do not have good measurements of in-house materials usage, particularly serials usage, this statistic helps libraries understand in-library use patterns that were heretofore difficult to measure.[22]

Indeed, this measure—probably more than any other currently provided measure—provides the best indication as to the use of an electronic journal. Most vendors of electronic journal packages will provide this type of data on a title-by-title basis, allowing librarians to see which titles are most used.

However, Hahn and Faulkner (2002) point out that it is important to not only collect and assess usage data but also to put that data in context and balance it against measures of quality, content, and price. Indeed, they argue that the provision of usage data by vendors is shaped by the ideal of what numbers are most useful for database evaluation, rather than electronic journals. The authors use Henry H. Barschall's print-based evaluation of the cost-effectiveness of journals as a base for developing new metrics to assess current electronic journal collections and to make decisions about which products to purchase. In doing so, they look not only at usage of a product but also at the *value* of content provided. The authors assert that content measures are essential to both librarians and publishers seeking to interpret and apply usage data. Part of the problem with developing effective metrics lies in the lack of information on electronic content for particular journals or collections . . . the tasks of counting the number of articles, pages, or words for a particular e-journal or collections of e-journals can be over-whelming. . . .[23]

They argue for looking at more than just usage data—use, content, and price are all used to develop the critical decision-making measures for electronic journals that are so needed by collections librarians. However, until vendors start providing information about the content provided (and in a standardized format) these measures will be difficult to implement.

Two key questions that arise in thinking about journal usage data are: what kind of use do we value, and what kind of use is the library willing to support? For example, in some ways, citation reports offer a more concrete measure of use than number of articles viewed. We *know* that the journal was useful because it was cited in a research paper, but a citation may be considered a kind of "end point" in terms of usage, one that may not always be reached, even though the article or journal may have been useful. In addition, undergraduate or graduate students (or faculty who are not as active in research) may not be publishing information, but should libraries not strive to meet their information needs as well? Even for users who are publishing, just because a journal is not cited does not mean that it did not provide some useful information to the user in terms of his or her general information in a particular field. If that journal was unavailable electronically or in print at the user's library, then he or she may not have bothered to go to the trouble of ordering it through interlibrary loan, but would research and/or knowledge of their field of study suffer as a result? These are questions that librarians must address when considering the incorporation of usage data into their collections decisions. A study that compares vendor-gathered statistics of the usage of electronic journal titles with an institution's ISI Local Journal Utilization Reports, to determine how similar or different these indicators really are, would be interesting and would help shed light on whether there is a relationship between these two measures.

PITFALLS OF USAGE DATA

We know that vendor usage statistics are far from standardized, which makes it difficult to compare statistics from different vendors. But suppose that usage data *was* standardized across all vendors and products—how should libraries use this new data, especially given the fact that many libraries are not used to having usage data for their journals? It is important to think carefully about the nature of this data as a whole and what it may or may not be telling us.

Usage data gathered from electronic resources is a kind of quantitative data, and it says nothing about the quality or type of use.[24] Our users may be using these journals, as indicated by the number of full-text articles displayed, but that does not mean they were satisfied with what they found. In his 1998 article on computerized monitoring of use, Thomas Peters notes that "Computerized monitoring alone is not a good indicator of the satisfaction levels of remote users . . . usually it is difficult to determine from logs alone if users are satisfied with the outcomes of their remote sessions with digital library information systems."[25]

In contrast, if vendor reports show that usage is low for a certain product or electronic journal, that may not necessarily mean that the journal is not useful to faculty and students. It may mean that the resource is simply not visible enough on the library Web site. Library Web sites can be large and difficult for users to navigate, and users may easily miss the most appropriate resource for their research. If usage data is low for a resource, it may mean only that users are not finding the product and not that the product is not useful. Perhaps the library needs to reconsider the design of its Web site, think about promoting the product in some other way, or, for electronic journal packages, consider how users are gaining access at the title level. Are they going through the catalog or other search tool or using another mechanism such as an alphabetical list of electronic journals? Are the electronic journals browsable by subject? Traditional print journals are fairly uniform in their organization and are relatively easy for users to find and browse, and librarians need to think carefully about the access routes for electronic journals and how these routes could be affecting use. Thus, it is important, in looking at usage data for consideration in collections decisions, for librarians to keep in mind the broader view of the electronic product being analyzed, consider the factors that may affect how someone arrives (or doesn't arrive) at an electronic journal, and acknowledge the role these factors may play in influencing usage.

The ability to easily access quantitative use data to make serials collections decisions may be new to many libraries, and at least one author has expressed concern about the overall practice of incorporating electronic journal usage data into serials collections decisions. In his article titled "Usage Statistics for Online Literature," Bernard Rous cautions:

> there is a fundamental problem with usage statistics in the context of business decisions about which online journals to acquire or drop. Just how is the value of scholarly research journals to be measured? It has never before been measured by usage, only by vaguely defined notions of "perceived value" or "importance," which include many factors: professional reputations of the Editor-in-Chief and Editorial Board, standing of the publisher's imprimatur, faculty recommendation, uniqueness, perhaps even citation indices. With the exception of the last, none of these factors is quantitative, and none, including the last, is a true, direct measure of usage. Heavy usage of research titles cannot measure their value to a discipline's advance. They might be a measure of the size of the research community devoted to a specific problem area, and perhaps a measure of writing density, i.e., how well translated the research results are for the broadest tier of that community. In this sense, they might provide a better measure of the value for education rather than research ... if statistical usage measures value against price, it is possible that less-used titles will be driven out, stultifying specialized research in narrow or newly defined fields.[26]

In addition to these concerns regarding the application of usage data to collection-making decisions, there are also ethical questions surrounding the collection of usage data. Thomas Peters asks: "Is unobtrusive uninformed computerized monitoring a fundamentally unethical unprofessional way to treat remote users?"[27] Although most tracking is done via IP address, which cannot easily be connected back to an individual user, should we be tracking our users at all, without their knowledge? Will librarians' and vendors' thirst for information about users grow to the point where we do start using more aggressive methods of tracking our users and gathering data about them? At the very least, librarians may want to consider posting information on their Web sites about the kind of data being gathered when users are on the library's site and when they venture onto a vendor site.

Obviously, librarians will have to think carefully about whether to incorporate usage data into their serials collections decisions and, if so, how much importance to give this data. Despite the drawbacks to this kind of data, it still does provide libraries with a measure of their collection's use, and some believe this kind of measurement to be the supreme test of the quality and utility of an institution's holdings. Indeed, as noted by Hahn and Faulkner, things are different on the electronic playing field:

> usage becomes even more important to assessing value in the electronic arena because libraries often pay for access and not ownership. In the ownership context, libraries can purchase materials just in case they prove useful in the future; it makes little sense to spend funds on access that is not used.[28]

The quantitative nature of current usage data, however, encourages the judging of a resource's value based on sheer volume of use; however, as Marshall Breeding points out, librarians must be careful not to judge on quantity of use alone: "The point is not to take too simple a view of the statistics, but to infer the more complex relationships of use by the specific user communities."[29]

PUTTING THE DATA TO WORK:
USING USAGE DATA IN ACADEMIC LIBRARIES

How has electronic resource usage data been used in academic libraries to date? It is important to begin this discussion by noting that although many libraries have started receiving and using usage reports from vendors within the last few years, information scientists have been using similar data to understand user information-seeking behavior for almost thirty years.[30,31] Historically, information retrieval (IR) researchers have been interested in this kind of remote use monitoring, using transaction log analysis—often from library catalogs—to determine use behavior. Now that many library resources are on the Web, however, the primary source for data collection on remote users has shifted toward Web server log analysis. It is interesting to note that although traditional IR research looked at the *pathways* of use, vendor-provided usage reports are highly quantitative in nature, giving only *totals* for searches, sessions, etc., instead of indicating the paths users took in their information searches. Granted, tracing the pathway of each user in a log file is a huge undertaking, but librarians need to be mindful of the kind of information being lost in our current quantitative usage reports.

Early research on the use of electronic journals and other Web-based products was often based on the manual review and analysis of Web logs. For example, in an early attempt to use usage data as a method of inferring user behavior in regard to journal usage, Alan Dawson looked at BUBL Journals' server log records.[32] He used Analog (a free Web log analysis program) to analyze the logs and produce aggregate figures for journal use within a six-month period. Dawson looked at the ways people accessed online journals (through a menu, looking at a text file, or accessing a search box) and then assumed their activity (browsing, reading, and searching, respectively). Dawson reported which journals were most used for which user activity and proposed that by measuring the "search-to-browse" ratio of a journal it was possible to determine which journals were being used for research and reference or for current awareness and casual browsing. This study was an early example of using data derived from Web logs to understand how electronic journals were being used.

In their study published in 2000, Morse and Clintworth compared use of print and electronic biomedical journals. The authors used Ovid transaction logs to determine how many full-text journal articles were viewed within a six-month period, and they then compared that number to how many print journals were reshelved in a similar time period. They found that during a six-month study period, there were approximately 28,000 viewings of full-text articles compared to only 1,800 uses of the corresponding print volumes, indicating a strong preference for electronic format.[33] The authors also found that overall usage patterns were similar for both print and electronic journals—that is, 20 percent of titles accounted for nearly 60 percent of usage for both print and electronic study sets.

Linda Mercer offered a unique approach in the early study of usage data. She looked at not only the use of electronic journals but also their value, for the purposes of making purchasing decisions. She examined usage data from HighWire Press as well as Ovid transaction logs and discussed the usefulness of the data for making decisions regarding purchasing of journals and training of users.[34] With the Ovid transaction logs, Mercer was able to pinpoint (using IP address evaluation) what departments and groups within the department (faculty, staff, residents, medical students) were using the journals, which she felt to be particularly important for assessing not only who uses certain journals but also the number of *different* users of a product. Mercer offered early arguments for creating good usage measures and setting standards for collection of data.

Charles Townley and Leigh Murray studied use-based criteria as decision-making factors in the selection and retention of electronic information. The authors looked at the usage of electronic resources in six different universities and also studied various factors affecting database usage. They found that usage of the products varied greatly across the six different institutions and did not appear to vary according to an institution's mission (e.g., liberal arts versus research institution). They also found that a number of factors positively influenced the use of electronic resources, including the length of time that an electronic resource had been available to users; a resource must be available to users for a minimum of twelve to eighteen months before heavy use will be observed.[35] This is an interesting finding, one that should be considered by librarians who are assessing the usage of electronic journals or other products.

In 1999, Carol Tenopir directed a two-phase study of academic libraries in which usage data was used to help identify patterns of database use and the factors that affect use. In one part of the study, usage data was captured from thirty-eight databases used in ninety-three academic libraries in the United States and Canada for a six-month period, and a survey was sent to each library asking questions about the factors that may affect use of electronic resources. The study found that the busiest time for online research by users at the academic institutions studied was between 11:00 a.m. and 5:00 p.m. on Mondays, and that November was the highest month of usage (the authors noted that April and/or May would likely also have been high-use months).[36] The study also found that although many of the databases were available remotely to users, usage of the databases was not very high during hours in which the library was closed.[37] It was also determined that simultaneous usage of reference databases was relatively uncommon, and the authors reported on how many simultaneous users would be required to fulfill the needs of most users, for various settings. In 1999, Tenopir and Green reported on other factors that might influence database use in academic and public libraries, including levels of instruction, availability of remote log-in, and placement of a database on the library's home page, but none of these factors was found to be statistically significant in influencing use.

In 2001, Blecic, Fiscella, and Wiberley reported on the results of a comprehensive analysis of vendor-supplied usage data for several electronic resources (representing fifty-one vendors including publishers, aggregators, and consortia). The authors determined how well vendors applied the ICOLC guidelines to their usage reports; in the fall of 2000, of the fifty-one vendors studied, only three reported all ICOLC elements relevant to their resources; twenty-eight supplied selected elements, and twenty offered none.[38] The authors identified five measures which they believe to have implications for collection management:

1. the variability of ICOLC data elements over time (measured by calculating the coefficient of variation);
2. the ratios of queries per session for searchable databases (this measure was determined to be the most stable measure in the study and as such acts as a good indicator for any major changes in the way a vendor is gathering its data);
3. hourly use;
4. uses of e-journal collections; and
5. the ratio of uses of Web-based resources per full-time equivalent students in the disciplinary population.[39]

The authors noted that the ways in which vendors collect and report data can change over time, and they recommend keeping documentation that accompanies usage reports, as well as conducting an annual review of the way each vendor counts the elements it reports. As part of their study, Blecic, Fiscella, and Wiberley also studied four e-journal collections (American Chemical Society, Karger, Project MUSE, and Ovid) from October 1999 to March 2000 to determine whether the "80/20" rule developed by J. M. Juran and introduced to the library literature by Richard Trueswell, who showed that 80 percent of library use is satisfied by 20 percent of materials, held true in the electronic realm.[40] They found that for all journal packages, more than 20 percent of the collection was required to satisfy 80 percent of use,[41] and that patterns could be seen according to the broad subject area of the journal packages. During their study, the authors found that several e-journal collections did not offer title-by-title use data, and the authors recommended that libraries consider negotiating with vendors for title-by-title use data when they are working on licensing agreements for electronic journal packages.

In 2002, Karla Hahn and Lila Faulkner published an article in which they used print journal evaluation techniques as a basis for developing metrics to evaluate electronic journals; indeed, this is one of the first studies to consider measuring the value of electronic journal titles, beyond simply looking at use. The authors note that "surprisingly few researchers have applied lessons from the assessment of print journals to the e-journal or collections of e-journals. This shortcoming in the literature seems to stem, in part, from the focus on evolving standards for e-journal statistics rather than on their application."[42] The authors developed three metrics to evaluate electronic journals and three benchmarks to help evaluate potential purchases.

Research studies on electronic resource usage data are hardly common in the literature, but they are appearing with more frequency. In addition, the type of tests and evaluations being performed in these studies tends to be more in depth as time progresses and librarians realize that significant research and work still needs to be done before usage data can be considered reliable and worth integrating into collections decisions.

COLLECTION AND DISSEMINATION
OF USAGE DATA

In order for usage statistics to be of value to the library, they must be made accessible to librarians involved in making decisions regarding the collection of, or access to, electronic resources; in addition, this data may also need to be distributed to administrators for reporting purposes. The collection and dissemination of usage statistics can be a difficult task for any library; this kind of data is new, unstandardized, and has never been collected before. Some key questions to consider when beginning to gather usage data in a systematic way include: Who will be responsible for collecting the data? Who will be responsible for communicating the data? How will the data be communicated and used? These are all difficult questions to answer, especially at a time when many libraries still do not have good management systems in place for their electronic resources or good decision-making processes for collecting and renewing electronic resources. Indeed, as noted by Charles Townley and Leigh Murray in their 1999 study, there have been few use-based models created for the selection and retention of electronic resources.[43]

Who Will Be Responsible for Collecting the Data?

Ideally, all libraries would have a position devoted to electronic resource management and/or assessment. This may be an "electronic resource librarian," a "database assessment librarian," or a similarly titled position. Someone who is familiar with electronic information providers and with the electronic products owned by the library would be preferable. A person who is already signed up to various provider e-mail lists and who is signed on as an administrator or technical contact for the library would be ideal, as he or she would have preexisting relationships with the providers and may already have access to the passwords and other information needed to gather the vendor usage data. If the library does not have an electronic resource management/assessment librarian in place, then other positions that may be considered for this type of data collection include acquisitions librarians (for example, the head of acquisitions or the serials librarian); a systems librarian could also be a good candidate, or the person in the library who deals with the licensing of electronic resources.

The person who collects the data will ideally be on all major vendor e-mail lists or other electronic resource communication circuits, so that they can be aware of any changes to the usage data reports. In addition, they should also try to sign up for at least one other messaging group that deals with electronic resources and that includes active discussions of usage statistics. Reading questions and discussions from people at other libraries can spark debates, and comparisons of data from different institutions can offer a library interesting insight on "where they fit" in terms of usage. Given that the collection and use of this type of data is still relatively new to most libraries and librarians, having a dialogue about usage statistics and their surrounding issues with others who are also involved in collecting and disseminating data can be helpful.

Collection of the data can occur in many different ways. For a library with numerous electronic resources, it is useful to keep a spreadsheet or database of information about each electronic resource and how to obtain its usage data. All vendors should be contacted, and information about how to obtain usage data for each product should be recorded. Libraries may want to consider drafting usage statistics policies—perhaps based on the ICOLC or E-Metrics measures—to include in their licensing negotiations with vendors.

Usage data can come in many different ways and formats (from the Web, usually with a user identification and password; on paper; via e-mail as attachments, or in the body of the e-mail; or upon special request only) so it is a good idea to keep all information organized in an electronic table. A simple database can be used to collect not only the information about how to access the statistics but also information about start and end dates of the data and what kinds of measures are reported. Then, application of a product such as ColdFusion can be used to create Web-based queries on the database. Having a simple Web form mounted on a library intranet, where all librarians can access information about vendor statistics, can be a useful communication tool. In addition to keeping track of how to get to the vendor statistics, the library may also want to keep a spreadsheet or database of the actual vendor data. Indeed, the *ARL E-Metrics Data Collection Manual* recommends keeping a spreadsheet or database of measures such as number of log-ins, queries, and items requested; they recommend calculating a monthly total of each type of measure for all electronic resources. Some libraries have developed in-house electronic resource management systems that have a usage statistics component (for example, Pennsylvania State University's Electronic Resources Licensing and Information Center); this approach would also be useful and would help to generally manage many aspects of electronic resources.

Communicating and Using the Data

Usage data can be sent to collection managers or other librarians as is—that is, in the format originally used by the vendor. Alternatively, the librarian responsible for collecting usage reports can use the data to format reports that summarize key measures in a standardized and more easy-to-read report format, which might include a summary analysis of the data. Another option is to make the data being kept in the spreadsheet or database available to librarians, either through the Web or by saving it on a common network drive. Ideally, of course, one would like to produce large reports that allow for easy comparison of values from different vendors, but this should really be avoided unless the person collecting the data is certain that all usage measures are being collected and reported in the same manner by all vendors. At this point, most usage data from different vendors is not comparable,[44,45] and thus these types of comparisons should be avoided.

Trying to systematically incorporate usage data as one of the decision-making criteria for journals or broader electronic products can be a difficult process, especially given the current unstandardized practices of data collection. In addition, the amount of data for each product can be overwhelming, especially for electronic journal packages. Should usage data be examined by librarians as it is updated by vendors (usually monthly), or will librarians realistically only be able to review it once a year, perhaps when electronic product renewal or serials collections decisions have to be made? These are all decisions that libraries need to consider and then put structures in place to encourage the appropriate review of usage data.

CONCLUSION

In his report on electronic resource usage, Marshall Breeding notes:

> Theoretically, the ability to measure access to electronic resources should be greater than traditional resources . . . Web servers can be programmed to record each and every time an item of content is requested. The obstacles to comprehensive measurement of use tend to be in the realm of coordination and organization, not in technical ability.[46]

This statement couldn't be more accurate. Much work needs to be done among libraries and vendors to coordinate and standardize the collection and reporting of current usage data. Then, as noted by Luther, and Hahn and Faulkner, vendors and librarians need to have further discussions on the appropriate context of usage data; the reporting of price and content would help librarians begin to create the tools with which to make important purchasing and renewal decisions. Intermingled among these challenges is the broader task of addressing these issues for *all* types of electronic resources—from online dictionaries to electronic journals; the complexity of pricing structures for electronic journals further complicates matters. Finally, ensuring that the organization of the library supports the effective collection and dissemination of data and integration into its decision-making models, will be another monumental challenge. Each library will need to determine how (or whether it wants) to assess the value of an electronic resource and its content, and what it deems to be acceptable costs for information.

NOTES

1. Thomas Nisonger, "Use of the Journal Citation Reports for Serials Management in Research Libraries: An Investigation of the Effect of Self-Citation on Journal Rankings in Library and Information Science and Genetics," *College and Research Libraries* 61 (May 2000): 263-275.

2. Deborah D. Blecic, Joan B. Fiscella, and Stephen E. Wiberley, "The Measurement of Use of Web-Based Information Resources: An Early Look at Vendor-Supplied Data," *College and Research Libraries* 62 (September 2001): 434-453.

3. Blecic, Fiscella, and Wiberley, "Measurement of Use," 449.

4. Rush Miller and Sherrie Schmidt, "E-Metrics: Measures for Electronic Resources. Keynote Speech Delivered at the 4th Northumbria International Conference on Performance Measurement in Libraries and Information Services," 2001. Available at: <http://www.arl.org/stats/newmeas/emetrics/miller-schmidt.pdf>.

5. Wonsik "Jeff" Shim, Charles R. McClure, Bruce T. Fraser, John Carlo Bertot, Arif Dagli, and Emily H. Leahy. "Measures and Statistics for Research Library Networked Services: Procedures and Issues: ARL E-Metrics Phase II Report," 2001. Association of Research Libraries, Washington, DC. Available at: <http://www.arl.org/stats/newmeas/emetrics/phasetwo.pdf>.

6. Jim Mullins, "Statistical Measures of Usage of Web-Based Resources," *The Serials Librarian* 36 (1999): 207-211.

7. JSTOR, "Web Statistics Task Force Establishes Guidelines for Electronic Resources," *JSTORNews* 2 (1998). Available at: <http://www.jstor.org/news/newsletter/no2/iss2/taskforce.html>.

8. International Coalition of Library Consortia Web site. 2002. Available at: <http://www.library.yale.edu/consortia/>.

9. Blecic, Fiscella, and Wiberley, "Measurement of Use," 436.

10. Shim, xii.

11. Judy Luther, *White Paper on Electronic Journal Usage Statistics* (Washington, DC: Council on Library and Information Resources, 2000).

12. NISO. 2002. Library Statistics Standards Committee AY. Available at: <http://www.niso.org/committees/committee_ay.html>.

13. Project COUNTER Web site. 2003. Available at: <http:www.projectcounter.org/about.html>.

14. Ibid.

15. Ibid.

16. Peter Shephard, "Keeping Count," *Library Journal* February 1, 2003: 46-48.

17. Ibid., 48.

18. Marshall Breeding, "Strategies for Measuring and Implementing E-Use," *Library Technology Reports* 38 (May/June 2002): 1-68.

19. Breeding, "Strategies for Measuring," 41.

20. Blecic, Fiscella, and Wiberley, "Measurement of Use," 437.

21. Shim et al., "Measures and Statistics," 61.

22. Ibid., 65.

23. Karla L. Hahn and Lila A. Faulkner, "Evaluative Usage-Based Metrics for the Selection of E-journals," *College and Research Libraries* 63 (May 2002): 217.

24. Luke Swindler, "Serials Collection Development." In Marcia Tuttle (Ed.), *Managing Serials* (pp. 65-100) (Greenwich, CT: JAI Press, 1996).

25. Thomas A. Peters, "Remotely Familiar: Using Computerized Monitoring to Study Remote Use," *Library Trends* 47 (1998): 11.

26. Bernard Rous, "Usage Statistics for Online Literature," *Professional Scholarly Publishing* 2 (Spring 2001): 3. Available at: <http://www.pspcentral.org>.

27. Peters, "Remotely Familiar," 1998.

28. Hahn and Faulkner, "Evaluation Usage-Based Metrics," 217.

29. Breeding, "Strategies for Measuring," 9.

30. Peters, "Remotely Familiar," 1.

31. Thomas A. Peters, "The History and Development of Transaction Log Analysis," *Library Hi Tech* 11(1993): 41-58.

32. Alan Dawson, "Inferring User Behavior from Journal Access Figures," *The Serials Librarian* 35 (1999): 31-40.

33. David H. Morse and William A. Clintworth, "Comparing Patterns of Print and Electronic Journal Use in an Academic Health Science Library," *Issues in Science and Technology Librarianship* (Fall 2000, Number 28). Available at: <http://www.library. ucsb.edu/istl/00-fall/refereed.html>.

34. Linda S. Mercer, "Measuring the Use and Value of Electronic Journals and Books," *Issues in Science and Technology Librarianship* (Winter 2000, Number 25). Available at: <http://www.library.ucsb.edu/istl/00-winter/article1.html>.

35. Charles T. Townley and Leigh Murray, "Use-Based Criteria for Selecting and Retaining Electronic Information: A Case Study," *Information Technology and Libraries* (March 1999): 32-39.

36. Carol Tenopir and Eleanor Read, "Patterns of Database Use in Academic Libraries," *College and Research Libraries* 61 (May 2000): 234-246.

37. Tenopir and Read, "Patterns of Database Use," 238.

38. Blecic, Fiscella, and Wiberley, "Measurement of Use," 436.

39. Blecic, Fiscella, and Wiberley, "Measurement of Use," 452.

40. Richard L. Trueswell, "Some Behavioral Patterns of Library Users: The 80/20 Rule," *Wilson Library Bulletin* 43 (January 1969): 458-461.

41. Blecic, Fiscella, and Wiberley, "Measurement of Use," 449.

42. Hahn and Faulkner, "Evaluative Usage-Based Metrics," 217.

43. Townley and Murray, "Use-Based Criteria," 32-39.

44. Shim et al., "Measures and Statistics," xv.

45. Luther, *White Paper,* 3.

46. Breeding, "Strategies for Measuring," 36.

Chapter 7

Case Study
in Claiming/Troubleshooting E-Journals: UCLA's Louise M. Darling Biomedical Library

Barbara Schader

Electronic journals have most of the problems of their print counterparts—and a whole host of new and unique problems. Librarians have been so preoccupied with acquiring e-journals, negotiating licenses, determining how to track and manage electronic journals and make them accessible to our patrons, that we have given little thought to issues of claiming or, more accurately, troubleshooting e-journal problems. In surveying the current literature on electronic journals, the author could find no article dealing with troubleshooting e-journal problems. However, the time has arrived when we must start looking at these problems and exploring any possible solutions. This situation is now even more critical in the electronic world than it was in the print world. Patrons are now becoming accustomed to and demanding instant access; if they cannot access a full-text article, then they expect immediate help. Patrons are no longer willing to spend the weeks or months that they had previously waited while we claimed print issues or obtained an interlibrary loan. Also, since fewer and fewer patrons are actually coming to the library, at times the only interaction librarians may have with patrons is when they

The individual(s) responsible for troubleshooting must be technologically adept, enjoy sleuthing, and also be good communicators. At the UCLA Louise M. Darling Biomedical Library, we are fortunate to have two superb troubleshooters, Richard Davidon and Robert Skinner.

call or e-mail regarding an access problem. How we handle our response to their problems may be the only information they have available for forming their opinion of a library staff's competence and value.

This chapter focuses on troubleshooting issues and how troubleshooting for electronic journals is accomplished at the UCLA Louise M. Darling Biomedical Library.

BACKGROUND

The Louise M. Darling Biomedical Library serves primarily the Schools of Medicine, Dentistry, Nursing, and Public Health, the life sciences divisions of the College of Letters and Sciences, related institutes in biomedicine, and the UCLA Medical Center. The collections are broad based in scope and designed to support the teaching, research, and patient care-related needs of its primary clientele. In addition, the collections are a resource for the health, life sciences, and psychology communities. The library contains over 605,800 print volumes and regularly subscribes to 4,456 current journals. Networked computers include sixty-eight workstations for staff, 164 workstations for library users, and twenty-six workstations for instructional use.

In 2000-2001 the library processed 8,532 items, cataloged 3,715 titles, circulated 98,920 items, processed 54,414 interlibrary loan and document delivery requests, answered 37,803 reference and information inquiries, and provided 105 instructional sessions and orientation tours.

UNIVERSITY OF CALIFORNIA SYSTEM

In 1996, the nine campuses of the University of California formed a tenth, electronic campus, known as the California Digital Library (CDL). This "campus" was charged with determining which digital products were most important to the other nine University of California (UC) campuses and then negotiating licensing agreements and access to these electronic resources. As of January 2002, the CDL had approximately 190 contracts, with seventy-one of these focusing on the sciences. As of June 2001, access has been provided to 5,797 electronic journals and 200 databases. UCLA has access to many more resources than we could afford on our own, due to the work of the CDL. UCLA participates in most of the CDL contracts. UCLA libraries also work with other UC campuses to sign more limited contracts, known as Tier 2 contracts. These are contracts that are not of interest to all nine campuses but are of interest to only three to six of the campuses. Since there are five medical schools among the nine campuses, there are several agreements in which the five health sciences libraries participate, within the Tier 2 arrangement. The UCLA Biomedical Library also negotiates individual licenses for products that are not feasible for Tier 2 or CDL licensing. Often these are contracts for which there is no price advantage to negotiate consortially, or for products not seen as a high priority systemwide, but which are important to UCLA Biomedical Library patrons. Having licenses that are UCLA only, Tier 2, and systemwide further complicates trouble-shooting issues.

UCLA'S LIBRARY E-RESOURCES MANAGEMENT

The UCLA Biomedical Library has been tracking electronic resources available to the UCLA health and life sciences disciplines and also for the physical sciences for the past five years in an *Access 97* database. In this database we track:

- E-resource title
- URL
- UCLA Library Catalog Record Number
- Call number
- Subscriber number
- Publisher/aggregator
- Vendor
- Cost
- Payment method (free with print, additional charge with print, online only, etc.)
- Availability (free to the world, UCLA only, or all nine UC campuses)
- Access (IP or ID/password)
- Simultaneous users, if applicable
- Licensing agreement, if applicable

- Coverage dates of our access
- Initial date of access
- Comments, if applicable

We also note whether information about new or updated records has been forwarded to our cataloging department to facilitate synchronization between this database and our library's catalog. We record whether the Internet domains of our resource providers have been registered with our campus proxy server so UCLA-affiliated users can have access from anywhere using any Internet service provider. We also note whether this data has been entered into our library's e-journals Web database. A ColdFusion interface allows our patrons to search this database from the library's Web site.

This has been the structure for over four years. However, the UCLA campus is now developing a more elaborate Electronic Resources database (ERdb), which will serve the entire campus library community and will drive all searches from the library Web pages. It will also act as a processing tool for technical services staff in each of our branch libraries. There are five technical processing screens in the Erdb: the resource screen (Figure 7.1), the bibliographic details screen (Figure 7.2), the descriptor screen (Figure 7.3), the licensing screen (Figure 7.4), and the troubleshooting screen (Figure 7.5). This chapter will deal with Figure 7.5, the *Troubleshooting Screen.* The public face of the ERdb can be seen at <http://www.library.ucla.edu/> under the option "Find online materials." Please keep in mind that this is all very new and may have changed by the time this book is published.

ORGANIZATIONAL STRUCTURE FOR E-RESOURCES CLAIMING/TROUBLESHOOTING

When the UCLA Biomedical Library began subscribing to electronic journals and dealing with their fascinating vagaries in the mid-1990s, most problem calls went to the Reference Division. However, Reference did not have much of the background information on these electronic resources and did not have access, at that time, to the Biomedical Library e-resources database. Reference had access only to what the patrons saw—the Biomedical Library e-journals Web page

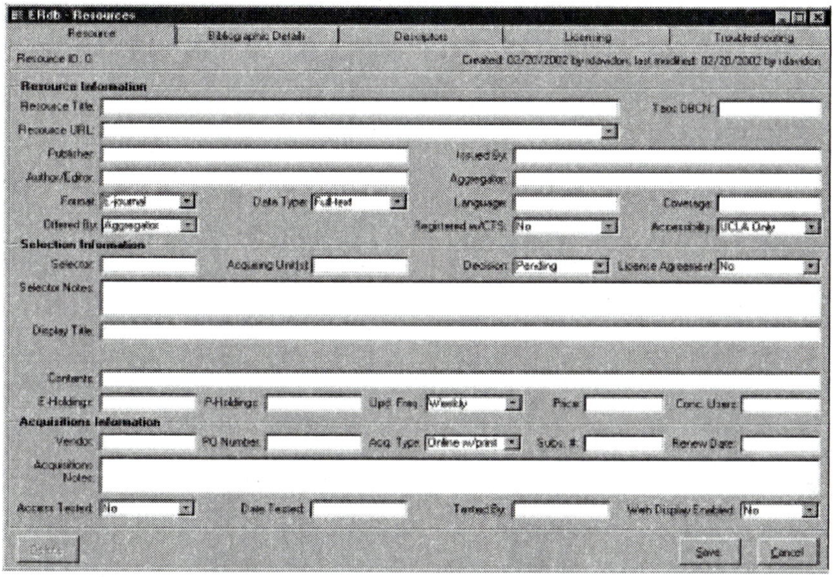

FIGURE 7.1. Resource Screen. The resource screen is the main data entry screen. The subject bibliographer or selector completes as many of the fields as he or she has data available. Acquisitions can then add additional data as necessary.

search feature. After much internal discussion, it was decided that many of the e-journal problems encountered were claiming-type problems, which should be referred to the Acquisitions Division. However, Acquisitions was in the midst of bringing a new system on line and did not have the staff to deal with another major task added to their already overloaded list of responsibilities. For that reason, the Collection Development Division took the lead on managing e-journal problems, with the understanding that eventually Acquisitions staff would take over the function.

The UCLA Biomedical Library currently subscribes to 5,000 electronic resources, 4,500 of which are provided via the California Digital Library contracts. The UCLA Library as a whole subscribes to 7,000 electronic resources. Again, most of these are provided via the CDL contracts. The UCLA Louise M. Darling Biomedical Library Collection Development and Acquisitions staff now spends at least twenty hours per week on troubleshooting/claiming electronic re-

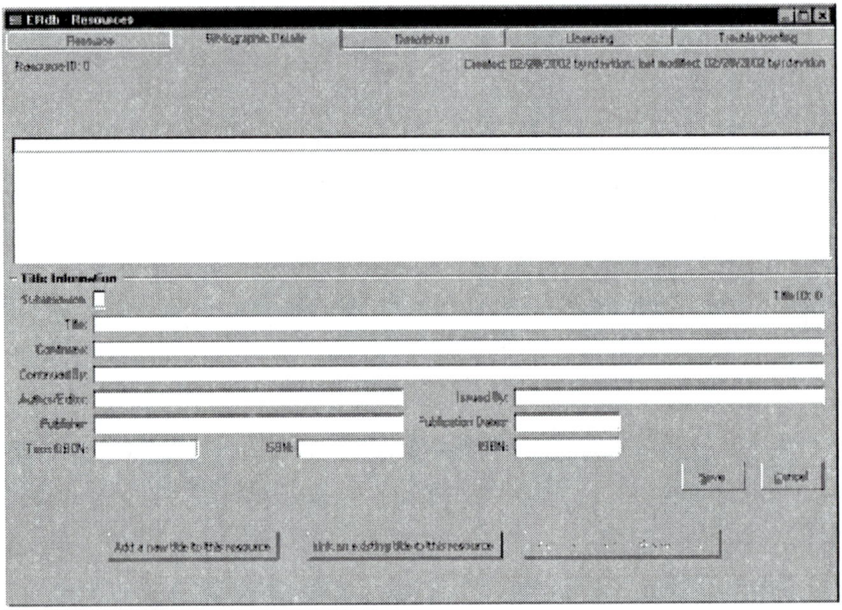

FIGURE 7.2. Bibliographic Details. Most of this information is automatically filled in by the data added to the Resource Screen.

sources. We do not anticipate this workload will lessen in the near future. Every year new, different, and more complex issues demand our attention.

E-Journal Troubleshooting

The Collection Development Division (CDD) is staffed by 1.5 professional full-time equivalents (FTEs), .8 support FTEs, and student workers equivalent to .3 to .5 FTEs. When the CDD staff became officially responsible for troubleshooting issues for electronic resources, we first provided our patrons with convenient ways to get in touch with us. One of the first priorities was to inform our Reference staff about the types of problems that were appropriate to refer to us. We also added a message to our e-journals Web page that displays before a title loads, stating: "If this e-journal does not load, please contact the Collection Development Division at x56498." After a few years,

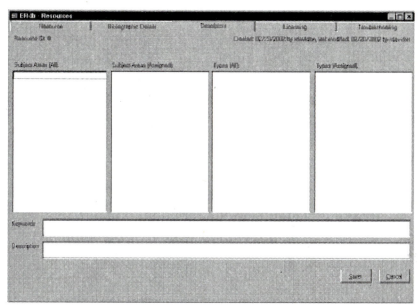

FIGURE 7.3. Descriptor Screen. "Subject Areas (all)" is a list of defined subject descriptors (which are not displayed, but would be in the left column). To add one of these descriptors to a particular resource, one double clicks on the descriptor and the word is copied into the "Subject Areas Assigned" column. The same applies to the "Types (all)" column. (The types are not shown either, but there is a defined list.) One double clicks on each type to copy it to the "Types (assigned)" column. The "Subject Areas (assigned)" and the "Types (assigned)" are mandatory fields. At least one subject and one type must be chosen for each resource.

Collection Development established a separate e-mail account to receive reports of e-journal problems and issues.

Our guiding principle in CDD is *communication*. We communicate regularly with Reference to alert them to known problems, such as when a particular site will be down or if a payment glitch has caused us to lose access. We also communicate with patrons via our Web site if we feel the problem will take several days or more to resolve. When patrons e-mail, call, or fax us regarding e-journal problems, we respond to them within twenty-four hours, letting them know we are working on the problem and when we anticipate a resolution.

We have found that each year brings new trends in e-journal access problems—often in addition to the previous year's problems. The

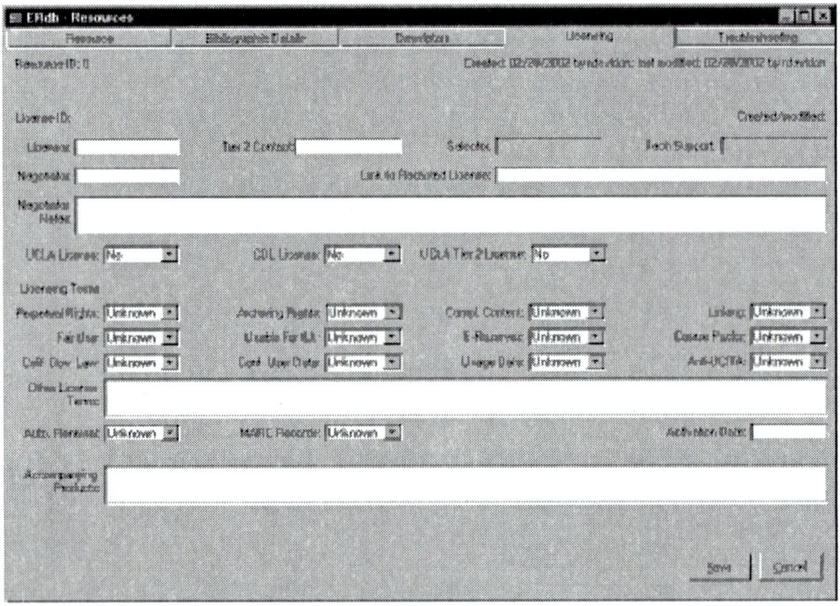

FIGURE 7.4. Licensing Screen. This screen is populated only by each library's licensing coordinators.

1999 theme was publishers shutting off access for long periods of time while hardware or software was retooled—often with no mention of this anticipated downtime to subscribers until access was suddenly denied to them. Then, 2000 was the year of free electronic trials suddenly becoming paid subscriptions. However, with no communication from the publisher, the fact was discovered only when access ceased and it was necessary to scramble to identify the problem and initiate an electronic subscription—often midyear. The year 2001 was characterized by publishers suddenly cutting off access on January 1 if they had not received vendor payments—which they frequently seemed not to have received in time! Fortunately, in 2001 there were enough complaints registered that in 2002 most publishers and vendors altered their deadlines and procedures. Also, 2001 brought us problems with embargoed issues, again with little explanation and no forewarning. The trend in 2002 was the sudden unbundling of print and electronic. Where once the electronic came free with print, one is now asked to

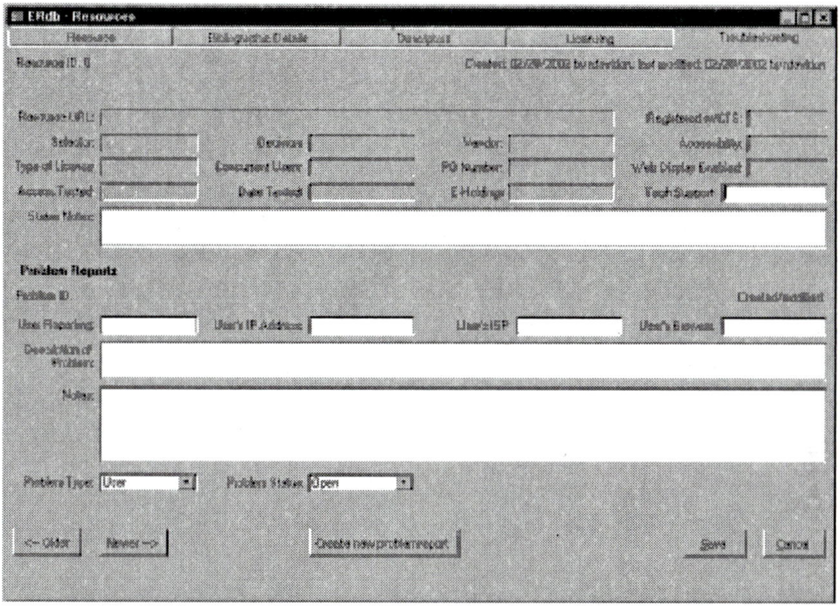

FIGURE 7.5. Troubleshooting Screen. Most of the top part of this screen, which is grayed out, is automatically populated with the field data from the Resource Screen. The remainder of the fields are completed by the individual doing the troubleshooting. This screen is accessible to all UCLA Library staff so anyone can check to see if a specific resource has already been identified as having problems and, if so, the status and who is working on the troubleshooting. If no problems have been recorded, then the problem is referred to one of the individuals doing troubleshooting for a specific library.

purchase each separately, and the electronic version is occasionally offered at greatly inflated prices. The pricing for the electronic is often based on campus or departmental FTE. This can result in paying several times more for print and electronic than in previous years. Finally, 2003 has brought huge price increases as some publishers start experimenting with the FTE pricing model. This model demands that organizations pay per the number of full-time employees, or full-time students, or full-time science faculty, etc. This model is a financial hardship to large institutions and unfair in that it does not allow one to pay for *actual* use. At UCLA we try to avoid signing any licenses that use the FTE pricing model, and we support the concurrent user or simultaneous user model instead. We believe the simultaneous user/concurrent user model is much more accurate in reflecting actual use by our patrons, and therefore we are paying for actual use and not publisher fantasies.

As time and technology have progressed, we are finding that the problems encountered with electronic journals have both increased and become more complicated. We have categorized here the most common problems that we are now encountering and offer the solutions that we are using. Some of the problems we encounter and the concomitant solutions are due to our unique situation as one of nine campuses in the University of California system. In these cases, the author will try to explain how the problem and its solution are unique to our situation.

CATEGORIES OF TROUBLESHOOTING ISSUES AND SOLUTIONS

Missing Volumes/Issues/Articles

Missing content is a discrepancy between the coverage as shown in our records and what is actually available. This is one of the most difficult problems because we have little control over the solution. We can only contact the publisher to request a resolution.

When Back Issues Are Accessible, but Not the Current Issue(s)

1. Check to see if this title has changed publishers. It seems lately that many journals are changing publishers, and often the previous publisher will retain the electronic access to older issues.
2. If the journal is still being produced by the same publisher, check to see if there is a publication delay. Has the entire editorial board departed? Was there a hardware crash and all of the new articles pending publication were lost or garbled?
3. Has the publisher gone to a new publishing schedule? For instance, is the publication now bimonthly instead of monthly, or quarterly instead of bimonthly, etc.?
4. Has the publisher started to embargo current issues? If this is the case, there is not much that can be done other than carefully ex-

plaining to the patron what has happened. I think it is absolutely critical that we explain these issues to our patrons and especially to our faculty. With the myth that everything is available on the Web, we need to be clear with patrons that because something is in an electronic format does not necessarily mean that the designated gatekeeper will allow unrestricted access and risk their revenue stream. Also, our faculty members are often on editorial boards, and thus are making decisions as editors and not thinking in terms of how these decisions will affect their access as patrons. The author has seen the situation happen frequently in which a faculty member will complain about an access problem; the author has then had to explain the problem, and then is told something to the effect that, yes, that faculty member had sat in on that decision and had voted for it, but had no idea about what the consequences would be. Educating our faculty and graduate students to these issues may solve some of our problems in the future.

When Volumes, Issues, or Articles Are Missing

It is critical to report missing material to the publisher. Librarians often feel that they are too busy to take this step, but it is essential this be done. If the publisher does not receive enough complaints, then they are not going to make the effort to load or reload the missing data. If this data is not loaded and is then electronically archived, then the archival copy will be incomplete. This is the reality of the situation, and it is happening every day (Inera Incorporated 2001; Henebry and Safley 2001). At UCLA, we also record this information on our troubleshooting screen. We keep track locally, and also notify the CDL if it is a CDL-negotiated title. When we negotiate for contract renewal, these missing data will be presented to the publisher a second time.

Access Denied

When There Is No Subscription, or It Is on Hold, or Expired (or About to Expire), or Patrons Are Being Asked to Enter a User Name and Password, or to Pay for Viewing Content

1. Check payment records to be certain payments are up to date.
2. If payments are up to date, check with the vendor to be certain they have forwarded the payment in a timely manner. At this

point, most vendors will take over contacting the publisher and straighten out the situation so access can be restored. Often the vendor must send a copy of the canceled check to the publisher as proof of payment. Even if the vendor agrees to handle this problem, keep checking on access. Some vendors are more conscientious than others. It once took our institution eleven months and five faxes of the same canceled check to convince a major university press that we were entitled to access a particular title.

When Access to Full Text Is Available but Has Not Been Activated

We occasionally find that because of our workload, we have neglected to activate the online version of a title which has been included in the cost of our print subscription or that comes to us by virtue of using a specific vendor. When these titles come to our attention, we quickly attempt to activate them. One complication that often occurs is obtaining the subscriber number. We attempt to keep all subscriber numbers in our electronic resources database. However, some publishers change subscriber numbers annually; and the subscriber number may also change if the library rewrites the title with another vendor. For certain titles, the publisher treats the subscriber number like classified data and one must write letters to obtain the number. For all of these instances, our first recourse is for Collection Development to call the publisher directly. We have stopped waiting for another department to make the call or for our vendor to obtain the number for us; often we can resolve this problem in minutes by making the call ourselves. We discovered this truism when we were alerted to the fact that a few savvy patrons were activating titles for us if they thought we were moving too slowly!

At times we do not activate a title to which we are entitled because of problems with the licensing agreement. If we negotiate the licensing agreement and the publisher will not remove clauses that are quite problematic to us, then we will not sign the agreement and therefore will not have access to the electronic version. In these cases, we put a note on our electronic journals Web pages so patrons are aware that we have attempted to obtain access but licensing problems are preventing this access. The phrase most often used on our Web site is "Currently unavailable. Unacceptable pricing/licensing model from publisher. Negotiations continue."

When a Site Demands a User Name/Password

The UCLA Biomedical Library usually signs licensing agreements that offer online access only via IP address authentication. There are, however, a few exceptions to this, such as *The Chronicle of Higher Education* and the *New England Journal of Medicine.* Again, this is noted on our e-journal Web pages, and if patrons need the ID/password, then they can ask at the Reference Desk. We do not have the ID/password available on our Web site as many institutions have opted to do. Having a page of ID/passwords is, in our view, a cumbersome process for all involved and is not as secure as we would prefer.

Occasionally patrons receive a request for an ID/password to a title for which we have IP access. Often this happens when we have purchased access for a certain number of simultaneous users of a specific resource. The request for ID/password is usually an indication that we have exceeded our number of simultaneous users. We advise patrons of the situation and the reason that they are receiving the ID/password request and suggest they attempt to access the resource during a less busy time. Prime time for resources often varies on a title-by-title basis. We scan the usage data for these resources on a regular basis so we know when prime use is occurring for each item.

Also, on occasion, the request for a user ID/password is an indication that there is a problem with our subscription and therefore our IP access. For titles to which we do have IP access, we check payment records to be certain that our subscription is current and follow the steps outlined in the previous section in this chapter, When There Is No Subscription . . . If this does not solve the problem, we call the publisher to be certain we are still registered and that our proxy server is also registered. There are times when publishers and aggregators change software or hardware and, despite their best efforts, some registered users do not make the transition. If this is the case, the publisher or aggregator for that site should be able to tell the librarian fairly quickly if it has "lost" the library's registration. Under these circumstances, we reregister and this will usually take care of the problem. (Note that this can also be the problem if a site fails to recognize an IP address—the site does not always ask for ID/password, it just denies access. Again, if this happens and the library has a current subscription and the publisher/aggregator acknowledges this, then check to see if it is necessary to reregister. Even properly registered IP addresses can occasionally be dropped from the providers' servers.)

When IP Addresses Are Not Registered on the Providers' Servers

Over time, online access has been activated by different staff members who have been using different address lists. Occasionally certain ranges have not been registered with certain providers. This is especially relevant when UCLA changes IP addresses. This has happened at least three times in the past five years. The UCLA Library has a designated person responsible for making these changes with the publishers/aggregators/providers. This usually proceeds smoothly since we have a designated communicator. It is important that one's institution maintain detailed records of IP address registrations.

Another "wrinkle" we have discovered is that some providers, such as the American Medical Association, do not allow one to register Class B networks over the Web. For these instances, library staff should contact the technical support staff, explain the problem, and have them register the Class B networks. This usually goes smoothly once the problem has been identified.

When a Site's Domain Is Not Registered to the Proxy Server

At UCLA, in order for our Bruin OnLine (BOL) proxy server to function, the domains of resource providers must be registered on the proxy server. Proxy server registration involves completing a form on the BOL Web site. It is important to know how to register library resources on the proxy server.

Patron's Web Browser Is Not Configured to Use the Proxy Server

At UCLA, affiliated individuals can use the BOL proxy server regardless of what Internet service provider they are using. In order to do this, they must properly configure their browsers. There are instructions for doing this on the BOL Web site. If a user does not have a similar set of instructions, they may want to set this up. It can save users an enormous amount of trouble. We often point patrons directly to this Web site if it appears this is the problem. Note, however, that sometimes these sites are not updated in a timely manner and some of the information may no longer be accurate. Data should be checked regularly for accuracy when referring patrons to another campus Web site. Currently one must have Microsoft's Internet Explorer (IE) Version 5.5 with Service Pack 2 or Version 6 to use our proxy server. Older versions of IE have had issues with page caching not working well. Netscape users must have Version 4.0 or newer. We instruct our patrons to use the latest available browser version.

When Providers' Servers Are Unavailable

Like all computers, Web servers occasionally fail. Patrons will fail to access some resources because providers' servers have gone offline due to technical difficulties. If one is really lucky, the publisher/vendor/provider will notify subscribers that downtime is imminent. However, in most cases, this is discovered by dumb luck or via patron complaints. Unfortunately, a librarian has usually gone through all of the steps discussed in the When There Is No Subscription . . . section before he or she discovers that the problem lies with the publisher/vendor/aggregator. Vendors can also be less than forthcoming as to when the downtime will be resolved. At UCLA, we put a note on our e-journals Web page if it appears that the problem will last more than three to four days. Again, it is important to educate users about the realities of electronic resources, and it is also critical that patrons/faculty realize that downtime is due to publisher/aggregator/vendor issues and not due to problems in the library.

When Maximum Number of Concurrent Users Is Reached

Some resource providers have contracted with the library to provide access for a limited number of concurrent users for their products. When this limit has been reached, patrons may see a message on the screen stating that access to this resource is currently unavailable. This message may or may not indicate that the maximum number of users has been reached. At other times, one sees only a message requesting the user ID/password. See the section titled When a Site Demands a User Name/Password.

Bad URLs

*When Records Contain Incorrect URLs
or URLs That Lead to Journal Sites
That Do Not Link to Actual Content*

Occasionally, our records contain URLs that are outdated, incorrect, or misleading. We have even discovered PID URLs that are no longer correct. (Persistent identifiers [PIDs] use a database to associate the URL for a resource with a permanent ID. If the URL changes, the database is updated to reflect the new location and associate it with the persistent ID.) Establishing the correct URL can be tricky. Occasionally a Google search is useful in finding a new URL that is viable for the resource in question.

For the UC system, we are attempting to establish PIDs for many of our resources, so if the PID is incorrect, we get in touch with the CDL help desk. If a PID problem is discovered, who is to be contacted to resolve the issue will depend on who is setting up the particular PIDs and who is administering that PID server.

Format Issues

*When Full Text Is Available in pdf Format,
but Patron Does Not Have Reader
and/or Has Difficulty Downloading/
Installing the Reader*

Many resource providers offer full text in a variety of formats. The Adobe Acrobat pdf format is one of the most popular, as it facilitates printing the document in exactly the same format one sees online. In order to open a pdf file one needs the current version of Acrobat Reader installed. The reader is a free program, and the latest version can be downloaded from the Adobe Web site, <http://www.adobe.com/products/acrobat/>. Some library patrons who are not familiar with downloading and installing software might need assistance. See the When Providers' Servers Are Unavailable section.

Again, as mentioned in When Providers' Servers Are Unavailable, having the appropriate browser (and the appropriate release for that browser) is becoming progressively more important. For example, pdf files created with the latest version of the authoring software do not display properly in older versions of the reader.

When Access to Full Text in pdf Format Is Denied

Some providers will restrict access to full-text content in the popular pdf format even though the option is visible to patrons. Usually the html version works, just not the pdf for the current articles. It is important while troubleshooting to try accessing articles by both the pdf and html versions if available. One must contact the provider to decipher why this is the case with a particular title.

Providers make these changes with little or no announcement to subscribers. During a given week, one can obtain full text via either pdf or html and the next week discover that full text is available only via html.

Linking Projects

PubMed

PubMed LinkOut is a very complicated and time-consuming linking project, but it can be tremendously useful to library patrons. Libraries that would like to participate should contact the National Library of Medicine and follow its instructions.

Other Linking Projects

Currently, the UCLA Biomedical Library has spent most of its linking project time setting up linkages with PubMed. When we are up to date on PubMed, we will start participating on other linking projects. Some patrons are very interested in our linking capabilities. It is important to let them know this is a complicated and time-consuming process that will probably need to be accomplished slowly due to staffing and time constraints.

USING THE TROUBLESHOOTING SCREEN

Identifying information such as resource title, URL, activation date, and relevant licensing data is already supplied to this screen from the original Resource Screen. Therefore, the only data that need to be added to this screen are those fields that identify the problem (see Figure 7.5).

- *Status notes*—this is where updates to the problem are provided. Each update has the name of the person doing the troubleshooting.
- *User reporting*—patron's name if a patron is reporting the problem.
- *User's IP address*—rarely completed unless it is suspected that the IP may be the problem.
- *User ISP* and *User Browser*—indicate which ISP, which browser and which version of the browser is being used if a patron is reporting the problem. This is how ISP and browser problems are identified and tracked.
- *Description of the problem*—this is where we record our first indication that there is a problem and exactly what the problem is so far. The person doing the troubleshooting adds his or her name after the problem description.
- *Notes*—this is where we record the steps that are being taken to resolve the problem or to indicate how long we think it will take for the problem to be resolved. This "notes" field is for longer, more ongoing messages than what we would include in the "status notes" field. Again, the individual completes this field or adds to this field his or her comments.
- *Problem type*—this is a pulldown menu that helps us to initially identify where the problem is originating. The choices here are: user, CDL, provider, UCLA.
   User would indicate that the problem lies with the patron—they may have been using old browsers, may not have configured their software correctly, may have been inept, etc.
   CDL indicates there is a problem with the activation or the licensing via the CDL and that they must resolve the problem.
   Provider indicates that the problem is out of our control and lies with whomever we obtain the resource from. It could

mean the provider has lost our registration, is experiencing downtime, etc.

UCLA indicates the problem is ours. Possible examples are that we have not registered our proxy server, do not have enough access for simultaneous users, did not renew the electronic subscription, etc.

- *Problem's status*—we have two choices here: *open* and *resolved.*

We can also create additional problem reports if a specific resource seems to have many problems or ongoing problems.

All Reference, Collections, and Acquisitions staff have access to the troubleshooting screens of the ERdb, but only the troubleshooting staff may add information to these screens. The screens are relatively new, but we are already finding these data useful. When a problem is identified in Reference, Collections, or Acquisitions, we can go first to the ERdb to see if anyone is already working on this problem. It saves time and confusion. At some point, we hope to be able to generate reports by publisher, title, or problem so that we can track trends and perhaps prevent anticipated problems.

CONCLUSION

These are the major troubleshooting problems we have encountered over the past five years. As the author has mentioned previously, there appear to be annual trends with some problems diminishing and new problems arising without warning. The expenditure of time for troubleshooting is approximately twenty hours per week, and we also do not see this time expenditure decreasing.

Communication is absolutely essential for troubleshooting—with the patron, with Acquisitions, and with Cataloging. Patrons may have very little contact with libraries and librarians, so we must therefore make each and every possible contact a positive and productive experience. Acquisitions must be kept in the troubleshooting loop if vendors are to be contacted to send copies of canceled checks to publishers, and to verify that we actually subscribe to a title. Finally, Cataloging must be notified if the OPAC URL is no longer valid or is not the best URL.

REFERENCES

Henebry, Carolyn and Ellen Safley. "Before You Cancel the Paper, Beware—All Electronic Journals in 2001 Are Not Created Equal." (Paper presented at the North American Serials Interest Group [NASIG] meeting, San Antonio, Texas, May 25, 2001.)

Inera Incorporated. "E-Journal Archive DTD Feasibility Study Prepared for the Harvard University Library Office for Information Systems E-journals Archiving Project" (Inera Incorporated, December 5, 2001).

Chapter 8

Electronic Reserve:
A Future in Transition?

Ebe Kartus
Susan Clarke

INTRODUCTION

This chapter describes Deakin University's current practice in dealing with journal articles destined for the reserve collection. The issues covered will include work flows, copyright compliance, and the ability to use aggregator articles. The chapter discusses the future viability and composition of a digital reserve (electronic reserve) collection within the library. It will provide an outline of how Deakin University might deal with these digital objects in the context of a university-wide digital object management system.

The Deakin University Library was able to digitize photocopies because of a change in Australia's copyright law due to the Copyright Amendment (Digital Agenda) Act 2000 and an agreement between the Australian Vice-Chancellors' Committee (AVCC) and the Copyright Agency Limited (CAL).

The term *e-journal* will be treated in its broadest sense. It could be either a journal that was born digital or one that has been digitized. Thus, an article from an e-journal could begin as a digital product, be digitized and made accessible by an aggregator at a later point, or be digitized locally within a university.

The authors' special thanks goes to Donna Runner, Digital Environment Manager, for her work in the joint conference paper which provides the foundations for this chapter. Thanks also to Dr. Peter Macauley, Campus Library Manager, Geelong Waterfront Campus; and Joan Moncrieff, Associate Librarian, Access and Information Resources, for their detailed comments.

DIGITIZATION AT DEAKIN UNIVERSITY

It has been Deakin University Library's policy to provide access to the library's collection through the online catalog. Electronic material (bought, leased, or locally digitized) is considered part of the overall collection.

Phase One

The first phase of digitization at Deakin University commenced in 1995. This consisted of scanning examination papers and linking these to course records in the library catalog.

The library does not accept any examination papers directly from lecturers. Since some examination papers are permanently embargoed, only those examination papers received from Academic Administrative Services Division (AASD), which is the university division responsible for conducting examinations, are made public. Access to the examination papers is facilitated via Deakin's Integrated Library Management System (ILMS) electronic materials scope. A 695 MARC tag (Deakin has designated this as our genre field) of "course code" and general subdivision of "exam papers" was added to the bibliographic course record (Figure 8.1). An image link provides the clickable link to the actual image (currently a pdf file) via the WebPAC (Web-based public access catalog). Examination papers up to the year 2000 have also been captured in text pdf format; from 2000 onward they have been processed through an optical character recognition (OCR) program. They will be proofread and then converted to tagged pdf documents.

Phase Two

The second digitization phase began in 1998. Academic staff were encouraged to submit their lecture notes, PowerPoint presentations, and any other material they had produced for in-class or off-campus presentation to the library, so that these materials could be made accessible via the ILMS reserve module. During this second phase, the electronic reserve contained only Deakin University-produced material.

LASH	eng	UNIT	U	LOCATION	rec	LAY DATE	-- --
BIB LVL	m	MAT TYPE	a	ENC LVL	q	COUNTRY	xx
RECORD #	b17163778	CREATED	12-03-1996	UPDATED	25-10-2001	REVISIONS	24

```
035     courseAIH232
092     940.40994 Ausswar
245   0 Australia's War, 1914-18
246     AIH232
247     335232|f-1993
490     R196/S1|xB30/031/X29 ; alex1 10.7.96
490     R196/S2|xR10 ; alex1 10.7.96
490     Reading list received|n1997 semester 1
490     Reading list received|n1998 semester 1
490     Reading list received|n1998 summer semester
490     Reading list received|n1999 semester 1
490     Reading list received|n2000 semester 1
490     Reading list received|n2001 semester 1
490     Reading list received|n2001/2002 summer semester
547     Enrolment 1997 Semester 1: B63/G93
547     Enrolment 1997 Summer semester: X140
547     Supplied by LRS 28/1/99; unit guide 1999 semester 1
547     Enrolment 1999 semester 1: B53/G24/X30
547     Supplied by LRS 7/2/00; unit guide 2000 semester 1
547     Enrolment 2000 semester 1: B70/G56/X58
547     Supplied by LRS 6/12/00; reprints 2001 semester 1
547     Supplied by LRS 13/2/01; unit guide 2001 semester 1 & summer semester
547     Enrolment 2001 semester 1: B51/G38/X43
547     Enrolment 2001/2002 summer semester: X100
695     AIH232|xexam papers
```

FIGURE 8.1. Sample MARC Tag for Electronic Materials

Phase Three

With the signing of the Australian Vice-Chancellors' Committee-Copyright Agency Limited agreement in March 2000 (retroactive to January 2000), the ability of the university to digitize materials, under the provisions of Part VB (five B) of the Copyright Act, was simplified. The third phase began during December 2000. In initial testing, items were scanned as tiff images and run through OCR software. The resulting file was saved as text (.txt), which was then coded into basic HTML. Consideration was given to saving the converted text as a Microsoft Word document and then converting this to HTML. This idea was discarded because Microsoft Word added excess HTML coding to the document. There were several reasons for preferring to supply electronic reserve materials as html files. First, these files can be read by Job Access with Speech (JAWS) software, one of the screen-reading software products, thereby making materials available to students with print disabilities. Second, with 43 percent of Deakin's students being enrolled off campus, it was preferable to keep file size as small as possible. Another consideration was to keep converted files "clean"; therefore, if at any time in the future it was decided to convert from HTML to XML, this could be done without further cleanup of the text. One disadvantage of using HTML is that it is not a faithful representation of the original document, which could be a very important factor. XML is able to give a better approximation of the original. The issue as to which will be the preferred format for electronic reserve files remains to be reviewed.

Retroactive Conversion

Due to the major time commitment implied by converting images to HTML, the decision was made at the end of January 2001 to scan the items as images, and then to link these to the bibliographic record. A fast document-feed scanner assisted this process. The photocopies were retrieved from the reserve areas in Deakin's campus libraries. The total number of items handled was approximately 2,500. Photocopies were scanned as tiff images and then converted to pdf. Both format files were burned onto CD-ROMs. The pdf files were copied onto the library's server. One reason for this two-step process was that no direct link existed from the document-feed scanner to the library's server.

In the initial rush to make this material available, we "image linked" the file to a simple preexisting bibliographic record. A function of the ILMS is the ability to use what is called an image link. The link appears as a 962 MARC tag in the bibliographic record, which is a local tag. The main difference between using a 962 MARC tag and using an 856 MARC tag (which is how most URLs are coded in a bibliographic record) is that in most cases it takes only a single click of the mouse to get to the image. The image link also allows the inclusion of extremely rudimentary rights management. We use the publisher subfield to indicate either from where the item has come, e.g., Web, Deakin, or under what agreement/license we have communicated the item, e.g., CAL, EBSCO. It should be noted that the ILMS supports both the 962 and the 856 MARC tags.

The image link dialogue box (Figure 8.2) has a field for the URL. To ensure that there were no errors in URL transcription, each image had to be opened in a Web browser. The address was copied and pasted into the relevant line. A secondary benefit of opening the image as part of the processing was that a check could be made to confirm that the image was visible and readable and that the required copyright notice had been appended.

Due to the time frame of the retroactive conversion, no attention was paid to the quality of the original photocopy. It was surprising to see the poor quality of some documents that had been judged to be acceptable in paper format. The standard for acceptability had risen dramatically in the digital environment.

Current Procedures

The standard for processing electronic reserve items is no more than five working days from the submission of an Online Communi-

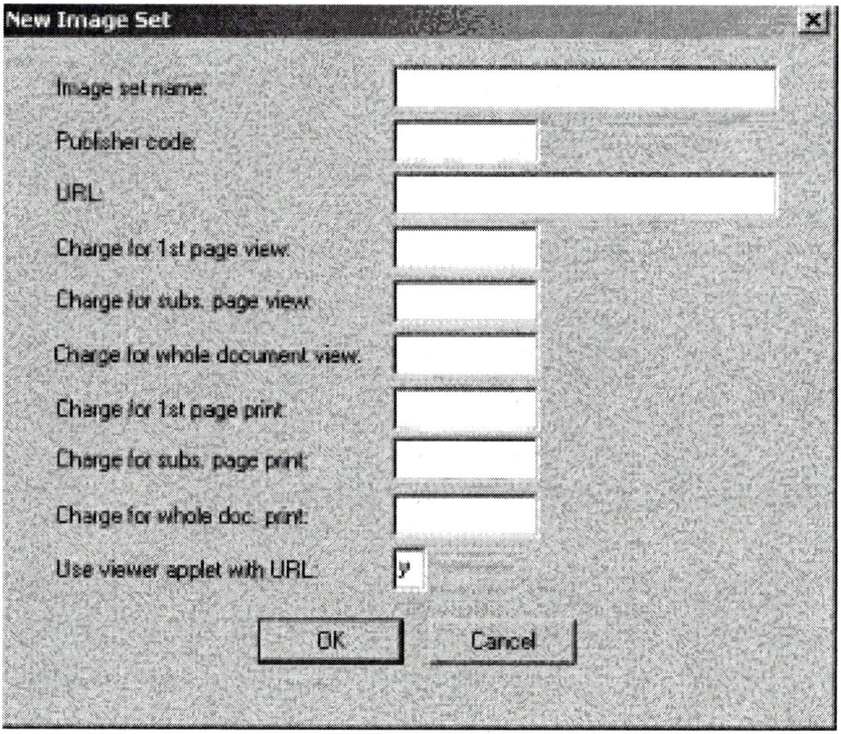

FIGURE 8.2. Image Link Dialogue Box

cation Compliance Application (OCCA) to the communication of the document. The work flow is shown in Figure 8.3. A variation on current procedures considered for 2002 is for campus libraries to scan from the original journals or books. This should improve both turnaround time and quality, compared to photocopying from the originals on the campuses and sending the photocopies through internal mail to the Digital Environment Unit (DEU). As a staff member so aptly stated: "Deakin University is geographically challenged with five campuses, some up to 200 kilometers apart."

During 2001, significant database cleanup projects were completed. These included:

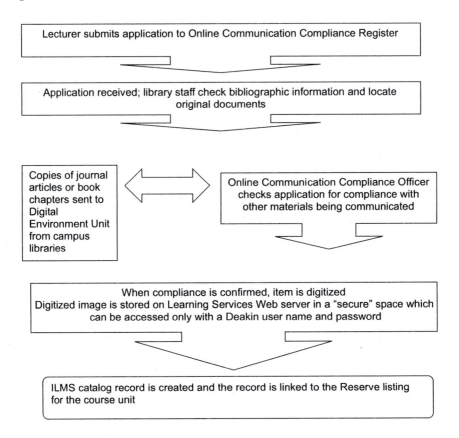

Lecturer submits application to Online Communication Compliance Register

Application received; library staff check bibliographic information and locate original documents

Copies of journal articles or book chapters sent to Digital Environment Unit from campus libraries

Online Communication Compliance Officer checks application for compliance with other materials being communicated

When compliance is confirmed, item is digitized
Digitized image is stored on Learning Services Web server in a "secure" space which can be accessed only with a Deakin user name and password

ILMS catalog record is created and the record is linked to the Reserve listing for the course unit

FIGURE 8.3. Simplified Work Flow for Processing of Electronic Reserve at Deakin University (*Source:* Copyright Donna Runner)

- Entering appropriate MARC records for Semester 2 material
- Deleting old lecture note links and files
- Removing duplicate bibliographic records for reserve items
- Merging some multicampus reserve records (an ongoing project as we need to examine each unit individually)
- General database cleanup projects

Generally, we have been pushing the boundaries of the ILMS reserve module. Unfortunately, it is not as flexible as we would like, especially in the area of digital object management. It is hoped that Deakin's new digital object management system (DOMS) will allow the flexibility that is required in the manipulation of these digital objects.

COPYRIGHT

Changes to Copyright Arrangements

For 2000-2002 the AVCC, on behalf of Australia's universities, negotiated a new license with CAL that permitted digitization of secondary source material, in addition to photocopying, under Part VB of the Copyright Act. As a result of the introduction of the new license, the library was able to start digitizing third-party copyright material for electronic reserve, and faculty and staff were able to digitize material without seeking permission of the copyright owner.

Digital copying, therefore, commenced through multiple means, for example, centralized for electronic reserve and for certain course materials handled by Learning Services (the university's teaching and learning support area), localized in faculties for course and supplementary materials prepared separately by academics. Awareness of copyright issues was high among academics experienced in Deakin's traditional flexible mode of delivery.

The introduction of the Digital Agenda Amendments in March 2001 saw a change in terminology from "digital copying" to "reproduction and communication" as a result of the introduction of the copyright owner's right of "communication to the public." The Digital Agenda Amendments had an impact in three main ways:

- Stricter (university-wide) limits for portions of a "work" that are communicated by being made available online. In other words, if a reasonable portion of a work is made available online for one unit, then no other reasonable portion of that same work can be made available online at the same time in compliance with Part VB.
- Need for the university to track copyright material being made available online because, although material can remain online indefinitely, there is deemed to be a fresh reproduction and a fresh communication at the end of each twelve-month period for which it is available. Some form of record keeping will be a requirement of the electronic use system that has yet to be agreed or determined.
- Obligation to attach the recommended Part VB notice before or at the same time as the material appears on the screen (Box 8.1).

Ensuring Academic Compliance with Copyright

Although the license permitting digital copying was greeted with enthusiasm by faculty and staff, the introduction of the new administrative obligations regarding Online Communication Compliance Applications (OCCA) was frequently regarded as an additional burden for already overloaded academics. Some faculties decided on a centralized administration approach to copyright checking and registration. One faculty opted to pay Learning Services to carry out the whole procedure, while another employed an administrative assistant to complete applications on behalf of academics.

Deakin does not have centralized digitization, but it has established a central database to record what has been digitized and what has been made available online whether through electronic reserve, faculty Web sites, or through our Teaching/Learning Management System (TLMS) and also to ensure copyright compliance prior to communication of the digitized works.

Online Communication Compliance Application

An OCCA must be completed for any material reproduced and communicated and made available online in compliance with Part VB through electronic reserve, faculty Web sites, or our TLMS.

Box 8.1.
Australian Copyright Notice

COMMONWEALTH OF AUSTRALIA

Copyright Regulations 1969
WARNING

This material has been reproduced and communicated to you by or on behalf of Deakin University pursuant to Part V B of the *Copyright Act* 1968 (**the Act**).

The material in this communication may be subject to copyright under the Act. Any further reproduction or communication of this material by you may be the subject of copyright protection under the Act.

Do not remove this notice.

The form, as shown in Figure 8.4, is the first screen that the applicant sees. As the applicant moves through the form, he or she must complete each section. As a section is completed, additional boxes will open to request more information depending on the answers given to the initial questions. The form is built in Lotus Notes. Figure 8.5 is an example of a completed form.

The online communication compliance officer (OCCO) uses a database to check that the requested item is not in breach of the Copyright Act and the CAL license to reproduce and communicate reasonable portions of copyrighted materials under Part VB of the Copyright Act. The OCCO will then either approve the material for communication online, ask for further information, or inform the applicant that the application cannot be approved. A significant reason for refusing an application would be that a reasonable portion of the copyrighted work is already being communicated elsewhere in the university. In this case, it is the OCCO's responsibility to try to negotiate an ar-

DEAKIN UNIVERSITY

ONLINE COMMUNICATION COMPLIANCE APPLICATION

APPLICANT:	
FULL EMAIL ADDRESS: (e.g. jblogs@deakin.edu.au)	
UNIT CODE: (e.g. ABC123)	
YEAR OF COMMUNICATION: (e.g. 2001)	
PERIOD OF COMMUNICATION: This includes year and semester or other dates you wish to make the material available	**Period:** ⦿ Semester 1 ○ Summer Semester ○ Semester 2 ○ Other **Dates to be Made Available** Start Date: [ ] -- End Date [ ]

ITEM INFORMATION

AUTHOR TYPE:	○ Author ○ Artist ○ Cartoonist ○ Musician ○ Photographer ○ Agency ○ Editor
AUTHOR NAME/S: Include all, last name/s first (e.g. Blogs Joe, Ramjet Roger)	
ITEM TITLE:	
ITEM TYPE:	Article ▾
LOCATION OF ITEM WITHIN SOURCE:	This relates to the page numbers, URL etc. within the source
MATERIAL TAKEN FROM:	○ Hardcopy ○ Off-Air Audio or Video ○ Electronic/Multimedia

SOURCE INFORMATION

SOURCE TYPE:	○ Book ○ Periodical ○ Video ○ Audio ○ Other
DO YOU KNOW THE COPYRIGHT STATUS OF THIS MATERIAL:	○ Yes ○ No

DEAKIN USE INFORMATION

IS THIS ITEM TO BE PLACED ON LIBRARY E-RESERVE:	○ Yes ○ No
ON WHICH CAMPUSES IS IT TO BE USED:	☐ Melbourne ☐ Geelong ☐ Waterfront ☐ Warrnambool
DO YOU HAVE THIS MATERIAL IN ELECTRONIC FORM:	○ Yes ○ No
IS THIS ITEM EMBEDDED WITHIN ANOTHER FILE ?	○ YES ○ NO

Click Here To Submit Form ▶

FIGURE 8.4. Blank Deakin University Online Communication Compliance Application Form

rangement whereby both parties can communicate the desired material or deliver it by alternative means.

If the application is approved, the reply indicates the dates between which the material may be communicated and provides the copyright notice that must be attached. The attachment of the notice is handled by the library staff in the case of electronic reserve. Compliance with communication dates is also handled by library staff members in the case of electronic reserve.

Offers to renew communication are sent out to relevant applicants just prior to the commencement of each period of communication.

DEAKIN UNIVERSITY

ONLINE COMMUNICATION COMPLIANCE APPLICATION

APPLICANT:	Lewis, Simon
FULL EMAIL ADDRESS: (e.g. jblogs@deakin.edu.au)	swlewis@deakin.edu.au
UNIT CODE: (e.g. ABC123)	SBC111
YEAR OF COMMUNICATION: (e.g. 2001)	2002
PERIOD OF COMMUNICATION: This includes year and semester or other dates you wish to make the material available	Period: ☒ 4th Feb - 28th June 2002 ☐ 8th July 2002 - 31st Jan 2003 If you need the material to be available all year, please tick both buttons.

ITEM INFORMATION

AUTHOR TYPE:	⦿ Author ○ Artist ○ Cartoonist ○ Musician ○ Photographer ○ Agency ○ Editor
AUTHOR NAME/S: Include all last name/s first (e.g. Blogs Joe, Ramjet Roger)	Ringnes Vivi
ITEM TITLE:	Origin of the Names of the Elements
ITEM TYPE:	Article
LOCATION OF ITEM WITHIN SOURCE:	731-738 This relates to the page numbers, URL etc. within the source
MATERIAL TAKEN FROM:	⦿ Hardcopy ○ Off-Air Audio or Video ○ Electronic/Multimedia

SOURCE INFORMATION

SOURCE TYPE:	○ Book ⦿ Periodical ○ Video ○ Audio ○ Other
	Title Journal of Chemical Education Volume 66 Issue 9 Year 1989
DO YOU KNOW THE COPYRIGHT STATUS OF THIS MATERIAL:	○ Yes ⦿ No

DEAKIN USE INFORMATION

IS THIS ITEM TO BE PLACED ON LIBRARY E-RESERVE:	⦿ Yes ○ No
ON WHICH CAMPUSES IS IT TO BE USED:	☐ Melbourne ☒ Geelong ☐ Waterfront ☐ Warrnambool
DO YOU HAVE THIS MATERIAL IN ELECTRONIC FORM:	○ Yes ⦿ No

If you wish to send this material to the library, please attach it in an email to: ereserve@deakin.edu.au
In the body of the email, refer to this application, please.
WILL YOU BE PROVIDING YOUR CAMPUS LIBRARY WITH A GOOD QUALITY COPY OF THE ITEM FOR SCANNING PURPOSES?
○ YES ⦿ NO

IS THIS ITEM EMBEDDED WITHIN ANOTHER FILE ?	○ YES ⦿ NO
IS THIS ITEM AVAILABLE IN THE UNIVERSITY LIBRARY:	⦿ Yes ○ No

IF SO PLEASE PROVIDE CALL NO (If Known)   540.705 Jou

DATE OF SUBMISSION:	13/02/2002
APPLICATION STATUS:	Approved
RENEWAL STATUS:	○ Yes ○ No ⦿ Pending
DATE CHECKED:	14/02/2002
DATE APPROVED:	14/02/2002
DOI:	
COMMENTS:	

FIGURE 8.5. Completed Deakin University Online Communication Compliance Application Form

Staff members wishing to submit lecture notes, PowerPoint presentations, and any other material that they produced for in-class or off-campus presentations to the electronic reserve are required to check whether these documents contain any secondary source material. If so, they must submit an OCCA for these items and indicate on the application where the items are embedded.

If materials cannot be communicated in compliance with Part VB, or any other license, application to copyright holders can be made through the university's copyright officer.

GENERAL COMMENTS

One of the greatest changes has been the concept of "communication" in the digital environment. Whereas photocopies, as long as they complied with copyright law, could be made available to students all year long on reserve, digital reserve items need to be more strictly controlled. The law as it stands allows, through special provisions, a greater degree of flexibility in photocopying material for off-campus students. It does not allow the full utilization of the current level of technology so as to provide access to these same materials in digital format for either on-campus or off-campus students.

The storage of noncommunicated digital images is also stricter. The library stores its unused images on CD-ROMs and not on its server. This makes it abundantly clear that this material is held for administrative purposes and cannot be, even accidentally, communicated.

AGGREGATORS

As explained previously, making material available via electronic reserve is not a simple process. There are two main components to the task. The first is legal, and the second is procedural. The legal requirements are the most problematic. This includes not only the legal requirements of copyright law but also the legal requirements of various aggregator contracts.

In any discussion of issues dealing with aggregators, it must be remembered that things are constantly in a state of flux.

It takes time, work, and money to digitize an existing photocopy to an acceptable standard. It would be much simpler to use articles from aggregators to which the library already subscribes, as the library has already paid for access to this material. Most aggregators allow only direct links to their databases. Only two that the authors are aware of allow copies to be stored, for a limited time, on the library's server.

Deakin University has a large off-campus student component. This creates numerous challenges that may not be faced by universities and colleges whose student populations are on campus and have access to the institution's network. One issue is that off-campus students connect to the university using commercial ISPs.

Currently, it is less trouble to digitize a paper article than it is to link to an article in an aggregator service. For user ease of access, it is simpler to store the article image on the library server. This bypasses problems of IP recognition, passwords for off-campus access, and the inability in some aggregators to link easily to individual articles. The Deakin University Library does not want to archive the aggregator image or "store" it for longer than it is required. A short (currently MARC) descriptive record is provided for each electronic reserve item. Information regarding which aggregator could provide access to a particular item can be added to the descriptive record. Thus, it would not be too difficult to reacquire an image that was needed again. An image could be deleted from the library's server and reacquired if and/or when it was required. This, unfortunately, appears not to be possible with the majority of aggregators.

Access to these same articles can be provided by digitizing the paper version in house and by communicating the image under Part VB of the Copyright Act. Therefore, the aggregators cannot bar access to a digitized copy of the articles. Ultimately, the university is paying twice—once for aggregator access and again to have the article digitized in house. In the age of the Internet, why is it easier and simpler to provide access to a paper reserve than to digital readings?

CHANGES IN THE CONCEPTION
OF A "RESERVE" COLLECTION

A reserve collection has normally been thought of as a collection of high-use and/or restricted access material. In the current environment, the journal articles and book chapters that form part of a reserve collection are digitized and referred to as electronic reserve. This distinguishes material from the remainder of the reserve collection. Often access to both paper and electronic reserve materials are provided using the same software.

The question that needs to be asked is whether the term *electronic reserve* is accurate. Materials are continuously available and can be accessed by any number of students. Thus, these are not on "restricted access" in terms of being available only on a short-term loan within a library building. These are "restricted" only in the sense of being available to university staff and students but, on the other hand, so are aggregator databases. These may or may not be high-use materials, but this is an inconsequential issue in the digital environment. Therefore, these materials are not different from any other digital library resource in any truly meaningful way. The differences are usually only in the way the materials are treated and their major points of access. Thus, it could be argued that electronic reserve describes a concept that is no longer applicable to the reality of an electronic library. These materials are just digital resources, like many others. An even more accurate description would be digital readings.

More and more courses, whether taught on campus or off campus, are being provided electronically. It is logical, then, that links to digital readings will be provided within the electronic course material. It must be stressed that these would be links to materials that reside in, for example, a DOMS, and would not be individual copies of the same resource stored in multiple course units.

Reserve is most often provided through the library's ILMS. These are quite efficient in dealing with paper reserve—something that can be held in the hand and barcoded. However, the ILMS is not yet able to deal with material that requires more than very minimal rights management. Various software packages have been, and are currently being, developed that have a more developed rights management component. In Australia, providing access, or communicating a digital reading, is integrally linked with rights management. With many

ILMS vendors developing a single front-end product (e.g., ENCompass, MetaLib, MAP), it is feasible to provide seamless access to paper reserve through the library's ILMS and to digital readings through an alternative product.

Even though more supplemental and required readings are being digitized, there will always be material that needs to be placed on paper reserve. This could be due to copyright or cost restrictions or to other types of access restrictions. Thus, the concept of reserve, as it is currently understood, is unlikely to disappear in the near future. The terminology that is used to describe the various types of material for which the library and/or university is providing access to will need to change to more accurately describe these resources.

THE FUTURE?

Deakin is investigating the feasibility of a DOMS. Since the final specifications have not yet been drafted, the following is only the authors' view of what a DOMS could be.

At its most basic level, it would be a central store for all of Deakin University's digital objects. These would include Deakin's intellectual property, items for which Deakin has purchased the copyright, and items for which Deakin has a license. It would need to store the metadata associated with each object and be able to handle numerous metadata schemas. It would need to have a well-developed rights management module. It should also be able to hold the images of the items that have been legally digitized and that comply with copyright law. Under the current legislative framework, it is questionable whether this would be possible.

Access to digital readings should be, in the majority of cases, via a link from the course in the TLMS to the DOMS. For those courses that have not been developed online, there would need to be the ability to link from either an ILMS or some other type of course outline to the digital readings in the DOMS.

To seamlessly incorporate access to aggregator databases into a TLMS, the following questions and/or issues will need to be addressed: deep linking to article level, stability of links, more manageable (i.e., shorter) URLs, ability to access these databases via a commercial ISP without constantly having to either authenticate or enter passwords (i.e., a student should only need to authenticate to gain access to his or her course).

Accessibility

In the digital environment, the issues dealing with different formats and accessibility to these become much more critical than in the paper environment. In trying to provide material that is accessible to students with print disabilities, texts are being reformatted so that the appearance bears no resemblance to the printed page. These texts are usually of smaller size so as to make them available, as the law allows, to off-campus students. This then raises the question of text integrity. In reformatting a text by processing it through an OCR program, is anything less than 100 percent accuracy legitimate? Should aggregator reformatted articles be acceptable?

CONCLUSION

The complexities and challenges increase remarkably in the digital environment. Deakin University has taken the first steps in coming to grips with these and in finding solutions to them. One of the major issues that needs to be addressed is that of digital rights management. Whether one agrees or disagrees with the implicit "locking up" of intellectual property, the technology and the various views need to be understood. Electronic reserve or, more accurately, digital readings is only one component in the digital environment, which is very much in transition.

Chapter 9

E-Books After the Fall:
A New Model

Vivian Lewis

After a few years of unrealistic expectations and lackluster sales, the dust is starting to settle on the electronic book trade. Usage statistics and survey results suggest that the digital book is not being embraced as readily as journal suites and aggregators have been. The electronic book clearly does have a future, but it will still require some work to be successful. Through a careful analysis of past and current e-book initiatives, the dimensions of the preferred model can be surmised. To succeed, the e-book of the future must first meet the needs of the reading consumer in terms of breadth of content, price, standardized file format, interface, and research tools. In addition, the model must protect the authors' and publishers' interests by providing reasonable economic return and a secure digital rights management environment. Finally, the chosen model must accommodate the library's needs for effective collection development tools, fair pricing models, multiuser access, reasonable archival provisions, full integration with other electronic resources, good statistics, and cobranding opportunities.

DEFINITION

The whole e-book concept is somewhat blurry, given the wide spectrum of products assuming the label. The term can be applied to any book-length text stored in one of a number of electronic formats (html, xml, pdf). Although many variations exist, e-books are typically divided into two broad categories: those that are served up on handheld readers (also called "appliances" or "devices") and those that are distributed via the Web for viewing on standard personal computers. To make matters more confusing, the term *e-book* is sometimes used to refer to the dedicated devices, rather than to the content.[1] The term *reader* has also been adopted by many companies to describe the software used to control access and to serve up content on the desktop.

The handhelds come in one of two forms: either as dedicated devices such as the Gemstar REB 1100 or 1200, or as multiuse Pocket PCs (combination personal digital assistant, mp3 player, e-book reader, etc.). Specifications vary considerably. The cheapest handheld on the market, the Franklin eBookMan, has a monochrome screen and no backlighting. Some of the palm screens are only 2.25 inches wide. On the other end of the spectrum, the top-of-the-line Gemstar features an 8.2-inch full-color touch-sensitive screen and is backlit to facilitate reading in the dark. The e-readers are often described as being the size of a large paperback. The e-book content, the actual files viewed on the readers, can be downloaded from numerous publisher and third-party vendor sites on the Internet.

The PC-based market includes both the large "library-like" collections (netLibrary, Questia, ebrary, etc.) and the new software solutions being released by multinationals including Microsoft and Adobe. The services vary considerably in terms of pricing, delivery models, and target audience. netLibrary and ebrary direct their services to the library market; Questia, Adobe, and Microsoft target the consumer. In both cases, titles are served up via the Web and can be viewed on any Internet-enabled PC.

BACKGROUND

The concept of electronic books has been around for decades. Project Gutenberg has been mounting free digital texts on the Internet since 1971, and libraries have been supporting CD-ROM-based books for many years. During the closing months of 1999 and early 2000, however, the new e-book models appeared poised to take over a major share of the publishing marketplace. Dedicated reading devices such as the SoftBook and the RocketBook were attracting lots of media attention. Over 500,000 copies of Stephen King's novella *Riding the Bullet* were downloaded in a single month. netLibrary, which opened its doors in March 1999, was billing itself as "the world's premier provider of electronic books."[2] The Boulder, Colorado, company reported raising over $100 million in venture capital and receiving over one million hits a week on its Web site during the first months of its operation. Its big competitor, Questia, began operations in January 2001 and marketed itself as the "world's largest online library of books."[3] The company targeted undergraduate students, with promises to help them save hours of research time and get better grades. In December 2000, Forrester Research predicted that by the end of the year 2004 electronic book sales would account for 14 percent of industry revenues.[4]

Libraries across North America were making cautious forays into the e-book world. Libraries of all sizes reported purchasing small numbers of the new readers. Staff members were developing circulation procedures and learning how to download new titles onto the equipment. At the same time, thousands of sites were entering into pilot projects with netLibrary for large collections of e-titles, either individually or as part of a consortium.

Even in hindsight, the euphoria surrounding e-books seems justifiable. Electronic books can be downloaded in a fraction of the time it takes to visit a bookstore or library. Several books can be downloaded onto one lightweight device, and most models allow searching, highlighting, and the creation of annotations. The concept seems to fit perfectly with the modern consumer's obsession with convenience, "edutainment," and "24/7 access" to resources.[5] Electronic commerce had been revolutionizing business processes. People were already banking, shopping, and corresponding via computers—so why shouldn't they also start reading books online?

Authors and publishers also had good reason to be excited. Creators were getting another platform to distribute their work. Publishers were securing an alternative to the inefficiencies of the traditional print (p-book) model. Estimates suggest that the e-book costs somewhere between 40 to 60 percent less to produce than its print counterpart and has a much shorter "time to market."[6] The e-book does not need to be printed, bound, warehoused, or shipped. It would never go out of print or be returned from the stores at the end of the season. E-books were opening up new sales channels as well: publishers could now market to the growing population of Internet users, some of whom were not regular bookstore customers.

Libraries were attracted to e-books as an exciting new service to offer local and remote users. Online journals (suites and aggregators) had become extremely popular with patrons, many of whom now shunned the paper formats at all costs. Libraries hoped that the e-book would be as well received as the online catalog, electronic reserves, or Web-based interlibrary loans. The ease of maintenance was also enticing. Electronic titles would never need to be bound or shelved. They would never go missing or require repair. In some cases, ready-made catalog records could be purchased along with the titles.

A mere two years later, however, the e-book seems to have fallen flat. Sales figures are suspiciously hard to come by, but reports indicate that the Gemstar readers have not sold very well, and even Microsoft and Adobe have not been able to conquer the resistance to e-book technology.[7] In September 2001, Contentville.com closed its doors after reportedly spending over $40 million in advertising. Two months later, both Random House and AOL Time Warner killed off their digital imprints. Just a few weeks after that, Princeton University Press closed down its e-book division, due to the "collapse of the market that never actually materialized."[8]

The large e-book "libraries" (netLibrary, etc.) have faced their own woes. Studies at major U.S. campuses indicate lower than expected use of netLibrary titles. At the University System of Georgia, only 800 out of several thousand potential users actually registered for accounts.[9] At the University of California at Berkeley, use of the 835 purchased titles was also disappointing. One staff member noted that "we just didn't see anybody beating down the doors." If anything, students seemed to browse the titles just long enough to decide whether they wanted to sign the print copy out.[10] Rumblings were heard about the company following a round of layoffs in early 2001. Publishers reported bounced royalty checks. The library world was not shocked when, in November 2001, netLibrary laid off most of its staff and filed for bankruptcy protection. The same month, Questia went through its second round of layoffs and hedged questions concerning the total number of paid subscribers that they had. The literature also became filled with detailed lists of the e-book's shortcomings, and dire warnings to libraries abounded about the risk of "jumping in" before the technology had stabilized.

General opinion now seems to be that the "paperless society" is largely a myth and that the e-book will probably *never* totally replace the printed text. Numerous studies have illustrated that online reading is slower, less accurate, and more physically demanding than traditional print reading.[11] Newer software (such as Adobe's CoolType and Microsoft's ClearType) use quarter pixels to smooth out the font, but the resolution is still poor in comparison to print. Contrast is also a problem, especially when the reader is held at certain angles or in certain lighting conditions. The "snuggle" factor also cannot be overlooked: many champions of the print book question whether anyone would want to cozy up with a computer before bedtime or at the beach. Using an e-book requires a bit of instruction, whereas most literate individuals can use a book without assistance. Finally, e-books, like any computer-based product, come with significant risks: devices may crash, servers can go down, and companies go out of business. As noted by Stephen Sottong, "a book in the hand is worth a whole database of books on a shut-down server."[12]

The success experienced with online journals did not appear to be carrying over to the e-book largely because of the length of the item and the amount of time required to read it. Several authors have noted that users seem willing to skim short "chunks" of material (e.g., articles) for specific facts or perspectives, but few will tolerate reading anything lengthier than about three paragraphs or 500 words.[13] Anyone working at the reference desk can attest that users are enamored with our electronic journal suites and aggregator databases, but most users will print, e-mail, or download even short articles rather than read them on the screen.

THE FUTURE

The future of e-books is likely to be neither as glowing as the preliminary predictions were nor as gloomy as some recent naysayers have claimed. The reality, as with most issues, is somewhere between the two. As stated in an October 2001 issue of *Publisher's Weekly,* "for all the pessimism, an aura of inevitability still surrounds electronic reading."[14] The bigger publishing houses, which were initially apprehensive about e-books due to concerns about security and the cannibalizing of print revenues, are continuing to invest (at least small amounts) in research and development. Third-party vendors such as Amazon.com continue to develop partnerships and to sign up new content. In many cases, the publishers are hedging their bets and signing multiple nonexclusive agreements with different distributors. In other cases, publishers are transforming themselves into retailers and setting up their own digital storefronts. In mid-September 2001, Random House, Penguin Putnam, HarperCollins, and Simon and Schuster inked a deal to sell books on the Yahoo! Shopping Internet site. That same month, Barnes & Noble announced the creation of a new digital book group division (Barnes & Noble Digital), with plans to issue ten to fifteen titles a month. Around the same time, Simon and Schuster launched an e-bookstore on its own Web site, <SimonSaysShop.com>.

Certain niche markets appear to have some real growth potential. Industry analysts often suggest that reference works (encyclopedias, dictionaries, etc.), which are meant to be consulted, rather than read in a linear fashion, will probably work as e-books.[15] Travel books, although not the gold mine originally envisioned by the industry, seem particularly viable as PDA or reader products to be carried around en route to a destination.[16] Certain kinds of fiction (e.g., sci-fi) might work in situations where graphics or special effects could facilitate the story.[17] The electronic textbook probably holds the most promise over the long term. A lightweight computer tablet which could hold a full semester's textbooks, with graphics, interactive multimedia, full-text searching, bookmarking, and annotation capability, would undoubtedly win over even the more skeptical reader.[18]

Other analysts have suggested that print on demand (POD) might be the real growth area, at least in the short term.[19] In this scenario, books are still converted or created in a digital format, but a print copy is made, bound in some kind of cover, and sent to the requestor. Sales account for at least 500,000 volumes per year. The publisher still realizes significant financial benefits. Books are not being printed in advance of anticipated demand (the traditional p-book model)— only to be returned a few months later if expectations are not fulfilled. The requestor is ultimately receiving a permanent paper copy of the work, which she or he could read in the bathtub, share with a friend, or annotate as she or he sees fit. The POD scenario works especially well for scholarly or obscure works with limited audiences and linear texts which are meant to be read from beginning to end and then pondered over time. Although not technically an e-book, POD might serve as a good bridge technology until a better model emerges.

THE NEW MODEL

Given the criticisms lodged against e-books and their poor performance to date, what is the real future of the electronic book? If a new model is required, what will it look like? A review of past and current e-book initiatives suggests that to be successful, an e-book model must satisfy, at least to some reasonable degree, the needs of all parties engaged in the transactions (the reading consumers, the authors and publishers, and the libraries). Courting certain parties at the expense of one or more others will jeopardize a new model's chances for ultimate acceptance.

The Consumer

Readers have certain expectations, which must be fulfilled before the electronic book will be widely accepted. In some cases, their demands are based on past experience with print. In other cases, the requirements are unique to the digital environment. As with most consumer products, content and price are the immediate concerns. In this case, reading consumers are also very interested in the standardization of file formats and the quality of the interface and search tools.

Content

Good content is absolutely essential to the e-book's success. Readers will tolerate some technological flaws, as long as they can gain access to the most popular titles or the highest caliber authors.[20] Content can be measured in terms of volume (the total number of titles), breadth (the span of subjects covered), and depth (the comprehensiveness within subjects). Currency (the number of frontlist titles or the ratio of front to backlists) and quality (the caliber of publishers and authors, the number of best sellers) are also important. Exclusiveness (the number of titles unique to the service) may also hold some merit.

There are currently hundreds of e-book sites on the Internet, some of them selling thousands of titles. That being said, e-titles represent only a small proportion of the total number of new releases—and certainly not the "critical mass" required to entice repeat customers. Precise numbers are almost impossible to obtain, but estimates suggest that Gemstar users have about 4,000 titles available to them through various channels. Microsoft Pocket PC users are less advantaged and frequently express frustration with the lack of content.[21] Microsoft and Adobe eBook readers for PCs can purchase titles from hundreds of "partners" but may still have trouble finding the title they want.

The large PC-based collections provide thousands of titles, but have still taken a lot of criticism for the "spotty" and "skimpy" nature of their holdings. For example, netLibrary's collection was described as an unpredictable "grab bag" of titles during its early months of operations. Publishers, we are told, cherry picked their backlists, selecting titles with only one author and no pictures in an effort to reduce the number of e-right permissions.[22] The criticism is more muted now: as of January 2003, netLibrary users have access to over 48,000 titles from 400 publishers.

Questia reports having 240 publishers under contract to provide content. The company originally aimed to have 250,000 titles by 2003, but financial difficulties have prevented it from getting anywhere close to that figure. As of February 2002, the service included 70,000 books; however, the company is often criticized for its lack of scientific and mathematical material. Mick O'Leary describes most of its titles as "obsolete items that would be discarded in any serious collection weeding effort."[23] In a 2001 study reported in *Library Hi Tech,* Susan Gibbons reports that of a random sampling of 100 Questia titles, the average publication date was 1973—with only one title published after 1999.[24]

The newest entrant in the institutional e-book trade, ebrary, is starting small but already looks like a serious contender. As of March 2003, 20,000 titles are available from 150 leading publishers. The caliber of its source materials sound fairly impressive. In July 2001, ebrary signed an agreement with twelve university presses, including Stanford and Columbia. At the same time, Springer-Verlag agreed to provide mathematical and statistics content, and the DSI Publishing Group signed on to provide its collection of early American history reproductions. In early February 2002, the company announced deals with Princeton University Press for frontlist and backlist titles, plus a deal with Elsevier Science for technical, medical, and business titles.

Pricing

Consumers are always looking for deals, and e-books are no exception. Digital texts must be priced inexpensively to attract first-time users, especially during the current period when the technology is still under development. Consumers, as a general rule, still seem reluctant to pay for content served up on the Internet.[25] In the post-Beta/VHS world, few people are willing to invest significant amounts of money on content until industry standards are in place.[26] The lack of content is also an issue: given the poor selection of titles, consumers will not always be purchasing their "first-choice" books.

To date, most vendors have accepted the necessity for some discounts, although few have dropped the prices as far as some analysts recommend. (Burk suggests less than 50 percent of print.)[27] Many, such as SimonSaysShop.com, regularly offer e-titles on par with or slightly below the print price. Sometimes very popular titles, such as the most recent Stephen King thriller, are offered at a deep discount for limited periods. Sites sometimes offer a few "freebies," but not as many as consumers would like.

Questia uses a subscription model. Readers pay $149.95 a year or $19.95 a month for unlimited access to its collections. Since opening, the company has tried many unconventional strategies to win business. In summer 2001, the company offered free subscriptions to over 100,000 students and faculty at four American universities. Later that fall, Questia inked a deal with AOL subscribers to offer free trials for all of their customers. The company has even been known to e-mail students' parents, suggesting that they buy a subscription for their son or daughter. The company has been very tight-lipped about the size of its paid subscription base, but industry analysts suggest the numbers are quite low. (Gibbons suggests not much more than 1,000 in a 2001 article.)[28]

Conversely, ebrary's consumer site uses a different and inventive business model. Users can view the books for free but must pay by the page to print or download. It is too early to tell right now, but this "photocopier"-type pricing model might be very successful with users who want only to read (and pay for) small portions of a work.[29]

Standardized File Formats

Ultimately, the e-book of the future should be "device-agnostic." Users should be able to download and view titles on the equipment of their choice. If their device fails or requires updating, they should be able to transfer the title to another machine. Users should be able to register for multiple downloads—for example, to have the same title on their desktop at work and on their portable device in their briefcase.

Historically, most e-books have been designed with proprietary software, which can only be read on a specific kind of equipment. Dennis Dillon suggests that as of 2001 twenty-one different e-book file formats were in use.[30] The restriction can be extremely frustrating to users: the book they wish to read may be digitized but not in a format appropriate for their equipment. E-books designed specifically for one brand of dedicated reader (e.g., Gemstar eBooks) are the most problematic. Why should someone spend $300 to $500 on a piece of equipment that can only be used to read a limited number of titles, especially given the generally inferior quality of the reading experience. The PC-based library collections (Questia, netLibrary, etc.) offer more flexibility (once the account is set up, users can search from any Internet-enabled station), but the titles still cannot be read on one of the portable readers.

The Open eBook Forum, a consortium of publishers and hardware and software manufacturers, has been working on the creation of industry-wide standards for several years. These standards would define a single format for all e-books. In theory, the standard would speed up the conversion of titles from print to electronic formats and allow e-books to be read on any platform.[31] Some momentum seems to be building for this (netLibrary recently adopted the standard), but so far no formal agreement has been reached. Some analysts suggest that the bigger players' commitment is less than sincere, given the financial benefits associated with proprietary products. As Dillon and others indicate, the big corporations seem to have their own agendas.[32] Companies such as Microsoft have adopted the standard but have layered proprietary rights management software on top. Adobe has been lobbying hard to have pdf accepted as the basis for the standard.[33]

At the same time, e-book distributors seem to be loosening up some of their restrictions on the transferability of e-titles. As of January 2002, Adobe allows customers up to four downloads of each title. Microsoft Reader 2.0 works on any Windows-based PC, laptop, or Pocket PC 2002 device. Users can now activate the reader on up to four devices.

Interface and Research Tools

The successful e-book model must present a fairly sophisticated interface and support effective and user-friendly research tools to meet the expectations of the more sophisticated online customers. At a minimum, users familiar with CD-ROM products or with the "open" Internet expect to be able to search full-text documents, bookmark or tag pertinent sections, and then print, download, or e-mail the selected material. However, they also expect a bit of flash: the e-book of the future must "wow" the reader with value-added hypertext linking to external sources (such as dictionaries, chronologies, maps, etc.). Readers should be enticed with interactive graphics and sound comparable to the CD-ROMs currently on the market.

The current slate of products has some ways to go: the dedicated readers allow searching, bookmarking, and highlighting. Some even allow users to make electronic notes to accompany the text. For the most part, however, the titles available are simply digitized reproductions of the printed page. The text is reformatted from the original, often with disappointing results (e.g., with inappropriate line breaks in poems or within mathematical formulas). The screen images are typically very flat—with poor resolution, low-grade graphics, and very few links to external material. Acrobat and Microsoft eBook reader software is considerably more sophisticated. Acrobat titles are served up true to the original. The latest version includes a "Read Aloud" button that simulates human speech.

netLibrary provides a fair number of good search tools but with some significant limitations. Users can search the full text of a single book or a whole collection by author, title, subject, etc. The site features a good online dictionary *(American Heritage)* and hypertext links between the text, the table of contents, and indexing. Printing and downloading, however, are supported only minimally: users can print or copy a single page at a time using their browser buttons, but transactions are monitored and users lose their accounts if excessive patterns are detected. Bookmarking, highlighting, and annotating were supported until January 2002 when the offline reader software was discontinued. As of March 7, 2002, bookmarking capabilities have been reinstated in a different form, and users now have the ability to open more than one e-book at the same time.

The Questia model is a bit slicker than netLibrary's. Users can search, then cut and paste chunks of text into their word processing program. Given its undergraduate focus, the product includes many useful student tools: for instance, readers can store notes on the server as part of a specific "project." Downloaded text is accompanied by complete citations in a choice of five standard formats (MLA, etc.). With Version 2.0, released in fall 2001, users can maintain a personalized bookshelf of favorite titles, as well as a customized home page. The screen display, however, is not ideal. Pages are served up as html files, so the original formatting is lost. Printing is supported, but only one page at a time.

ebrary offers a full selection of tools including searching, annotation, highlighting, and bookmarking. In addition, the service supports links to maps, biographical information, and other digital resources owned by the specific library. ebrary serves up books as pdf documents, so the pages retain the exact look of the original, including column configuration, fonts, and graphics. Page numbering, table of contents, and indexing is left intact. Page-by-page printing is also supported.

Authors

Creators play a strangely minor role in most discussions of the electronic book—except perhaps for prominent authors such as Stephen King, who actually have a say in how their books are marketed. No firm models are yet in place for distributing royalties for e-book offerings. As E. A. Vander Veer indicates in a recent issue of *Writer,* authors currently face difficulties negotiating proper advances for e-books, given that no one yet knows what the true value of the product is. Publishers, we are told, are trying to claim the lion's share of the rights by routinely including clauses demanding "other rights to be developed in the future, throughout the universe."[34] The control lies primarily in the hands of the publishers. In many cases, the publishers and creators may share the same interests—but not always.

Publishers

Publishers bring their own requirements to the electronic book trade. For them, two issues are of paramount importance: First, they need to receive a fair economic return on their investment. Second, they require a secure environment in which their intellectual property rights are fully protected.

Reasonable Profits

Publishers, like creators, must be adequately compensated for their efforts. Many were initially reluctant to get involved in the e-book trade for fear of encroaching on their print book sales.[35] The e-book costs less to make, but if it is discounted too deeply on the vendors' sites, users would opt to purchase the e-book instead of the print, thereby reducing the publishers' overall revenues. As Burk notes in a recent issue of *Library Hi Tech,* publishers seem to fear success and the "disruptive innovation" that success might cause.[36] Poor sales have reduced this anxiety to some degree, but the sentiment still lingers.

Some publishers, on the other hand, are turning the whole price issue on its head. These houses, primarily university and nonprofit presses, are actually exploring the revolutionary concept of putting their e-books up on the Internet for free—as a sales catalog for their print publications.[37] Project Gutenberg has been mounting public domain titles on the Internet with free downloading for thirty years. The National Academy Press made headlines when it disclosed that it had its full list (2,100 books in full-text page images) on its Web site and had actually increased sales of its print versions. Brookings Institution Press has 100 books up on its site. MIT, University of Illinois, and Columbia University Press are all testing the idea of putting some titles up for free.

Security

A successful electronic book model must satisfy the publishers' and creators' needs for secure digital rights management (DRM).

E-book piracy is a major international concern to the trade: estimates suggest that over $8 billion worth of U.S. books were pirated in 2000.[38] One publisher surmised that for every piece of content sold, another six copies are stolen, often by people who aren't aware that what they're doing is illegal.[39] In a post-mp3 world, mechanisms are required to restrict access to only those individuals and institutions that have paid for service, and then to prescribe the specific transactions allowed while on the site. Rights management has become big business: estimates suggest that there are currently over 100 companies in the United States providing DRM services.[40]

To date, the various digital rights management strategies (encryption, watermarking, locking, etc.) have not always been successful in restricting access to authorized individuals. Pirated copies of Stephen King's *Riding the Bullet* were posted to the Net less than one month after it was released. *Harry Potter and the Goblet of Fire* was pirated in less than one hour. In July 2001, Dmitry Sklyarov, a Russian hacker, was arrested under the U.S. Digital Millennium Copyright Act (DMCA) of 1998 for producing and selling hardware that cracked the code on Adobe's eBook Reader. (Note: Very few copies were actually sold, and Mr. Sklyarov's intentions were not considered by many to be malicious.)

More important, these mechanisms frustrate and alienate a lot of potential users. Analysts frequently describe overly cumbersome DRM practices as the chief obstacle to the e-book's popularity.[41] Users expect to be able to read an e-book on various devices and to be able to share a particularly enjoyable title with their friends. netLibrary users are often annoyed by the inability to print or to save large chunks of text to disk.

LIBRARIES

Libraries are important players in the e-book trade, as they purchase a significant portion of the electronic titles being released. In many cases, they provide customers with their first introduction to digital texts. They train users in basic navigation and then support the titles on the floor. Finally, they are familiar with and respect intellectual property rights, and so can be trusted to work within the digital rights management guidelines laid out by vendors.

Given this key role, libraries should be treated as partners, not as competitors for the limited consumer trade.[42] Most vendors seem to understand that reality, and have gone out of their way to develop good customer relationships with libraries. netLibrary and ebrary, in particular, have courted the library market by attending conferences, visiting sites, and preparing customized materials. Questia, on the other hand, has rankled many in the profession by marketing directly to university deans by offering forty-eight-hour subscriptions to panic-stricken students around exam times and by taking out fairly "low-brow" advertisements in student newspapers. One library reported finding yellow sticky notes on OPAC stations reading, "Try Questia next time, it's faster."

Libraries share many of the individual consumer's concerns regarding electronic books. In evaluating new products for purchase, content, price, interface, and search tools are all taken into consideration. In addition, libraries require e-books to integrate themselves with the complex buffet of collections and services already on the floor. Libraries require good collection development tools, adequate archiving provisions, quality cataloging records, meaningful statistics, and cobranding opportunities.

Collection Development Tools

Like the end users they serve, libraries require good content. When selecting collections, the sheer number of titles is of some interest, but the scope, depth, and quality of those titles is of primary importance. Libraries are looking for high caliber publishers and prominent authors. Depth of coverage is vital: selectors are often looking for classic works from publishers' backlists, as well as the more notable best-sellers. Currency tends to be a very important factor in certain fields such as medicine, science, and business.

The mechanisms for choosing content are also crucial. Libraries need effective tools for wading through large numbers of titles and for communicating their selections to the vendor. Sites need the option of picking and choosing only the content they want, rather than blindly accepting preselected slates. Notification systems, electronic or paper, must be in place to help grow e-book collections. Once usage patterns have been established, libraries should be able to create profiles with the vendors to customize future offerings. The entire process must parallel or be fully integrated with the mechanisms already in place for traditional books.

To date, netLibrary has supported collection development very well. The company employs teams of professional librarians to evaluate content and to identify gaps in its collections. Libraries are able to browse lists of titles by subject and to generate lists of new titles on the administrative Web site. Selections can be made on a one-by-one basis. In April 2001, partnerships were set up with book distributors such as Coutts Library Services to sell netLibrary titles. Libraries can set up approval or new titles plans and receive notification (via e-mail or slips) when items matching their profile become available.[43] On January 19, 2002, netLibrary announced the availability of Title Direct, a new tool to facilitate collection development. Staff in different departments will have access to specific areas of the site to review titles, create and store lists on the server, share the lists with colleagues, and then submit orders for processing.[44]

Pricing Models

Libraries require fair and reasonable pricing models before they can invest significant portions of their budgets on e-books. To date, few libraries feel confident enough in the new technology to be able to rely on e-books as replacements for print titles and often find themselves paying twice for the same content.[45] Titles designed for dedicated devices are not, in themselves, expensive, but the readers required to view them add significantly to the overall cost of the program. netLibrary purchases are especially painful: libraries purchase "perpetual access" to a preselected slate of titles for a one-time fee of 150 percent of the print price, with no discount offered for second or subsequent copies. ebrary was originally planning to sell its product on a strict "page-per-view" basis but has abandoned that strategy for the institutional market in favor of a flat annual license fee (based on full-time equivalent students [FTE]), plus a small fee for blocks of print/copy transactions (which can either be paid by the library or passed on to the user). The transaction fees range from fifteen to fifty cents per page, as set by the publisher.

Gary Brown suggests that in the future libraries will demand new pricing models based on chapters or sections of books. These "chunks" can be used for reserve reading rooms, printed in course packages, or included in course management programs such as WebCT.[46] (ebrary might prove to be a good fit in this regard.) Others suggest print on demand as a preferred alternative to the standard e-book. The titles can be ordered online or from special kiosks set up on the library floor.

Multiuser Access

When purchasing collections, libraries require multiuser access models similar to those currently in use for electronic journals.[47] Computer-savvy users expect to be able to access and read all of the titles in an e-book collection—even if someone else is viewing them at the same time. Publishers, however, are more comfortable with the traditional print (p-book) model whereby one user reads one book at a time. This model safeguards their intellectual property rights and encourages the purchase of multiple copies by large sites.

Questia and ebrary have chosen to support multiple-user access, but to date netLibrary has not. Individual netLibrary users must register on the site for a personal account. Once registered, they can "borrow" titles for a specific period of time (as determined by their institution), but only one user can "check out" the same book at the same time—unless their library purchases an additional copy—at the same undiscounted price. If five libraries negotiate a consortium purchase, their users are sharing a single copy across five institutions. (As an interesting note, the single-user model has shown some signs of crumbling. A much-publicized article in *The Chronicle of Higher Education* reported that netLibrary was involved in a pilot project with California State University, whereby about half of the 1,500 titles they purchased could be circulated to an unlimited number of users at the same time.)[48]

Archiving

The successful e-book model must assure that a library's users have access to purchased titles in perpetuity. Until these assurances are in place, e-books can be little more than accessories to the permanent collections. Books published on acid-free paper have been proven to last for hundreds of years, but no one really knows what the shelf life of an e-book is. The content and the data file may last for many years, but the hardware used to read it on may disappear from the market. The server could crash or the company could go out of business.

netLibrary's financial woes served as a wake-up call to librarians across North America. Customers started to wonder what "perpetual access" actually meant, when the files were stored on the company's own servers and could vaporize at any moment. Had we been snookered into purchasing the equivalent of a lifetime membership in a fitness club—only to have it go under the following month? In June 2001, netLibrary started offering "escrow" agreements, whereby OCLC would supply CD-ROM versions of books if it went out of business.[49] Some librarians were skeptical that the backup versions would function outside netLibrary's DRM environment. Publishers questioned whether they had the legal right to make such promises given that they had signed over rights only for sale of content via Internet. Some publishers disclosed as well that they had signed on for a set number of years and had the legal right to pull their content after that date.[50]

Integration with Other Electronic Resources

E-book collections must be fully integrated into the library's electronic landscape to facilitate seamless access by users and to streamline work processes for staff.[51] The cornerstone of this integration process is the OPAC. Studies indicate that e-book usage increases once MARC records have been loaded.[52] Users are able to search for known titles or browse lists of related works by subject, author, etc. If full URLs are added, the users can move directly from the OPAC to the e-book itself. Given that libraries often purchase hundreds or thousands of e-books at a time, vendors should be able to sell MARC records along with their collections.

Both netLibrary and ebrary succeed in this regard. Libraries can obtain netLibrary titles via OCLC, or ftp them directly from the company's Web site. Arrangements have been made with major library management systems (such as epixtech and Innovative Interfaces) to facilitate the additions. The purchasing library still needs to do some editing (adding notes, reflecting print holdings, etc.), but the bulk of the work has already been done. Reports indicate that the record quality is very good.[53] The recent purchase of netLibrary by OCLC bodes well for the level of catalog support in the future.

The OPAC is really just the beginning. E-books should link to other electronic resources owned by the library. In late 2001, ebrary announced that it would support the linking concept. The company will be using proprietary linking middleware rather than adopting the OpenURL standard but promises that the systems will integrate smoothly.[54]

Statistics

Libraries require meaningful and regular statistics on e-book use to determine future buying decisions and to justify costs. netLibrary has recognized this need and has committed significant resources toward providing good data. Six reports are available on the company's site to help individual libraries track the most and least popular titles, turnaway statistics, etc.[55] ebrary also provides usage statistics, but the details were not readily available.

Branding

Electronic books should support "branding," the prominent placement of the funding library's logo and/or name in key spots on the collection's Web site. Such placements help the libraries in their efforts to create a digital place for themselves. These markings also help educate the user about the value of Internet-based resources and the fact that their institution has purchased these resources on their behalf. So far, netLibrary and ebrary recognize the importance of this concept and have incorporated good branding opportunities in their products.

CONCLUSION

Publishers and individual readers aren't giddy with excitement over e-books anymore, but the technology cannot and should not be dismissed. The electronic book may never completely replace print or be as widely accepted as e-journals, but it definitely does have a future. The new model must balance the interests of the reading consumer, the authors and publishers, and the libraries. From the reader's perspective, the chosen model must supply a critical mass of titles, with sufficient breadth, scope, and quality to satisfy a mass audience—and at a reasonable price. Users should be able to download and view titles on the equipment of their choice and to transfer the title to a reasonable number of other machines. The e-book should feature an attractive, intuitive interface and also support a good selection of research tools. From the publishers' and the authors' perspectives, the e-book must supply a reasonable economic return on their investment and also protect their intellectual property rights. For libraries, content is still paramount but must be accompanied by good collection development tools, fair pricing models, and reasonable archival provisions. The e-book must also be able to integrate with other electronic resources already owned by the library, support multiuser access, and provide good statistics and cobranding opportunities. The list of tasks is, admittedly, daunting, but the potential benefits to all parties will undoubtedly be worth the effort.

NOTES

1. Ronald Jantz, "E-Books and New Library Service Models: An Analysis of the Impact of E-Book Technology on Academic Libraries," *Information Technology and Libraries* 20(2) (June 2001): 104.

2. "netLibrary Launches the World's Most Comprehensive Digital Library on the Internet," press release available on the Web at <http://www.netlibrary.com/about_us/company_info/press_releases/march291999-1.asp>. Retrieved February 16, 2002.

3. "What We Offer: The World's Largest Online Library of Books," available on the Web at <http://www.questia.com/aboutQuestia/about.html>. Retrieved February 16, 2002.

4. Goldie Blumenstyk, "Publishers Promote E-Textbooks, but Many Students and Professors Are Skeptical," *The Chronicle of Higher Education* 47(36) (May 18, 2001): 35.

5. Bruce Barton, "Publishing Books in the Electronic Environment," *Collection Management* 20(3/4) (1996): 25.

6. Judy Luther, "Innovations Affecting Us: eBooks—the Next Generation," *Against the Grain* 10(6) (December 1998/January 1999): 74.

7. Roberta Burk, "E-Book Devices and the Marketplace: In Search of Customers," *Library Hi Tech* 19(4) (2001): 327.

8. Michael Rogers and Mirela Roncevic, "E-Book Aftermath: Three More Publishers Fold Electronic Imprints," *Library Journal* 127(1) (Winter 2002): 4.

9. Goldie Blumenstyk, "Companies Find Academic Libraries a Key Target and a Tough Sell," *The Chronicle of Higher Education* 47(36) (May 18, 2001): 37; see also Diana Ramirez and Suzanne D. Gyeszly, "netLibrary: A New Direction in Collection Building," *Collection Building* 20(4) (2001): 163.

10. Blumenstyk, "Companies Find Academic Libraries," 37.

11. Michael Jensen, "Academic Press Gives Away Its Secret of Success," *The Chronicle of Higher Education* 48(3) (September 14, 2001): 24; Stephen Sottong, "E-Book Technology, Waiting for the 'False Pretender,'" *Information Technology and Libraries* 20(2) (June 2001): 74-76.

12. Sottong, "E-Book Technology," 76.

13. Thomas Mann, "The Importance of Books, Free Access, and Libraries As Places—and the Dangerous Inadequacy of the Information Science Paradigm," *Journal of Academic Librarianship* 27(4) (July 2001): 270.

14. Steven Zeitchik, "Screen Time or Smokescreen?" *Publisher's Weekly* (October 1, 2001): 25.

15. Sottong, "E-Book Technology," 78.

16. Zeitchik, "Screen Time or Smokescreen?" 26.

17. Ibid., 26.

18. Blumenstyk, "Publishers Promote E-Textbooks," 35.

19. Ruth Ellen Fischer and Rick Lugg, "E-Book Basics," *Collection Building* 20(3) (2001): 121; Glen M. Secor and Helmut Schwarzer, "A New Beginning: Distribution of Scholarly Monographs in an Electronic World," *Collection Management* 20(3/4) (1996): 6.

20. Secor and Schwarzer, "A New Beginning," 4.

21. Burk, "E-Book Devices and the Marketplace," 328.

22. Janet L. Flowers, "netLibrary.com: Cautious Optimism/Views from a Research Library and a University Press," *Against the Grain* 11(5) (November 1999): 22.

23. Mick O'Leary, "New Academic Information Model Bypasses Libraries," *Online* 25(4) (July/August 2001): 72.

24. Susan Gibbons, "Growing Competition for Libraries," *Library Hi Tech* 19(4) (2001): 363.

25. Dennis Dillon, "E-Books: The University of Texas Experience, Part 2," *Library Hi Tech* 19(4) (2001): 361.

26. Burk, "E-Book Devices and the Marketplace," 329.

27. Ibid., 331.

28. Gibbons, "Growing Competition for Libraries," 367.

29. O'Leary, "New Academic Information Model Bypasses Libraries," 72.

30. Dillon, "E-Books: The University of Texas Experience, Part 2," 354.

31. "Open eBook Forum," available on the Web at <http://www.openebook. org/>. Retrieved February 16, 2002.

32. Dillon, "E-Books: The University of Texas Experience, Part 2," 354; see also E.A. Vander Veer, "The Revolution That Wasn't," *Writer* 115(1) (January 2002): 18.

33. Dillon, "E-Books: The University of Texas Experience, Part 2," 354.

34. Veer, "The Revolution That Wasn't," 18.

35. Matthew Nauman, "Book Pricing Update—eBooks and Publishing: Developing a New Business Relationship," *Against the Grain* 12(2) (April 2000): 34.

36. Burk, "E-Book Devices and the Marketplace," 330.

37. Jensen, "Academic Press Gives Away Its Secret of Success," 24.

38. Mike Goodwin, "Napster for Novels," *Reason* 33(8) (January 2002): 61.

39. Thomas Pack, "Keeping Digital Text Safe," *Econtent* 24(9) (November 2001): 20.

40. Fischer and Lugg, "E-Book Basics," 122.

41. Rachel L. Wadham, "E-Book Explosion," *Library Mosaics* 11(5) (September/October 2000): 23.

42. Rogers and Roncevic, "E-Book Aftermath," 4.

43. "E-Books," available on the Web at <http://www1.couttsinfo.com/uk/index.htm>. Retrieved February 16, 2002.

44. "netLibrary Announces New eBook Profiling Service," available on the Web at <http://www.netLibrary/com/about_us/company_info/press_releases/january192002-1.asp>. Retrieved February 16, 2002.

45. Blumenstyk, "Companies Find Academic Libraries," 37.

46. Gary J. Brown, "Beyond Print: Reading Digitally," *Library Hi Tech* 19(4) (2001): 391.

47. Flowers, "netLibrary.com: Cautious Optimism," 22.

48. Goldie Blumenstyk, "Cal State Throws Its Weight Around in Negotiating an E-Book Deal," *The Chronicle of Higher Education* (September 7, 2001): 50.

49. "OCLC and netLibrary Update Content Storage Agreement," press release available on the Web at <http://www.netlibrary.com/about_us/company_info/press_releases/June061601pr1.asp>. Retrieved February 16, 2002.

50. Michael Rogers, "OCLC Purchases netLibrary," *Library Journal* 126(20) (December 1, 2001): 15.

51. Lynn Silipigni Connaway, "Web-Based Electronic Book (e-Book) Library: The netLibrary Model," *Library Hi Tech* 19(4) (2001): 348.

52. Dillon, "E-Books: The University of Texas Experience," 357.

53. William A. Garrison, "E-Books in the Catalog: CU-Boulder, netLibrary and the Colorado Alliance of Research Libraries," *Colorado Libraries* 27(2) (Summer 2001): 51.

54. David Dorman, "ebrary at Bat," *American Libraries* 33(1) (January 2002): 96.

55. *Learning netLibrary: User Manual, Version 2.0.* (Boulder, CO: netLibrary, 2000): 56.

Chapter 10

Open Access and Retrieval: Liberating the Scholarly Literature

Gerry McKiernan

An old tradition and a new technology have converged to make possible an unprecedented public good.[1]

BUDAPEST OPEN ACCESS INITIATIVE

On February 14, 2002, the Budapest Open Access Initiative (BOAI) was formally launched.[2] The BOAI is a public statement and plan of action that calls for "open access to peer-reviewed research articles in all academic fields and the preprints that might precede them."[3] The initiative is the outcome of an international conference held in Budapest, Hungary, in early December 2001 convened by the Open Society Institute (OSI).[4] The BOAI was authored by representatives affiliated with the university research community, for-profit and nonprofit publishing, and the philanthropic sector. Among the members were Michael Eisen, the Public Library of Science; Rick Johnson, director, Scholarly Public and Academic Coalition (SPARC); Peter Suber, professor of philosophy, Earlham College, and editor of *The Free On-*

We are grateful to the following individuals and organizations for their permission to reproduce selective screen prints from their respective project Web sites: Figure 10.1: eprints.org; Figure 10.2: Dr. Stevan Harnad, Professor, Intelligence, Agents, Multimedia Group Department of Electronics and Computer Science, University of Southampton, United Kingdom; Figure 10.3: Dr. Kurt Maly, Kaufman Professor and Chair, Department of Computer Science, Old Dominion University, Norfolk, Virginia; Figure 10.4: Timothy D. Brody, postgraduate student and researcher, Intelligence, Agents, Multimedia Group, Department of Electronic and Computer Science, University of Southampton, United Kingdom.

line Scholarship Newsletter; and Stevan Harnad, professor of cognitive science, University of Southampton (United Kingdom) and a noted proponent of author self-archiving. Other authors included Leslie Chan, Bioline; Fred Friend, director scholarly communication, University College London; István Rév, Open Society Institute; and Jan Velterop, publisher, BioMed Central.[5]

The authors characterize *open access* as the free availability on the public Internet of peer-reviewed journal articles, as well as nonreviewed preprints of potential interest to the scholarly community, that permit users to:

> read, download, copy, distribute, print, search, or link to the full texts of these articles, crawl them for indexing, pass them as data to software, or use them for any other lawful purpose, without financial, legal, or technical barriers other than those inseparable from gaining access to the internet itself. The only constraint on reproduction and distribution, and the only role for copyright in this domain, should be to give authors control over the integrity of their work and the right to be properly acknowledged and cited.[6]

Although focused on peer-reviewed journal articles and preprints, BOAI could be extended to include scholarly monographs on specialized topics, conference proceedings, theses and dissertations, government reports, and other writing for which an author does not expect payment.[7]

The BOAI endorses two strategies for achieving the overall goal: (1) the establishment of "a new generation of journals" and (2) authors self-archiving and commitment to offering open access to their full content.[8] The first strategy calls for the founding of new research journals that do not charge for a subscription or impose access fees, and the second advocates that authors deposit a digital copy of their publications or prepublications in a publicly accessible Web site.[9]

In that it also advocates the creation of open access electronic journals, the BOAI is similar to the vision of the Public Library of Science (PLoS) initiative.[10] However, although similar in this and other respects, the BOAI differs significantly from the PLoS in the breadth of the literature to be included and the nature and scope of access. Unlike PLoS, BOAI encourages open access to the peer-reviewed literature for all academic fields, not just the sciences, and, perhaps most important, BOAI seeks to promote author self-archiving, thus providing immediate access to current research results in contrast to the months postponement accepted by PLoS.[11]

NEW GENERATION JOURNALS

In an effort to provide and promote open and wide dissemination of articles, the BOAI journal model proposes that new journals no longer invoke copyright to restrict access or use of journal content. Copyright and other tools are instead recognized as a system for ensuring permanent open access to published articles. As price is an inherent barrier to access, such alternative journals would not charge a subscription or access fee. To cover the necessary costs of production and access, the BOAI advocates other funding strategies, including organizational and institutional support, endowments, gifts, page charges, or use of monies that would be made available by the demise or cancellation of journals charging traditional subscription or access fees. Significant savings can be expected for open-access journals by publishing only online and by dispensing with the costs associated with managing subscriptions of authorized and unauthorized access.[12]

Among the titles and organizations cited as exemplary alternative journals or publishers are *Algebraic & Geometric Topology* (<http://www.maths.warwick.ac.uk/agt/>), BioMed Central (<http://www.biomedcentral.com/>), *Geometry & Topology* (<http://www.maths.warwick.ac.uk/gt/>), HighWire Press (<http://highwire.stanford.edu/lists/freeart.dtl>), *Journal of Insect Science* (<http://www.insectscience.org/>), *Journal of Machine Learning Research* (JMLR) (<http://www.jmlr.org/>), *Living Reviews in Relativity* (<http://www.livingreviews.org/>), *New Journal of Physics* (<http://www.njp.org/>), and *Psycoloquy* (<http://psycprints.ecs.soton.ac.uk>).[13]

Free or affordable software for electronic journal publishing would also reduce the cost and expedite the production of open-access journals.[14] Among the available commercial and noncommercial packages and vendors are AllenTrack (<http://www.allentrack.net/>) from Allen Press, EdiKit (<http://www.bepress.com/services.html>) from Berkeley Electronic Press, ESPERE (<http://www.espere.org/>), Bench> Press (<http://benchpress.highwire.org/>) from HighWire Press, International Consortium for Alternative Academic Publication (ICAAP)

(<http://www.icaap.org/services.html>), PaperCutter (<http://www.
miracd.com/>) from Mira Digital Publishing, and Manuscript Central
from ScholarOne (<http://www.ScholarOne.com/>).[15]

Although BOAI advocates the establishment of alternative online-
only journals, it does not advocate that peer review—the core strength
of the scholarly journal—be abandoned. For BOAI, open-access
journals "do not differ from toll-access journals in their commitment
to peer review or their way of conducting it, but only in their cost-
recovery model. . . ."[16] For the BOAI, "peer review is medium-inde-
pendent, as necessary for online journals as for print journals, and no
more difficult."[17] Indeed, it emphasizes that:

> the quality of scholarly journals is a function of the quality of
> their editors, editorial boards, and referees, which in turn affect
> the quality of the authors who submit articles to them. Open-
> acccess journals can have exactly the same quality controls work-
> ing for them that traditional journals have. The main reason is
> that the people involved in the editorial process, and the stan-
> dards they use, do not depend on the medium (print or elec-
> tronic) or the cost (priced or free) of the publication.[18]

In addition to promoting and supporting open access for peer-
reviewed literature, BOAI also endorses open access for the electronic
preprints, preliminary versions of publications that are "put online
prior to peer review but which are intended for peer-reviewed journals
at a later stage in their evolution." Self-publishing on the Internet that
bypasses peer review, however, is not endorsed by the BOAI.[19]

SELF-ARCHIVING

Preprints

A variety of studies[20] have documented preprints as a predominant
source of information and medium of communication. As summa-
rized by Kramer:

> [T]he role of the preprint in the informal information exchange
> among scientists is a major one. It may well be the most vital

link that the scientist has on a worldwide basis to keep up-to-date on current progress in any field.[21]

Although there are various interpretations on the nature of the preprint,[22] it is perhaps described best as "a record of research distributed among scientists prior to formal publication."[23]

EPRINTS

Electronic mail was the first formal method by which preprints were distributed electronically. The inherent limitations of this distribution method, however, led Paul Ginsparg, a particle physicist then at the Los Alamos National Laboratory, New Mexico, to develop a more efficient system for storing and providing access to electronic preprints from a central location. Ginsparg wrote software that automated the process by which authors could submit electronic preprints on a central server and enabled them and others to search and retrieve the full text of this document collection.[24]

Since its implementation more than a decade ago, the Los Alamos National Laboratory (LANL) eprint service (<http://arXiv.org/>) has revolutionized scholarly communication within many scholarly communities.[25] The success of the LANL eprint service has also inspired others to advocate the adoption of author self-archiving as a viable and beneficial publishing option in other academic fields[26] and led others to develop improved software to facilitate the establishment and creation of institutional archives.[27]

EPrints is a free software package developed at the Electronic and Computer Science Department of the University of Southampton, United Kingdom, that facilitates the creation of an electronic archive of departmental or institutional publications (see Figure 10.1). The first version of EPrints (EPrints 1) has been available since the end of 2000. To coincide with the launch of BOAI, a new version of the eprints.org self-archiving software, EPrints 2, was released in February 2002.[28]

The EPrints software is made available through eprints.org, a Web site that is part of the Open Citation Project, a DLI2 International Digital Libraries Project funded by the Joint Information Systems Committee (JISC) of the Higher Education Funding Councils, in collaboration with the National Science Foundation. eprints.org was

Figure 10.1. eprints.org Logo

previously supported by CogPrints, itself funded by JISC as part of the Electronic Libraries (eLib) Programme (UK).[29]

Software Features and Functionalities

EPrints 2 offers a variety of user-friendly features and function-alities,[30] including:

- An installation script that automates much of the installation process
- Storage of individual research papers (or eprints) in one or more than one document format
- Organization of eprints in a "configurable, extendible" subject hierarchy that can be used to view and search the archive collection
- Submission of documents using a simple Web-based interface; documents can be uploaded as files, in compressed file format (e.g., zip), or mirrored from an existing Web site by specifying a URL
- Inclusion of associated metadata for authors
- Web-based or e-mail subscription as author or reader
- Web-based moderation option for administrative review and approval

- Automatic data integrity checks without administrator intervention
- Web-based system maintenance

An EPrint archive can use any metadata schema. Through a systematic process, an archive administrator selects the metadata fields and the level of access. Activities include the selection of metadata fields (e.g., authors, title, journal, etc.), determination of eprint type (e.g., refereed journal article, technical report, unpublished preprint, etc.), and designation of interoperability with open archives search engines.[31] Although the system is preconfigured to operate as an institutional eprint archive, it can be reconfigured with different metadata fields.[32]

Software and Hardware Requirements

A major objective of eprints.org is to offer a highly functional system at minimum cost. The major expense of managing an EPrints archive could be limited to hardware purchase. The following software and hardware are required for establishing an EPrints service:[33]

- a Unix computer platform
- a Unix (<http://www.bell-labs.com/history/unix/>) operating system
- Linux (<http://www.linux.org/>), the advanced and free Unix implementation, was the development platform and is highly functional
- an Apache WWW server (<http://www.apache.org/>), a professional-quality free software product, often included with commercial Linux, such as Red Hat (<http://www.redhat.com/>)
- the Perl programming language (<http://www.perl.com/>)
- mod_perl module for Apache (<http://perl.apache.org/>), which significantly increases the performance of Perl scripts
- the MySQL database software (<http://www.mysql.com/>), a database system that is free for noncommercial use
- the EPrints software itself

Special software such as wget, tar, gunzip and unzip that allow users to upload documents in compressed file formats (e.g., tar, gz, or zip), or to capture them from a URL, are also required.[34]

Once the prerequisite software has been loaded, the installation of the EPrints software is simply a matter of editing configuration files and activating an installation script. The software can then be modified to suit the needs of the local institution.[35] EPrints 2 is strictly internationalized with all metadata being stored as Unicode,[36] in accordance with the Unicode Standard, the "character coding system designed to support the worldwide interchange, processing, and display of the written texts of . . . diverse languages."[37]

EPrints 2 was developed under the GNU General Public License (GPL)[38] and is made available free of charge subject to the GPL.[39, 40] EPrints 2 was developed by Christopher Gutteridge, system administrator with the Systems Group, Department of Electronics and Computer Science, University of Southampton with the assistance of Mike Jewell. EPrints 1.0 was designed and implemented by Robert Tansley with enhancements and corrections by Christopher Gutteridge.[41]

In late 2002, a new version of EPrints (2.2.1) with additional configuration options and corrections was released.[42]

EPrints Sites

Many archival collections, in a variety of disciplines, have been established using versions of the EPrints software,[43] and include:

- AKT Prints <http://eprints.aktors.org/> (EPrints 2)
  The AKT project is an interdisciplinary research collaboration funded by the Engineering and Physical Sciences Research Council (United Kingdom) that seeks "to develop and extend a range of technologies to provide integrated methods and services through the knowledge life cycle of capture, modeling, reuse, publishing and maintenance; services taking knowledge."
- Arquivos Abertos da Sociedade Brasiliera de Genética, Instituto Brasiliero de Informação em Ciência e Tecnologia (IBICT) (Brazil) <http://www.sbg.ibict.br/> (EPrints 1)
- Behavioral and Brain Sciences (BBSPrints) <http://www.bbs online.org/bbsprints.html> (EPrints 1)
  An interactive archive for the journal *Behavioral and Brain Sciences*. Registered users can submit papers, commentaries, responses, and edit user registration information.

- Caltech Computer Science Technical Reports <http://caltechcstr.library.caltech.edu/> (EPrints 1)
- Caltech Library System Papers and Publications <http://caltechlib.library.caltech.edu/> (EPrints 1)
- CogPrints Cognitive Science Eprint Archive <http://cogprints.soton.ac.uk/> (EPrints 2)
  CogPrints is an electronic archive of papers in various areas of psychology, neuroscience, and linguistics, and many areas of computer science (e.g., artificial intelligence, robotics, vision, learning, speech, neural networks), philosophy (e.g., mind, language, knowledge, science, logic), biology (e.g., ethology, behavioral ecology, sociobiology, behavior genetics, evolutionary theory), medicine (e.g., psychiatry, neurology, human genetics, imaging), anthropology (e.g., primatology, cognitive ethnology, archaeology, paleontology), as well as any other portions of the physical, social, and mathematical sciences that are pertinent to the study of cognition (see Figure 10.2).
- DLIST (Digital Library of Information Science and Technology) <http://dlist.sir.arizona.edu/>
  The objective of DLIST is to serve as a repository of electronic resources in the domains of library and information science (LIS) and information technology (IT). Creators of materials in all areas of LIS and IT are encouraged to deposit their materials, regardless of format. Although all subject areas are encouraged to deposit materials there are two initial areas of emphasis: information literacy and informetrics. At this time, DLIST is able to accept only materials in English.
- CAV 2001: Fourth International Symposium on Cavitation <http://cav2001.library.caltech.edu/> (EPrints 1)
  The conference papers presented at CAV2001, the Fourth International Symposium on Cavitation held at the California Institute of Technology on June 20-23, 2001. The symposium proceedings includes invited lectures and papers presented by engineers and scientists addressing the state of the art, new developments, and new ideas in the basic and applied fields of cavitation.
- Iowa State University Computer Science Technical Reports <http://archives.cs.iastate.edu/> (EPrints 1)
- PhilSci Archive <http://philsci-archive.pitt.edu/> (EPrints 1)

An electronic archive for preprints in the philosophy of science offered as a free service to the philosophy of science community to promote communication in the field by the rapid dissemination of new work.

- Sammelpunkt. Elektronisch archivierte Theorie <http://sammelpunkt.philo.at:8080/> (EPrints 2)
- E-prints Prototype Archive (Università degli studi di Firenze) <http://biblio.unifi.it/indexeng.html> (EPrints 1)

OPEN ARCHIVES INITIATIVE

Mission

The Open Archives Initiative (OAI) seeks to develop and promote interoperability standards to facilitate the efficient dissemination of

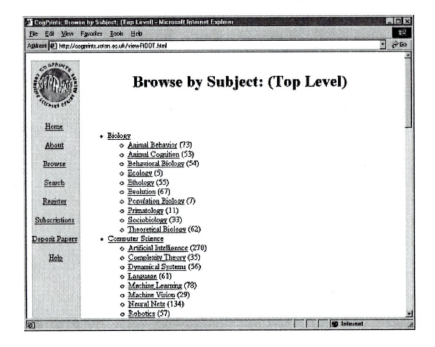

Figure 10.2. Selected Top and Subordinate Level Subject Categories in the *CogPrints* EPrint Service

digital content. OAI is based on efforts to enhance access to eprint archives as a cost-effective means of facilitating and increasing the availability of scholarly research, and the support of this activity remains a cornerstone of the open archives movement.[44] Within the eprints community, the term *archive* refers to a repository for stored information,[45] and the term *open* is used in an architectural sense for "defining and promoting machine interfaces that facilitate the availability of content from a variety of providers."[46] Although the initial work in the OAI has been focused on interoperability for eprint collections, the conceptual foundation of the OAI interoperability framework has applications beyond the eprint community, and the OAI has adopted a broader mission statement to open access to a range of other digital materials.[47]

Participation

The OAI invites participation in its interoperability framework at two levels: as *data provider* and/or *service provider.* Data providers can support the initiative by using the OAI protocol and registering their archive through the OAI data provider registration Web page;[48] service providers, which develop and offer services that harvest metadata from data providers that utilize the OAI protocol to build value-added services, can register via the service provider registration page.[49] In each case, both providers publicize their collections or services. As the OAI protocol provides a "mechanism for exposing metadata in multiple forms" via Internet and the Web, it offers unprecedented opportunities for knowledge sharing and publishing alternatives. As the service framework is implemented and adopted, it is hoped that over time content will become more visible and accessible to a broader community.[50]

Support for Open Archives Initiative activities is provided by the Digital Library Federation and the Coalition for Networked Information; additional funding has been provided by the National Science Foundation (Grant No. IIS-9817416) and the Defense Advanced Projects Agency (Grant No. N66001-98-1-8908).[51]

OPEN ARCHIVES INITIATIVE PROTOCOL
FOR METADATA HARVESTING

The generic version of the EPrints software is fully interoperable with all eprint archives that have implemented the Open Archives Initiative Protocol for Metadata Harvesting (OAI-PMH). Using this protocol, documents in registered OAI-compliant archives can be "harvested" into a global *virtual archive* by open archive services providers.[52] The OAI protocol provides access to metadata from OAI-compliant repositories; a *repository* is defined as a network-accessible server to which OAI protocol requests can be submitted.[53]

The current OAI technical infrastructure that specifies the OAI-PMH defines a mechanism for data providers to expose their metadata through an HTTP-based protocol. Although the OAI mission is not limited to the use of metadata, it is guided by the goal "to define a low-barrier and widely applicable framework for cross-repository interoperability," and strongly promotes the use of metadata as a "plausible route to such a goal." In the future, it plans to explore and define other mechanisms for interoperability.[54]

Dublin Core

The OAI-PMH defines a mechanism for harvesting records containing metadata from repositories. However, the protocol does not mandate the means of association between that metadata and related content. As some providers may wish to access the content associated with harvested metadata, data providers may want to link metadata to content. The Dublin Core format[55] offers the "identifier" element that can be used to associate metadata and content.[56] As the Dublin Core has become a de facto standard for simple cross-discipline metadata, it is considered an appropriate choice for a common metadata set.[57] The OAI-PMH is not limited, however, to the use of the Dublin Core; the protocol also supports parallel metadata sets, allowing research communities to use formats that are specific and most appropriate to their applications and domains. The OAI technical framework does not limit the nature of such parallel sets, other than that the metadata records be structured as XML data.[58,59]

The OAI-PMH was extensively tested prior to its public release in January 2001. It was subsequently upgraded to accommodate XML

Schema changes made in May 2001 (version 1.1). A new version of the protocol (v. 2.0) was publicly released on June 14, 2002.[60]

Data Providers

In addition to the various EPrints archives, there are several dozen other OAI registered data providers. These collections cover a variety of subjects and formats [61] and include:

- arXiv (Los Alamos National Laboratory)
- Chemistry Preprint Server (ChemWeb)
- CIMI Metadata Harvesting Working Group Demonstration Repository (CIMI Consortium)
- Comparative Bantu Online Dictionary (CBOLD) (University of California at Berkeley)
- ConoZe: intelligere ut credas, credere ut intelligas (<http://conoZe.com/>)
- Elektronisches Dokumenten-, Archivierungs-, und Retrievalsystem der Universität Dortmund
- Ethnologue: Languages of the World (SIL International)
- Hong Kong University Thesis Online
- Library of Congress Open Archive Initiative Repository
- Mathematics Preprint Server (Elsevier Science)
- NACA Technical Reports (National Advisory Committee for Aeronautics)
- OCLC Online Computer Library Center Theses and Dissertations Repository
- Open Video Project (University of North Carolina at Chapel Hill)
- Resource Discovery Network (RDN) (United Kingdom)
- Schoenberg Center for Electronic Text and Image (University of Pennsylvania)
- Universidad de las Américas (University of the Americas), Puebla (Mexico) Tesis Digitales project
- University of Michigan Library Digital Library Production Service
- Uppsala (Sweden) University Digital Archive
- Virginia Polytechnic and State University Thesis and Dissertation Collection

Service Providers

Although there are fewer service providers than data providers, the current registered service providers offer a range of retrieval options and functionalities [62] and presently include:

- Arc (Old Dominion University): A federated search service based on metadata harvested from several OAI-compliant repositories
- Citebase (Southampton University): A search service provides users with the ability to search across multiple archives with results ranked by a variety of criteria, such as citation impact
- DP9 (Old Dominion University): An open source gateway service that allows general Internet search engines such as Google (<http://www.google.com/>) to index OAI-compliant archives
- Networked Computer Science Technical Reference Library (NCSTRL) (Old Dominion University, University of Virginia, Virginia Polytechnic Institute and State University): An OAI-based implementation of the NCSTRL project that provides unified access to technical reports and eprints from computer science departments
- Repository Explorer (Virginia Polytechnic Institute and State University): An interactive Web-based tool to test repositories for compliance with the Open Archives Initiative Protocol (versions 1.0 or 1.1)
- Torii (International School for Advanced Studies, Trieste, Italy): A service that provides unified access to various open archives in physics and computer science that offers filtering, personalization, and other advanced features

Among the most comprehensive service providers is Arc (<http://arc.cs.odu.edu/>), a cross-archive searching service developed by faculty associated with the Department of Computer Science at Old Dominion University, Norfolk, Virginia. The search interface supports both simple and advanced search functionalities, as well as results sorting by date stamp, relevance ranking, and archive. The simple search option allows the user to search free text across the search archives, while its advanced search feature permits the user to search in specific metadata fields. Users can also search or browse specific archives and/or archive partition (see Figure 10.3).[63]

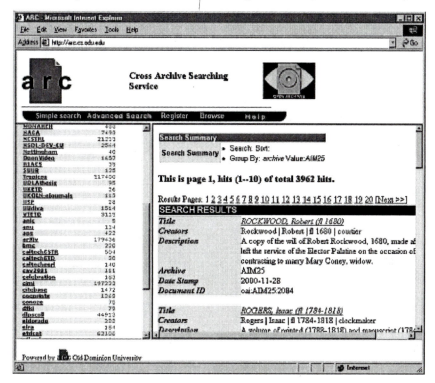

Figure 10.3. The Arc Cross-Archive Searching Service Browse Interface Screen

Another service provider, Citebase (<http://citebase.eprints.org>), offers cross-archive searching for two major OAI-compliant eprint archives: arXiv.org and CogPrints. Search results can be ranked according to various criteria, notably citation impact. Citebase is a prototype intended to demonstrate open access citation linking and harvesting and was created and is maintained by Timothy D. Brody, a postgraduate student and researcher with the Intelligence, Agents, Multimedia Group of the Electronic and Computer Science Department at the University of Southampton (United Kingdom).[64] Citation data has been extracted computationally from the arXiv.org collection using software developed under the Open Citation (OpCit) Project, an international cooperative project based at the University of Southampton (United Kingdom) directed by Stevan Harnad (see Figure 10.4).[65]

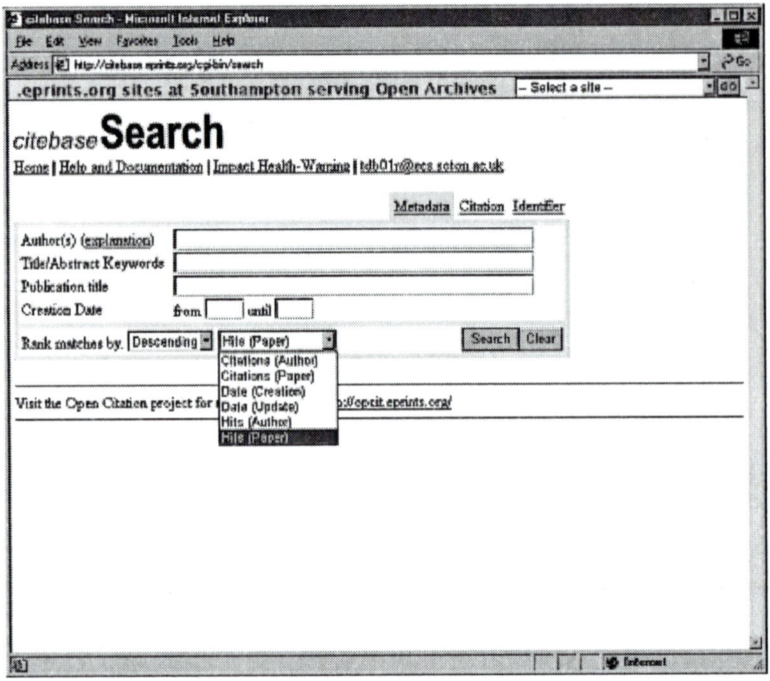

Figure 10.4. Citebase Search Page with Pull-Down Menu Listing Rank Display Options

ROLES AND RESPONSIBILITIES OF SELF-ARCHIVING

In a major review on self-archiving and its associated implications and ramifications, Harnad outlines the roles and responsibilities that stakeholders should have in the liberation of the research literature.[66]

Researchers

For Harnad, "the freeing of their present and future refereed research from all access- and impact-barriers forever is now entirely in the hands of researchers." From his point of view, distributed, institution-based self-archiving is "a powerful and natural complement to central, discipline-based self-archiving" that will "broaden and accelerate the self-archiving initiative."

Universities

Harnad advocates that "universities should create institutional eprint archives . . . for all their researchers" and mandate that their faculty adopt this publication option. As he observes,

> it is already becoming normal practice for faculty to keep and update their institutional CVs online on the Web; it should be made standard practice that all CV entries for refereed journal articles are linked to their archived full-text version in the university's Eprint Archive.

For researchers "who profess to be too busy, tired, old, or inexpert to self-archive their papers for themselves," Harnad proposes "a modest start-up budget to pay library experts or students to do it for them." For him such an investment " . . . will only be needed to get the first wave over the top; from then on, the momentum from the enhanced access and impact will maintain itself, and self-archiving will become as standard a practice as e-mail."

Libraries

For Harnad, "[l]ibraries are the most natural allies of researchers in the self-archiving initiative to free the refereed journal literature" as they have been affected most by the ever-increasing costs of institutional journal subscriptions in the past two decades. He believes the self-archiving paradigm offers librarians and libraries an opportunity "to establish a new digital niche for themselves" by "facilitating the all-important start-up wave of self-archiving" and maintaining the eprint archives. Through such initiatives as SPARC (<http://www.arl.org/sparc>) and "their collective, consortial power," Harnad believes that "libraries can also facilitate a stable transition" by leveraging support for publishers who are prepared to provide open access and offer the key feature of formal publication, the peer-review service.

Students

Harnad advises students "to keep doing what they do naturally: favor material that is freely accessible on the Web."

Publishers

Harnad believes that "publishers should concede graciously on self-archiving as the American Physical Society (APS) has . . . and not try to use copyright or embargo policy to prevent or retard" its adoption. From his point of view, "such measures are in direct conflict with the interests of research and researchers, ... are destined to fail, . . . can already be legally circumvented, and . . . only make publishers look bad." For Harnad, a better policy would be for publishers "to concede on the optimal and inevitable for research," and plan to separate their quality control and certification functions from the access and needless "added-value" features.

Government and Society

As much of research and its associated publication has been supported by public funding, Harnad strongly believes that public archiving of public research worldwide should be mandated:

> Government and society should support the self-archiving initiative, reminding themselves that most of this giveaway research has been supported by public funds, with the support explicitly conditional on making the research findings public.

> The beneficiaries will not just be research and researchers, but society itself, inasmuch as research is supported because of its potential benefits to society.

> Researchers in developing countries and at the less affluent universities and research institutions of developed countries will benefit even more from barrier-free access to the research literature than will the better-off institutions, but it is instructive to remind ourselves that even the most affluent institutional libraries cannot afford most of the refereed journals!

> . . . And on the other side of barrier-free access to the work of others, all researchers, even the most affluent, will benefit from the barrier-free impact of their own work on the work of others.

Furthermore, Harnad believes that "a freed, interoperable, digital research literature will not only radically enhance access, navigation, . . . and impact, [but] will also spawn new ways of monitoring and measuring . . . [the] impact, productivity and quality [of research]."

Foundations and Funding Agencies

Among the alternative funding options proposed for the establishment of open-access journals are subsidies from foundations and other granting agencies.[67] To accelerate the adoption and use of institution-based self-archiving, as well as the establishment of open-access electronic journals, the Open Society Institute (OSI) provided a multimillion-dollar grant to launch the Budapest Open Access Initiative in February 2002.[68] The OSI is the private granting agency "established . . . to promote the development and maintenance of open societies around the world"[69] and is one of several that form the Soros Foundations Network, the private operating and grant-making organization established by George Soros, the billionaire philanthropist.[70] Although other donors have been approached, to date the OSI remains the major benefactor, committing one million dollars per year for three years. As the costs of establishing an institutional eprint archive or alternative electronic journal are low ($10,000 and $50,000 respectively), this grant is expected to assist in the establishment of a significant number of archives and "new generation" journals.[71]

"THE FUTURE OF IDEAS"

The desire of Harnad and others to liberate the research literature by utilizing the potential of the Internet and associated technologies is representative of many current open-access movements, from the collaborative development and use of open source software to the widespread adoption of peer-to-peer networking for exchanging music files and other media. A recent review of *The Future of Ideas: The Fate of the Commons in a Connected World* [72] by Lawrence Lessig, professor of law, Stanford Law School, clearly articulates the inherent benefits of the Internet for creativity and innovation:

The explosion of innovation we have seen in the environment of the Internet was not conjured from some new, previously unimagined technological magic; instead, it came from an ideal as old as the nation. Creativity flourished there because the Internet protected an innovation commons. The Internet's very design built a neutral platform upon which the widest range of creators could experiment.

The legal architecture surrounding it protected this free space so that culture and information—the ideas of our era—could flow freely and inspire an unprecedented breadth of expression.[73]

Although Lessig focuses on a disturbing trend that seeks to extend and apply restrictive copyright and patent protection, his overall concern is not unlike that of Harnad and his colleagues who seek barrier-free access to the research literature; each recognizes the detrimental effects of stringent copyright and restrictive access on the open exchange of ideas. For Lessig, aggressive copyright protection "has allowed the media and software giants . . . to monopolize our cultural, intellectual, and political life,"[74] while for Harnad, barriers to author research imposed by the prevalent publishing model are both paradoxical and unwarranted.

In June 1995, the Association of Research Libraries (ARL), Office of Scientific and Academic Publishing, published an edited volume of "an Internet discussion about scientific and scholarly journals and their future" that ensued in response to a "subversive proposal for electronic publishing" made in June 1994 by Harnad, then at Princeton University. The volume provides a synthesis of views, with relevant commentary, on the future of scholarly publishing in the Internet era by various proponents and opponents of alternative publishing models such as the eprints service established by Ginsparg in 1991.[75]

In their conclusion, the volume editors, Ann Shumelda Okerson and James O'Donnell, make several observations that are as valid now as they were then for those considering participation in open access and retrieval initiatives:

Ideas can change the world. Will these? The uncertainties are many. The model that Paul Ginsparg has already brought to life is one that clearly can work, at least under specific conditions.

Where a well-defined group of users, all acclimated to the same kind of discourse and even familiar with standard software packages that transmit well by network, concentrate on producing rigorously analytical material, the relatively unobtrusive preprint server can be a powerful tool. Does it scale up?[76]

Although limited at this time, use of the generic EPrints software by a range of institutions for a variety of subject collections indicates that self-archiving can indeed enhance and broaden access to the research literature. Whether the self-archiving model becomes the new paradigm for scholarly publishing as envisioned by its proponents will depend not only on improved archiving and retrieval software and systems but also, and more importantly, on the degree to which all stakeholders endorse and embrace its potential as a viable and sustainable publishing alternative.

As of late March 2002, nearly 3,000 individuals and organizations, representing major universities and fields of research, have signed the Budapest Open Access Initiative; others who wish to endorse the initiative can do so by signing a Web-based petition[77] and by engaging in activities that support its philosophy and vision.[78]

NOTES

1. Open Society Institute, "Budapest Open Access Initiative," 2002. <http://www.soros.org/openaccess/read.shtml> Accessed March 16, 2002.

2. Ivan Noble, "Boost for Research Paper Access," *BBC News. Sci-Tech* (February 14, 2002). <http://news.bbc.co.uk/hi/english/sci/tech/newsid_1818000/1818652.stm> Accessed March 16, 2002.

3. Peter Suber, "The Budapest Open Access Initiative," Posting to VPIEJ-L electronic discussion list, February 15, 2002.

4. Peter Suber, "Budapest Open Access Initiative: Frequently Asked Questions," 2003. <http://www.earlham.edu/~peters/fos/boaifaq.htm> Accessed March 3, 2003.

5. Open Society Institute, "Budapest Open Access Initiative."

6. Ibid.

7. Suber, "The Budapest Open Access Initiative: Frequently Asked Questions."

8. Open Society Institute, "Budapest Open Access Initiative."

9. eprints.org, "Self-Archiving FAQ," n.d. <http://www.eprints.org/self-faq/> Accessed March 17, 2002.

10. Public Library of Science, "Public Library of Science," n.d. <http://www.publiclibraryofscience.org/> Accessed March 18, 2002.

11. Suber, "The Budapest Open Access Initiative."

12. Suber, "Budapest Open Access Initiative: Frequently Asked Questions."

13. Budapest Open Access Initiative, "Open Access Journals," n.d. <http://www.soros.org/openaccess/journals.shtml> Accessed March 24, 2002.

14. Suber, "Budapest Open Access Initiative: Frequently Asked Questions."

15. Scholarly Publishing and Academic Resources Coalition, "Publishing Resources for Journals and Repositories," 2002. <http://www.arl.org/sparc/core/index.asp?page=h16> Accessed March 24, 2002.

16. Suber, "Budapest Open Access Initiative: Frequently Asked Questions."

17. Ibid.

18. Ibid.

19. Ibid.

20. Ruth Kramer, "The Role of the Preprint in Communication Among Scientists," a paper prepared in fulfillment of the requirements for Library Science 571, Northern Illinois University, Department of Library Science (1985): 14-22. ED 261685.

21. Ibid., 38.

22. Ibid., 3-4.

23. Ibid., 4.

24. Gary Taubes, "Publication by Electronic Mail Takes Physics by Storm," *Science* 259 (5099) (February 26, 1993): 1246-1248.

25. Gerry McKiernan, "arXiv.org: The Los Alamos National Laboratory E-Print Server," *International Journal on Grey Literature* 1(1) (2000): 127-138.

26. Stevan Harnad, "The Self-Archiving Initiative," *Nature* 410 (6832) (April 26, 2001): 1024-1025. Also available at <http://www.nature.com/nature/debates/e-access/Articles/harnad.html> Accessed March 25, 2002.

27. eprints.org, "eprints.org Home," 2002. <http://www.eprints.org/> Accessed March 3, 2003.

28. Ibid.

29. Ibid.

30. eprints.org, "GNU EPrints 2," 2002. <http://software.eprints.org/> Accessed March 4, 2003.

31. Ibid.

32. eprints.org, "eprints.org Home."

33. eprints.org, "GNU EPrints 2."

34. eprints.org, "EPrints 2.2 Documentation—Required Software," 2003. <http://www.eprints.org/docs/php/reqsoftware.php> Accessed March 3, 2003.

35. eprints.org, "About the eprints.org Software."

36. eprints.org, "eprints.org Home."

37. Unicode, Inc., "The Unicode Standard," 2003. < http://www.unicode.org/unicode/standard/standard.html> Accessed March 3, 2003.

38. eprints.org, "eprints.org Home."

39. eprints.org, "GNU EPrints 2 Software Download," 2002. <http://www.eprints.org/download.php> Accessed March 24, 2002.

40. GNU Project, "The GNU General Public License," 2003. <http://www.gnu.org/licenses/licenses.html- GPL> Accessed March 3, 2003.

41. eprints.org, "GNU EPrints 2 Software Download."

42. Ibid.

43. eprints.org, "eprints.org Home."

44. Open Archives Initiative, "Frequently Asked Questions," 2001. <http://www.openarchives.org/documents/FAQ.html> Accessed March 24, 2002.

45. Ibid.

46. Ibid.

47. Ibid

48. Open Archives Initiative, "Registering as a Data Provider. OAI-PMH 2.0," 2002. <http://www.openarchives.org/data/registerasprovider.htm> Accessed March 3, 2003.

49. Open Archives Initiative, "Registering as a Service Provider," n. d. <http://www.openarchives.org/data/registerasprovider.html> Accessed March 3, 2003.

50. Open Archives Initiative, "Frequently Asked Questions."

51. Ibid.

52. eprints.org, "eprints.org Home."

53. Open Archives Initiative, "Open Archives Initiative Protocol for Metadata Harvesting," 2002. <http://www.openarchives.org/OAI/openarchivesprotocol.html> Accessed March 3, 2003.

54. Open Archives Initiative, "Frequently Asked Questions."

55. Dublin Core Metadata Initiative, "Dublin Core Metadata Initiative," 2002. <http://dublincore.org/> Accessed March 24, 2002.

56. Open Archives Initiative, "Frequently Asked Questions."

57. Ibid.

58. Ibid.

59. World Wide Web Consortium, "Extensible Markup Language," 2002. <http://www.w3.org/XML/> Accessed March 24, 2002.

60. Open Archives Initiative, "Open Archives Initiative Protocol for Metadata Harvesting, Protocol Version 2.0," 2002. <http://www.openarchives.org/OAI/2.0/openarchivesprotocol.htm> Accessed June 14, 2002.

61. Open Archives Initiative, "Registered Data Providers," n. d. <http://oaisrv.nsdl.cornell.edu/Register/BrowseSites.pl> Accessed March 24, 2002.

62. Open Archives Initiative, "Registered Service Providers," 2002. <http://www.openarchives.org/service/listproviders.html> Accessed March 24, 2002.

63. Xiaomong Liu, Kurt Maly, Mohammad Zubair, and Michael L. Nelson, "Arc—An OAI Service Provider for Digital Library Federation," *D-Lib Magazine* 7(4) (April 2001) <http://www.dlib.org/dlib/april01/liu/04liu.html> Accessed March 24, 2002.

64. eprints.org, "CiteBase Services," n.d. <http://citebase.eprints.org/> Accessed March 24, 2002.

65. eprints.org, "OpCit: The Open Citation Project," 2002. <http://opcit.eprints.org/> Accessed March 24, 2002.

66. Stevan Harnad, "For Whom the Gate Tolls: How and Why to Free the Refereed Research Literature Online Through Author/Institution Self-Archiving, Now," n.d. <http://www.cogsci.soton.ac.uk/~harnad/Tp/resolution.htm> Accessed March 24, 2002.

67. Suber, "The Budapest Open Access Initiative: Frequently Asked Questions."

68. Richard Poynder, "George Soros Gives $3 Million to New Open Access Initiative," *InfoToday News Breaks and Conference Reports* (February 18, 2002). <http://www.infotoday.com/newsbreaks/nb020218-1.htm> Accessed March 24, 2002.

69. Soros Foundation Network, "Open Society Institute," n.d. <http://www.soros.org/osi.html> Accessed March 24, 2002.

70. Soros Foundation Network, "Soros Foundation Network," n.d. <http://www.soros.org/> Accessed March 24, 2002.

71. Ivan Noble, "Boost for Research Paper Access."

72. Lawrence Lessig, *The Future of Ideas: The Fate of the Commons in a Connected World* (New York: Random House, 2001).

73. Stanford Center for Internet and Society, "About *The Future of Ideas*," n.d. <http://cyberlaw.stanford.edu/future/> Accessed March 24, 2002.

74. James Surowiecki, "The Financial Page: Righting Copywrongs, " *The New Yorker* 77(44): 27. (January 21, 2002). <http://www.newyorker.com/PRINTABLE/?talk/020121ta_talk_surowiecki> Accessed March 24, 2002.

75. Ann Shumelda Okerson and James J. O'Donnell, eds., *Scholarly Journals at the Crossroads: A Subversive Proposal for Electronic Publishing* (Washington, DC: Office of Scientific & Academic Pub., Association of Research Libraries, 1995). Also available at: <http://www.arl.org/scomm/subversive/toc.html> Accessed March 25, 2002.

76. Okerson and O'Donnell, *Scholarly Journals at the Crossroads,* 225.

77. Budapest Open Access Initiative, "Sign On," n.d. <http://www.soros.org/openaccess/sign.shtml> Accessed March 25, 2002.

78. Budapest Open Access Initiative, "What You Can Do To Help," n.d. <http://www.soros.org/openaccess/help.shtml> Accessed March 25, 2002.

Chapter 11

E-Serials and Regional Accreditation

Cheryl McCain
Karen Rupp-Serrano

E-serials are a relatively new wrinkle to libraries and a particularly vexing one. Since their inception, they have been providing numerous challenges to library professionals. First, librarians tried to figure out how to afford them, and later how to continue to afford them. Once libraries had acquired e-serials, librarians tried to determine how best to offer and promote them. As libraries continue to build e-serial collections, they are still looking to find the most effective ways to manage, organize, and account for them.

One area in which accounting for e-serials has been a consideration is regional accreditation. When librarians prepare reports for their college or university self-study documents, how should these new and costly resources be represented? Should they be counted and reported? What about the issue of title duplication among providers? Should distinctions be made between large aggregators, whose e-serial offerings vary frequently, and smaller, more specialized aggregators? How can librarians best demonstrate the value of e-serials to the overall educational mission of the institution? Do the regional accreditation agencies' guidelines require, suggest, or in any way support the reporting of e-serial holdings?

The goal of this chapter is to provide assistance to librarians who are trying to answer these questions. An investigation was conducted by the authors between November 2001 and February 2002 to determine (1) what, if anything, regional accreditation guidelines say about reporting e-serials; (2) how some libraries have recently presented their e-serial holdings in self-studies; and (3) what are some of the unresolved issues concerning the reporting of e-serials for the institutional accreditation process.

REGIONAL ACCREDITATION'S PERSPECTIVE
ON E-SERIALS

Much has been written about regional accreditation standards in the past decade. Authors have explored topics such as how and why standards have been revised; how the various standards compare in regard to specificity in certain areas such as serials; and what guidance standards provide for libraries seeking to link electronic resources to educational outcomes. Writing about the growth and expense of information technology in libraries, Ronald Leach (1992) concluded, "changes occurring in academic libraries generally have not been acknowledged by regional accrediting bodies in their criteria" (291). In a 1993 research report, Mark McCallon found that "most agencies do not provide much information concerning serials requirements in their published accreditation standards" (10-11), and "very little information is available concerning the extent to which the use of serials in an electronic format satisfies accrediting agencies" (10). Joan Worley noted, "as of spring 1994, none of the standards have definitive statements on access to electronic or on-line resources" (1994, 73).

Accrediting agencies may not have been adding specific guidelines pertaining to electronic library resources, but their overall focus was in a state of flux during the 1990s. Delmus Williams reported in 1993, "libraries are now being asked to focus on why they do what they do and what they expect to accomplish within the university while keeping with the spirit of outcome measurement" (35). Ralph Wolff also noted this trend, saying, "accrediting agencies are placing more emphasis on assessment and outcomes data" (1995, 80). More recently, Arlene Lucio (2000) reported that regional standards continue to be "worded generally so as to leave room for an institution to interpret them and tailor them to fit its mission. The regional agencies are more interested in qualitative assessment" (12).

In the past few years, the six regional accrediting bodies[1] have clearly shifted their focus from specific input measures to a more outcomes-oriented evaluation of an academic institution's standing. Beth McMurtrie (2000) reported, "all of the six regional associations will have rewritten their standards in the next two to three years" (A29). One trend she identified is the increasing emphasis on demonstration of educational outcomes and information literacy in self-studies and less concern about the exact methods used to accomplish this directive. Institutions and libraries must show that they are accomplishing their educational missions and goals. What are the implications for the reporting of e-serials? How do we account for e-serials in the changing accreditation scene? If the standards do not specify what (if anything) should be reported in regard to e-serials, can librarians cease to be concerned about accounting for them? By looking more closely at the various standards and their overall objectives, it appears that the answer may very well be: "it depends."

Each regional accreditation agency has its own criteria/guidelines/standards, or information about the same, posted on its Web site. These documents were located and searched for any explicit or implicit references to e-serials. None of the six has specific requirements for the reporting of e-serials. However, each provides ample opportunities for an institution to include information on its e-serial holdings, within a larger context. In order to explore this option, one representative from each of the six regional accreditation bodies was contacted in regard to the reporting of e-serials for accreditation. During the interviews, several of these individuals indicated that they either held an MLS degree, had prior experience as a librarian, or both. Questions were asked to determine (1) what impact e-serials might have on the evaluation of a university as a whole, (2) if their guidelines had changed, or would be changing, specifically in regard to e-serials, and (3) any issues related to accreditation that pertain specifically to e-serials.

SOUTHERN REGION

The Commission on Colleges of the Southern Association of Colleges and Schools (SACS-COC) is the accrediting body for eleven U.S. southern states. The association's *1998 Criteria for Accreditation* (SACS-COC 2000) makes several references to libraries. The SACS-COC criteria place libraries within "educational support services." As such, they call for institutions to ensure that "adequate library and other learning resources and services" are available to faculty and students wherever they are. In some cases, e-serials may meet this requirement better than traditional resources. These resources and services "must be evaluated regularly and systematically." Quality, relevance, accessibility, availability, delivery, and use are of greater importance in regard to resources than scope, type, or variety. Collections must be "cataloged and organized" and effective access must be provided, as well as adequate physical facilities and equipment. On this point, a library could note how its e-serial titles are made accessible through the online catalog, the same way that other cataloged materials are.

Library collections must "provide access to essential references and specialized program resources for each instructional location." Institutions may supplement a traditional library with electronic access, but must provide evidence of the incorporation of "technological advances into its library and other learning resource operations." Cooperative agreements with other libraries may be used to enhance resources and services but cannot be used to "avoid responsibility for providing adequate and readily accessible library resources and services."

E-serials are not specifically mentioned in the SACS-COC documents, but it is clear that they have a role to play in the provision of resources. Ralph Russell, an associate executive director of SACS-COC, further emphasized this point during a telephone conversation with the authors on November 29, 2001. He stated that site-visit teams need to make connections between library resources and student or faculty needs, so it is incumbent upon libraries to make clear what resources they are providing and how they are being provided in order for site-visit teams to make an assessment. Russell went on to discuss changes currently under way within the SACS-COC criteria. The strong language and more prescriptive tone in the 1998 criteria (in effect until January 2004) will soon be giving way to a document more in line with current trends in accreditation. The document now taking shape, *Principles of Accreditation* (SACS-COC 2001), places an emphasis on relevance and currency, how students are being taught, and how they are learning. Librarians and teaching faculty will have to demonstrate how they are meeting these objectives to site-visit teams.

WESTERN REGION

The Western Association of Schools and Colleges (WASC) is pushing the envelope of change in accreditation. In its *Handbook of*

Accreditation (WASC 2001a), libraries fall primarily under Standard 2, "Achieving educational objectives through core functions." In regard to teaching and learning, it states that "the institution's expectations for learning and student attainment are clearly reflected in its academic programs and policies. These include . . . the use of its library and information resources." In regard to support for student learning, "student support services—including . . . library and information services—are designed to meet the needs of the specific types of students the institution serves and the curricula it offers."

The library could also be construed to fall under Standard 3, "Developing and applying resources and organizational structures to ensure sustainability." In regard to fiscal, physical, and information resources,

> the institution holds, or provides access to, information resources sufficient in scope, quality, currency, and kind to support its academic offerings and the scholarship of its members. For on-campus students and students enrolled at a distance, physical and information resources, services, and information technology facilities are sufficient in scope and kind to support and maintain the level and kind of education offered.

How to Become Accredited (WASC 2001b), the procedures manual accompanying the *Handbook of Accreditation,* provides guidelines to use in demonstrating that "the institution holds or otherwise provides long-term access to sufficient information and learning resources to support its purposes and all of its educational programs." Recommended sources of documentation include a profile of holdings and resources, including descriptions of computing facilities' availability and usage; copies of agreements for access to external resources; student training for institutional and external library and computing facilities; and a plan for library and computer development. These examples of statements in WASC's standards do provide contexts in which e-serials can be addressed if a library chooses to do so.

E-serials have no specific mention; libraries are never even separately categorized in the WASC documentation. A telephone conversation on December 5, 2001, with Stephanie Bangert, an associate director of WASC, explored this. Bangert noted that the previous WASC accreditation document had nine standards; the current one (adopted in 2000) has four and is oriented toward outcomes. Institutions address how resources and services are integrated holistically and how they speak to learning outcomes.

Under the current WASC configuration, accounting for e-serials, or for that matter going into any great numeric detail, would be unnecessary unless the university chooses to emphasize such in the documentation they prepare for WASC. Rather, the institution selects a few issues on which it wishes to focus, develops an approach to them, and sets intended outcomes. Once that is agreed upon with WASC, a brief portfolio is prepared addressing institutional capacity to deliver its educational programs. E-serials might show up as one of any number of figures in this regard. After the institution has successfully negotiated this preparatory review, a second review occurs within a year focusing on educational effectiveness in regard to the previously selected issues. WASC considers libraries critical to an institution's capacity to fulfill its educational mission, and accreditation reviews do incorporate an examination of information and learning resources. However, only if an institution chooses to focus on a specific issue under whose rubric libraries fall, will the library receive more than a basic examination to ensure it meets institutional capacity demands.

NORTHWEST REGION

The Commission on Colleges and Universities of the Northwest Association of Schools and Colleges addresses libraries in its *Standards* (NASC-COC 1999). Standard 5, currently under revision, calls for libraries to support teaching, learning, and research consistent with the institution's mission and goals. Holdings, equipment, and personnel should be sufficient. The core collection, information resources, and services should be sufficient in quality, depth, diversity, and currency. Resources should be readily accessible to all eligible users, and cooperative arrangements with other libraries or information resources may be pursued. Supporting documentation includes statistics on the use of the library and other learning resources, statistics on library collections, assessment measures to determine the adequacy of holdings, information resources and services to support educational programs, budget information, written agreements with other libraries, computer usage statistics related to the retrieval of library resources, and studies or documents describing the evaluation of library and information resources.

E-serials are not specifically mentioned in the NASC-COC standards, but it is again clear that they fall within the concept of information resources, a fact emphasized in a telephone conversation on November 29, 2001, with Ronald Baker, an associate executive director of NASC-COC. The real question, says Baker, is whether or not institutions provide students, faculty, and staff access to adequate and appropriate resources, for this is what they will be held accountable for. Toward this end, Standard 5 is being revised to meet current practice and eligibility requirements. Previously, NASC-COC eligibility requirements called for a library to have

> at least a core library and learning resources needed for independent work in the fields and at the levels represented by its offerings. If it depends in part on other institutions for specialized library and learning resources, it can demonstrate that they are adequate, easily accessible, and used.

That statement now reads, "the institution provides library resources, technology and services for students and faculty appropriate for its mission and for all of its educational programs wherever located and however delivered" (Baker 2002, 6).

NEW ENGLAND REGION

The Commission on Institutions of Higher Education New England Association of Schools and Colleges (NEASC-CIHE), has standards that "are essentially qualitative criteria that measure the institution's current state of educational effectiveness" (NEASC-CIHE 2001). Standard 7—"Library and Information Resources"—makes no specific reference to e-serials. However, the standard does include several statements that can pertain to e-serials: "The institution makes available the library and information resources necessary for the fulfillment of its mission and purposes," and "ensures that students use these resources as an integral part of their education." Both statements in Standard 7.1 are open doors to including e-serial holdings and usage statistics.

Standard 7.2 allows for either ownership of or guaranteed access to "sufficient collections, information technology systems, and services [that are] readily accessible to students wherever programs are located or however they are delivered." The library could also include information on how its e-serials support the institution's off-campus educational programs under "appropriate support for distance learning students and faculty" (Standard 7.5). Standard 7.6—"the institution regularly and systematically evaluates the adequacy and utilization of its library, information resources, and services and uses the results of the data to improve and increase the effectiveness of these services"—provides another option for reporting e-serial usage statistics.

NEASC-CIHE has produced an additional document, *Student Learning Assessment Cues for Self-Studies* (NEASC-CIHE 2001), to assist institutions. For Standard 7, libraries can demonstrate institutional effectiveness by showing that "library staff and faculty collaborate on assessment of information literacy competencies, with feedback to both the library and the academic departments" and that "library staff provide data on student use of collections . . . and electronic resources" (NEASC-CIHE 2001, 2). In addition to providing data on student assessment and use of library resources, here the library might include anecdotal information obtained informally from faculty or student participation through surveys or focus group feedback regarding the use and value of e-serials.

In a telephone conversation December 10, 2001, Barbara Brittingham, deputy director of NEASC-CIHE, emphasized that the commission's site-evaluation teams are not trained to look specifically at e-serials. They look for evidence of consistent financial commitment to providing materials (in any format), appropriate orientation and training in the use of electronic resources, evidence of use of all resources, and evaluative data that show how libraries are involved in the education of students.

MIDDLE STATES REGION

The Middle States Commission on Higher Education (MSCHE), published its revised *Characteristics of Excellence in Higher Education: Eligibility Requirements and Standards for Accreditation* in 2002. The document includes fourteen standards, none of which deal solely with libraries. Under "optional analysis and evidence," Standard 9, "Student Support Services," states that an institution may choose to provide "analysis of support services available to students, including . . . library/learning resources support . . ." (MSCHE 2002, 27), in addition to other required documentation. Standard 11, "Educational Offerings," states that accredited institutions are characterized by: "learning resources, facilities, instructional equipment, library services, and professional library staff adequate to support the institution's educational programs" (34). Standard 13, "Related Educational Activities," lists as optional evidence in support of branch campuses and additional instructional sites, the "analysis of the adequacy and appropriateness of library/information and other learning resources" (45).

Oswald Ratteray, an assistant director of the MSCHE, confirmed that their standards do not specifically mention e-serials (e-mail to Karen Rupp-Serrano on November 28, 2001, and a telephone conversation on November 29, 2001). Site evaluators are not trained to look at them specifically, but they might make a judgment "based on their professional expertise" as to "what is appropriate given an institution's mission, goals, and resources." He also noted that "the standards recognize that there are a variety of delivery systems now in place, and [the standards] allow flexibility in determining what is appropriate." In a follow-up e-mail on March 5, 2002, Ratteray emphasized that the standards "focus on student learning rather than the particular resources an institution should have in order to achieve that result." If an institution identifies e-serials as being fundamental to the support of its programs, "then Middle States requires that they be adequately supported and staffed," and will review them more closely.

Another document published by MSCHE is *Designs for Excellence: Handbook for Institutional Self-Study,* Seventh Edition. Chapter 4 of the handbook includes a section on "Library and Learning Resources." It states that

> the effectiveness of library, information, and other learning resources which support the programs and services offered by the institution is defined by the range of resources available to meet the needs of students, faculty, and staff, as well as by the manner in which they are delivered, their accessibility, and their utilization. (MSCHE 2000, 29)

The *Designs* document summarizes references to libraries in the *Characteristics* document, stating that "the need for broad and convenient access, as well as the effective use of resources, are recurring themes in all discussions of library, information, and other learning resources," and claims that the publication

> stresses that the concept of library and other learning resources should not be limited explicitly by narrow definitions of space (facilities such as libraries or campus versus off-campus locations) and media (print, non-print, or electronic), or limited implicitly by narrow definitions of time (hours of service or electronic access) or location . . ." (MSCHE 2002, 30)

E-serials could certainly find a place in each of these assertions.

NORTH CENTRAL REGION

The Higher Learning Commission of the North Central Association of Schools and Colleges (NCA-HLC) accredits educational institutions in nineteen states. Its *Policies on Institutional Affiliation* (revised February 2002) contains criteria for accreditation. Criterion 2 says that "the institution has effectively organized the human, financial, and physical resources necessary to accomplish its purposes," and "in determining appropriate patterns of evidence for the criterion, the Commission considers evidence such as . . . academic resources and equipment (e.g., libraries, electronic services and products, learning resource centers, laboratories and studios, computers) adequate to support the institution's purposes" (NCA-HCL 2002).

Steven D. Crow, executive director of the NCA-HCL, confirmed in an e-mail correspondence dated December 3, 2001, that NCA-HCL does not have a standard dealing specifically with e-serials. However, he acknowledged that "some programs would simply fail without lots of access to and use of serials . . . and electronic serials can be used in place of hardcopy and still be considered appropriate." He noted that site evaluators "will make some judgments about how any library is creating and managing its collections, and in that mix investment in electronic resources becomes important." Teams pay attention to imbalances in spending for resources, and "usually they are not pleased when investment in electronic resources means a net loss of investment in learning resources."

NCA-HCL's *Addendum to the Handbook of Accreditation,* Second Edition, contains a specific reference to online journals in its section

"Best Practices for Electronically Offered Degree and Certificate Programs." It recognizes that "library resources appropriate to the program, including . . . remote access to data bases, online journals and full-text resources . . ." (NCA-HCL 2001, 53) are necessary to support students enrolled in electronically offered programs. It is expected that distance education programs will require the provision of electronic resources, and a library would have no problem addressing their e-serials in this context.

HOW SOME LIBRARIES INTERPRETED
AND RESPONDED TO STANDARDS

It is clear from reviewing the regional accreditation standards that the associations are moving away from prescriptive "thou shalts." Rather, the new emphasis is more like Missouri mule "show me." In other words, if an institution has X, Y, and Z resources, then they need to demonstrate how those various resources impact educational outcomes. Next, the authors will turn to the libraries themselves and examine what they have been producing in terms of self-studies for the site visits of regional accrediting teams, and in particular look to see if and how they have been addressing the thorny question of accounting for e-serials.

Librarians representing one university from each of the six regional agencies were contacted and interviewed to learn how they accounted for e-serials in the reports for their institutions' self-studies.[2] Each person responded to questions about whether they did or did not specifically mention e-serials in their self-study. If they did mention e-serials, what did they say about them, and in what context? If not, why not? Further conversation focused on any issues and questions they had on the role of e-serials in accreditation.

The University of Georgia-Athens (UGA) was recently reaccredited by SACS-COC. Speaking with the authors via telephone on February 7, 2002, William Potter, director of libraries, stated that e-serials were not separated out in UGA's self-study. Individual e-serials were counted as subscriptions, just as print would be. Aggregators, which tend to be more fluid in the titles they provide, were counted, but no attempt was made to provide detailed information on the serials within them. The usefulness of e-serials to the provision of enhanced service and distance education were emphasized in the narrative of the self-study but without any hard evidence. Some sparse usage statistics were also included. Potter noted the difficulty in providing evidence that relates e-serials to learner outcomes.

California Polytechnic State University, San Luis Obispo (CalPoly), was reaccredited by WASC in 2000. CalPoly chose to utilize the new WASC standards document and focus on itself as a "center for learning" with three integrated components: the intellectual environment, the physical environment, and the campus climate (sociological and psychological environment). Hiram Davis, dean of library services, indicated to the authors in a telephone conversation on February 1, 2002, that no special effort was made to account for e-serials in the self-study; full-text databases were pointed to but not examined in detail. Overall, the library portion of the self-study emphasized how the library is meeting the mission of the university.

The University of Alaska-Fairbanks (UAF) was recently reaccredited by NASC-COC. Lisa Lehman, electronic resources librarian, stated during a telephone conversation with the authors on January 18, 2002, that in the library's report for the self-study there was an emphasis on having more e-serials than ever before. This is of particular value in Alaska, where distance education is, by necessity, extremely important. Serials were addressed in the narrative of the self-study; they emphasized that e-serials were of great benefit because they were accessible twenty-four hours a day, seven days a week to students at UAF's remote campuses. UAF's Elmer E. Rasmuson Library and its BioSciences Library provided numbers for serials but no breakdown by format. For large aggregators, the approximate number of individual titles supplied by each provider was given. Efforts to develop alternate access to journal information were cited, noting joint arrangement and consortia.

The NEASC-CIHE recently reaccredited Southern Connecticut State University (SCSU). In a telephone conversation on January 22, 2002, Susan Cirillo, director of library services, stated that the library's report provided the number of electronic databases to which it had access but not the number of e-serial titles. The report did provide the number of print serial subscriptions. According to SCSU's self-study document, the library conducts faculty and students surveys and collects data on journal use (including e-serials). "Detailed data on the use of online resources continually informs decisions on elec-

tronic subscriptions" (SCSU 70). The self-study indicates that anticipated growth in the library's materials budget will result in "particular emphasis on electronic resources to provide greater access to
distance learners" (SCSU 74).

MSCHE reaccredited Kean University (Union, New Jersey) in
2001. Barbara Simpson Darden, director of library services at Kean,
explained how the library reported its total number of periodical subscriptions and gave separate numbers for print and online serials
(January 17, 2002, telephone conversation with the authors). They
were able to also note the number of titles that were available in more
than one format or having more than one online access point. This
was possible because they created a comprehensive database of their
6,000 plus serial titles (in all formats). In the narrative for the self-
study, they emphasized the benefits of having both print and
electronic journals. Some listed benefits of e-serials included their
availability to multiple, simultaneous users; support for distance
education programs; indestructibility (pages cannot be torn out of
online journals!); and their availability when the library building is
closed.

The University of Oklahoma (OU) was reaccredited by NCA-HCL
in 2001. In its section of the self-study, the library reported having
"access to 14,637 electronic serials through full-text databases and
subscriptions" (OU 2001). This number was calculated by counting
the access points for every full-text serial title that could be identified
either through a database, aggregator, or publisher's site. Many titles
had multiple access points, so the actual number of e-serial titles
held would have been lower. One of the authors of this chapter was
assigned the tedious task of counting e-serial access points, and
wondered at the time what would come of the exercise. Upon reading the library's section of the self-study document, it was evident that
e-serial access points were mentioned in the larger context of what resources the library provides in support of the institution's purposes.

UNRESOLVED ISSUES RELATING TO E-SERIALS
AND ACCREDITATION

During this investigation into the role of e-serials in the accreditation process, several issues were brought to light through e-mail cor-

respondence and telephone conversations with persons from the regional agencies and the recently reaccredited institutions. Due to the nature of some of the discussions, the individuals who enlightened us with their comments, complaints, and frustrations will not be identified.

A frequently mentioned concern was that librarians are not sure how to generate "hard data" that will demonstrate the library's contribution to the institution's mission and to the education of information-literate, lifelong learners. Wolff suggests ways in which librarians should *continually* pursue the collection of evaluative data. He lists focus groups, exit interviews, syllabi reviews, and student "library portfolios" as some of the methods that libraries might employ to create a "culture of inquiry, data collection, and analysis" that will provide "the proper basis for an outcomes-oriented self-study" (1994, 131). Evaluations of students' ability to locate, use, and cite e-serials after attending bibliographic instruction and online research classes would also provide evidence of the library's teaching role.

Financial pressures were noted by another individual as a continuing problem for libraries. Since most lawyers and legislators do not understand the necessity or value of electronic serials, they do not understand that the "cost to buy" electronic resources is continual, not a one-time expense. This individual noted that some librarians believe accreditation standards are "too watered down," which in some cases leaves libraries without leverage to lobby for sufficient funding for electronic materials from administrations and state legislatures. Librarians should be making an argument for funding each and every year with university administrators; counting on feedback from an accrediting agency's site-visiting team to make that argument for them is a risky roll of the dice.

Another individual spoke about the problematic nature of distance education, saying that it greatly impacts funding, yet it is difficult to define and assess the clientele. Some are alarmed that libraries will suffer funding decreases as the regional accreditation bodies focus more on results "rather than counting heads and library books . . . they are holding colleges accountable while giving them the flexibility to experiment with new forms of education, such as Web-based courses or partnerships with for-profit institutions" (McMurtrie 2000, A29). Bonnie Gratch-Lindauer's perspective on funding concerns is that "most of the standards revised in the last three years have strengthened the teaching role of libraries and made the connections clearer between the use of libraries and information resources and an excellent learning environment" (2002, 16).

CONCLUSION

Regional accreditation agencies will continue to revise their standards to reflect changes in higher education. Baker (2002) advances this point by saying, "changes in accreditation standards and policies are intended to preserve the values and principles of quality and effectiveness while allowing the criteria for institutional evaluations to adapt as appropriate and warranted" (6). As noted earlier in this chapter, the answer to the question "what, if anything, do we need to report about our e-serial holdings for the accreditation self-study?" can vary. Just as "accreditation has always had some difficulty determining what a good library contributed to a university" (Williams 1994, 27), librarians will continue to struggle with how to assess the role of e-serials in the institution's overall mission.

It appears that the advice gleaned from the literature, representatives from the accrediting bodies, and librarians who are collecting, organizing, and reporting on their e-serial collections boils down to: stay focused on demonstrating quality improvement in light of the institution's missions and goals, and make certain that learning is driving technology, not the other way around. In short, do as Ralph Wolff suggests, and "use the accrediting process to stimulate fundamental rethinking of the mission, role, and operation of the library" (1995, 77).

NOTES

1. Middle States Association of Colleges and Schools; New England Association of Schools and Colleges; North Central Association of Colleges and Schools; Northwest Association of Schools and Colleges; Southern Association of Colleges and Schools; Western Association of Schools and Colleges.

2. Recently reaccredited institutions were identified using information obtained on the regional associations' Web sites. The authors represented the institution accredited by NCA. Librarians who were involved with providing information on the library at institutions accredited by the other five regional associations were identified through e-mail and telephone queries.

REFERENCES

Baker, Ronald L. 2002. Evaluating Quality and Effectiveness: Regional Accreditation Principles and Practices. *Journal of Academic Librarianship* 28(1): 3-7.

Gratch-Lindauer, Bonnie. 2002. Comparing the Regional Accreditation Standards: Outcomes Assessment and Other Trends. *Journal of Academic Librarianship* 28(1): 14-25.

Leach, Ronald G. 1992. Academic Library Change: The Role of Regional Accreditation. *Journal of Academic Librarianship* 18(5): 288-291.

Lucio, Arlene. 2000. Accreditation in the Electronic Age: A Qualitative Study. *Alabama Librarian* 50(2): 11-16.

McCallon, Mark. 1993. *Meeting Serials Requirements of Accrediting Agencies Through Electronic Databases: An Exploratory Study.* Washington, DC: U.S. Department of Education. Available: ERIC Document Reproduction Service No. ED 364230.

McMurtrie, Beth. 2000. Accreditors Revamp Policies to Stress Student Learning. *The Chronicle of Higher Education* 46(44) (July 7): A29.

Middle States Commission on Higher Education (MSCHE). 2000. *Designs for Excellence: Handbook for Institutional Self-Study,* Seventh Edition. Online. Available: <http://www.msache.org/msadesig.pdf>. Accessed February 26, 2002.

———. 2002. *Characteristics of Excellence in Higher Education: Eligibility Requirements and Standards for Accreditation in 2002.* Online. Available: <http://www.msache.org/charac02. pdf>. Accessed February 26, 2002.

New England Association of Schools and Colleges, Commission on Institutions of Higher Education (NEASC-CIHE). 2001. *Standards for Accreditation.* Online. Available: <http://www.neasc.org/cihe/stancihe.htm>. Accessed February 26, 2002.

———. *Student Learning Assessment Cues for Self-Studies.* Online. Available: <http://www.neasc.org/cihe/self-study_cuespdf>. Accessed February 26, 2002.

North Central Association of Colleges and Schools (NCA-HCL). 2001. *Addendum to the Handbook of Accreditation,* Second Edition. Online. Available: <http://www.ncahigherlearningcommission.org/resources/HandAddendMarch2001.pdf> Accessed February 26, 2002.

———. 2002. *Policies on Institutional Affiliation* (revised February 2002). Online. Available: <http://www.ncahigherlearningcommission.org/resources/policies/edinstia.html>. Accessed February 26, 2002.

Northwest Association of Schools and Colleges, Commission on Colleges and Universities (NASC-COC), 1999. *Standards.* Online. Available: <http://www.nwccu.org/policyprocedure/standards.html>. Accessed February 26, 2002.

Southern Association of Colleges and Schools, Commission on Colleges (SACS-COC). 2000. *1998 Criteria for Accreditation.* Online. Available: <http://www.sacscoc.org/criteria.asp>. Accessed November 29, 2001.

————. 2001. *Principles of Accreditation* (approved December 11, 2001). Online. Available: <http://www.sacscoc.org/accrrevproj.asp>. Accessed February 26, 2002.

Southern Connecticut State University (SCSU). 2001. *Self-Study for Reaccreditation: Submitted to the Commission on Institutions of Higher Education of the New England Association of Schools and Colleges, August 2001.* New Haven, CT: SCSU.

University of Oklahoma. 2001. *Realizing the Possibilities: Reaccreditation in a Time of Renewal.* Online. Available: <http://www.ou.edu/ncaselfstudy/2001_ Reaccreditation.pdf>. Accessed February 26, 2002.

Western Association of Schools and Colleges (WASC). 2001a. *Handbook of Accreditation.* Online. Available: <http://www.wascweb.org/senior/handbook.pdf>. Accessed February 26, 2002.

————. 2001b. *How to Become Accredited.* Online. Available: <http://www. wascweb.org/senior/eligibility.pdf>. Accessed February 26, 2002.

Williams, Delmus E. 1993. Accreditation and the Academic Library. *Library Administration & Management* 7(1): 31-37.

Williams, Delmus E. 1994. Challenges to Accreditation from the New Academic Library Environment. In E. D. Garten (Ed.), *The Challenge and Practice of Academic Accreditation* (pp. 23-31). Westport, CN: Greenwood Press.

Wolff, Ralph A. 1994. Rethinking Library Self-Studies and Accreditation Visits. In E. D. Garten (Ed.), *The Challenge and Practice of Academic Accreditation* (pp. 125-138). Westport, CT: Greenwood Press.

Wolff, Ralph A. 1995. Using the Accreditation Process to Transform the Mission of the Library. In Beverly P. Lynch (Ed.), *Information Technology and the Remaking of the University Library* (pp. 77-91). San Francisco: Jossey-Bass.

Worley, Joan H. 1994. The Practical Librarian's View of Accreditation. In E. D. Garten (Ed.), *The Challenge and Practice of Academic Accreditation* (pp. 69-74). Westport, CT: Greenwood Press.

Chapter 12

Managing E-Resources:
A Database-Driven Approach

Sarah Robbins
Matthew Smith

INTRODUCTION

Much has been written about the problems associated with managing access to electronic resources. Indeed, they are some of the biggest problems currently facing libraries across the country. Large libraries often subscribe to hundreds of databases, providing access to thousands of e-journals. Finding an ideal way to present such a large base of information to users is often problematic; many libraries simply decide to present alphabetical lists of resource titles or to allow keyword searches. Libraries that have provided subject access to these resources are faced with the intimidating task of not only initially assigning subject categories to them but also of maintaining those subjects as the resources change or as new resources are acquired. Further complicating these issues is the fact that users tend to settle for the first resource they find which looks like it might be useful to them, rather than to diligently search for the best resource to meet their needs. Users would much rather read through an alphabetical listing of titles than to try to fumble their way around the online catalog and the detailed subject access that it provides.

The problems that are associated with e-resource management do not end after having found a way to present the resources to which a library subscribes. Often resource providers depend on IP recognition in order to grant access to subscribing university patrons, but for universities with large numbers of users located off campus or on satellite campuses, other measures must be employed to allow distance-education users to access these resources, as well as those users who are attempting to gain access from off-campus locations. Once a system has been put into place to handle such issues, the library must find a method to authenticate users before allowing them access to the system, and then must also disseminate information about how to use this system to remote users. Libraries are also confronted with the problem of how to permit remote users to access resources through the online catalog.

In an attempt to resolve the problems associated with e-resource access and management, the University of Oklahoma Libraries developed LORA (Library Online Resource Access) to handle all of its electronic resources. LORA (<http://libraries.ou.edu/LORA>) provides patrons with one easy-to-use interface for databases and electronic journals, as well as for selected local resources and links to subject-related Internet sites, search engines, government documents, and e-books. LORA has multiple interfaces—a public interface used by patrons and several private interfaces posted on the library's intranet that are utilized by library personnel for updating information and accessing administrative information.

The LORA interface is composed of a set of scripts written in ASP and HTML. These scripts handle both the public interface and the intranet interface that allows staff to modify the data within LORA. External system calls are made through operating system and API calls when necessary. Database connectivity is achieved through ADOs within the ASP scripts. With over 35,000 records and over fifty subject areas, LORA is one of the most comprehensive and ambitious e-resource management systems currently in use.

LORA PUBLIC INTERFACE

The public interface to LORA currently provides users with three search methods; users may access electronic resources through alphabetical listings of the resources, keyword searches of resource titles, and subject area lists. The alphabetical listing of resources is currently the most familiar portal to users, since this method was in place before the switch to LORA. Keyword searching of resource titles was also previously available but did not function reliably enough for users to become confident in it; search capabilities improved drastically with the implementation of LORA. Subject access to electronic resources is a new service provided to users that increases the visibility of specialized databases that were previously buried in long lists of resources.

There are currently seven resource classifications for resources available through LORA. These include databases, e-journals, local resources, search engines, Internet links, government documents, and e-books. The inclusion of databases, e-journals, and e-books was part of LORA's original concept; however, the decision to add local resources, search engines, Internet links, and government documents came about in the planning and development stages of LORA. There were initially some concerns that listing local resources in LORA would be a duplication of effort with what was available through the catalog, but it was finally decided that the added value of listing these resources in LORA, and allowing them to be added to individual subject guides by librarians with the inclusion of usage notes or additional location information, made it worth the effort.

When utilizing LORA, users have three search options. After selecting a search option and performing a search, the number of results found for each type of resource meeting the search criteria and links to those lists of resources are displayed. The user may then select the type of resource that he or she is interested in viewing, and the results within that category are then displayed in alphabetical order by the resource title or under subheadings assigned by subject librarians. The user may then click on the resource title to gain access to the resource. The user may also view descriptions, coverage dates, or other descriptive information, such as resource provider, physical location within the library, or usage information depending on the type of resource being viewed.

Next to each database and e-journal title, an icon may be selected for information about reporting technical problems, and there is also a link to the "e-mail a librarian" service provided by the library, should the user need assistance in searching the resource. Licensing information is also available on this page if there are special restrictions about the resource, such as a limited number of simultaneous users, restrictions on who can access the resource, etc. If the database or e-journal supports the Z39.50 protocol, users may download an Endnote connection file from this page. Links to usage guides and announcements—such as training dates—are also presented if available.

LORA STAFF INTERFACE

With the implementation of LORA, the library sought to not only provide more efficient management of databases and e-journals but also to standardize the way librarians went about adding resources to their subject areas. In addition to providing an easy-to-use public interface, LORA also has several interfaces on the staff intranet that allow librarians to update the publicly displayed information, track licensing agreements, locate vendor and provider contact information, find statistical data about the usage of the electronic resources, and maintain the plethora of administrative passwords and user names necessary for updating subscription information.

Once logged onto the intranet, the subject librarians may add databases, e-journals, or e-books to their subject areas from a list of those to which the library subscribes, or they may add other related resources that fit into one of the established categories. For each resource they add, librarians may include a description of the resource, coverage dates, and other relevant information. They may also use the intranet interface to create usage guides for databases and e-journals; only a select group of librarians, however, is designated to handle the general information about these resources, such as the description and coverage dates, since this information is used across all subject areas. This group of librarians is also able to add newly acquired databases to LORA. E-journals are added automatically with data obtained from an external vendor.

Licensing and administrative information is also available through the staff interface. The signed site licenses for the databases and e-journals are scanned in and saved as pdf files so that they are accessible to all librarians and a single point of access exists for all site licenses. Attempting to keep track of the paper licenses had become an overwhelming task, as many librarians throughout the system negotiate various types of licenses and file their copies in different locations. In the past, when a librarian needed to view the signed license, it had become a lengthy endeavor to locate the license's filed location. In addition to site license information, the intranet also provides administrative user names and passwords associated with each of the resources needed for viewing the usage statistics and maintaining the subscription. Contact information for vendors, providers, and publishers is also accessible through this interface.

IMPLEMENTATION

LORA consists of several different subsystems. Most are custom built, but some commercial software has also been integrated into it. LORA's subsystems include a Web server (IIS 5), a database, an e-journal management component, public and private interfaces, a remote-access management system, and a system for ensuring the permanence of LORA URLs. The noncommercial subsystems were developed in-house by the library's technical staff.

Data Storage

All electronic resource data is stored in a database, and information is added, deleted, and manipulated within this database. Although a full discussion of the advantages of using a database is beyond the scope of this paper, utilizing such a database yields numerous benefits including the following:

- It allows content to be separated from the methods used to display the content. This permits much more flexible interface possibilities and a dynamic Web presentation rather than a static list or a set of lists.
- It allows librarians to use Web-based editing pages to update data without going through the technical staff. This puts less of a burden on technical personnel, and it allows the librarians to have direct control over their content at their own convenience, rather than being forced to wait until others have time to update the data.
- The data integrity improves, since updates occur in only one location, and the changes are immediately replicated across all data sets.
- Flexibility in generating reports for the staff is greatly enhanced.

The data are currently stored in a Microsoft Access database. MS Access was chosen as a temporary solution, and the system is scheduled to migrate to Oracle in the near future. Although Access was useful for prototyping and was acceptable for initial deployment, it proved not to be a robust-enough relational database to be able to be an acceptable long-term solution. With approximately twenty librarians who can change data through the intranet interface, and thousands of end users accessing the data, concurrency and locking issues have been known to arise while using Access. To solve this problem temporarily, several Access databases are used by the library and synchronized hourly.

Maintaining the E-Journal List

As the library continued to increase the number of electronic resources to which it subscribed, it became increasingly difficult to maintain accurate information about e-journals. Necessary information included which e-journals could be found in which databases, or through which publisher, and the coverage dates for each of the titles, as well as the URL through which the resource could be accessed. It was also impractical to expect subject librarians to assign subjects to over 20,000 e-journals, or to expect the technical staff to maintain URLs to these titles within various aggregators. To resolve this situation, the University of Oklahoma Libraries outsourced the management of most of the e-journal data to an external vendor. University of Oklahoma librarians utilized the vendor-provided Web interface to generate a list of subscribed databases and a list of those e-journals accessed directly from the publisher. The vendor then used this list to generate a list of journal titles, URLs, journal vendors, aggregators, providers, ISSNs, coverage dates, and subject classifications for the journals. That data was then loaded into LORA using custom scripts that automated the process. Since the initial loading process, the vendor has provided weekly updates that included recently added or dropped titles within an aggregator, as well as e-journals that have changed coverage dates, subject assignments, or URLs. Custom scripts automatically retrieve the data files from the vendor that detail these changes and process any necessary modifications to the LORA database on a weekly basis. These changes are made while still preserving any additional adjustments that librarians might have made to the e-journals, such as alterations of the default subject classifications.

If the subject librarians do not want an e-journal listed that has been automatically assigned to their area by the vendor, they may manually remove it. Likewise, they may add e-journals not automatically assigned to their subject area. However, the bulk of the updating and classification work is automated. With over 20,000 e-journal records, the process of ensuring accurate information in the ever changing world of e-journals would be a difficult feat to undertake using only library staff, but outsourcing this task allows the most current information to be displayed with minimum demands on library staff time.

Licensing information is also stored for each e-journal. Although the number of databases is relatively small and, therefore, easy to maintain, the number of e-journals is daunting and can raise problems in data maintenance. LORA eliminates as much of the maintenance work as is currently possible. Most of the e-journals are accessible via a subscription through an aggregator or other provider. These aggregators or providers already have associated license information contained in LORA. LORA allows e-journals to inherit the license information from the e-journal's associated aggregator or provider unless otherwise instructed. Occasionally, a single e-journal will have unique licensing information or restrictions that other e-journals provided by the same aggregator do not have enforced. In those situations, a librarian may override the default licensing information and enter new information to ensure accuracy. Instead of having to enter information for 20,000 to 30,000 e-journals, this method allows all but a few hundred to automatically be assigned accurate licensing information.

Remote Access Capability

In order to allow off-campus users to access databases and e-journals another piece of commercial software was integrated into LORA—EZProxy (<http://www.usefulutilities.com/>). EZProxy is a pass-through proxy server. It acts as an intermediary, passing client requests on to remote resources and then relaying the resources' response back to the client who originated the request. In this way, all traffic originating from off-campus users who are accessing resources through LORA comes from the EZProxy server, which resides within the campus IP range for which the resource subscription is active. Unlike traditional proxy systems, EZProxy does not require users to modify their browser settings or operating system files.

Code sections within LORA will automatically detect off-campus users; instead of passing them directly to the database, it will pass them through the proxy server. The only difference off-campus users notice is that they are prompted for a user name and password when accessing databases and e-journals from remote locations. Three obstacles were overcome when initially deploying EZProxy, but none of them were technologically problematic; careful planning was required, however, to ensure the elimination of all these barriers before launching LORA.

The first obstacle to overcome was configuring a URL list for EZProxy to use. Instead of allowing any URL to be proxied, a text-based configuration file is required that explicitly specifies each URL that should be proxied. In order to ensure off-campus accessibility, each resource available through an IP-based subscription must have its URL entered into this file; each resource must also have some metadata associated with its URL to identify the destination servers where the remote resources are located. Not only is manual entry of this information a tedious task, but any mistakes in data entry would deny access to resources. In addition, each time databases or e-journals are added, this file must be manually updated. To solve this problem, custom scripts were written to automatically update the configuration file whenever databases or e-journals are added, removed, or altered within the database. This allows the configuration file to remain accurate and to still conform to the tenet that the system should have only a single location that requires updates.

Authenticating users was the second problem. At the time of implementation, EZProxy had no built-in method of authenticating users that was suitable for large environments such as universities. Accounts could be manually configured, but for a population with over 60,000 expected users, this solution was not feasible. To solve this problem, the campus-wide LDAP authentication system that was already in place was utilized. The preexisting LDAP system required no extra workload for library staff, and since patrons already used this system, no additional user name and password combinations were required to generate or disseminate to the users. A tie-in to the LDAP system was implemented via a custom LDAP filter, and this filter authenticates users before they are granted access to EZProxy functionality.

The third obstacle to overcome was a problem specific to the ISP used by the University of Oklahoma. The ISP uses a caching server to speed Internet access. Since the caching server acts in many ways like a proxy server, the use of this hardware meant that any request coming from the University had a nonuniversity IP address and was thus rejected by database and e-journal vendors who restrict access by IP address. When the ISP launched its caching server, it effectively denied the use of any remote resource to qualified university patrons.

The library overcame this problem through negotiations with the ISP. An exclusion list was established at the ISP, and any resource subscribed to must be communicated to the ISP for addition to the caching server exclusion list. Since this is functionally similar to the text-based configuration file generated for EZProxy, it was a simple task to automate the delivery of this information to the ISP.

Permanent URLs

One of the most important features is the permanence of the URLs that allow off-campus users to access databases, e-journals, and e-books. LORA builds links to resources by sending a numeric resource identifier to a separate ASP page, where all of the work of detecting off-campus users and passing off those users to an authentication page is handled. This allows the construction of links that will move a user directly to a resource, from inside or outside LORA, and that also still retains all of the benefits LORA provides for off-campus users. In the event that LORA is ever moved to a different server, a new root URL to our Web server was aliased through the university's domain controller for use exclusively with LORA.

LORA URLs are created in the form: <http://connect.ou.edu/access.asp?id=resourceid>, where "resourceid" represents the unique resource numeric identifier. Once established, this URL will always lead a user (on or off campus) directly to the corresponding resource, as long as the library has access to the resource. A university patron selecting a URL will either be taken directly to the resource if on campus, or be prompted for authentication if accessing the link from off campus. If their authentication is accepted, they will then be taken directly to the resource. In this way, the LORA functionality of remote user access can be used even if a patron is not explicitly using LORA to access that resource.

Before LORA, links within the catalog went directly to the database or to the e-journal, allowing the link to work only for on-campus users. Once this method of permanent URLs was established, however, it became possible to replace URLs in the 856 fields of the MARC records with these new links within the catalog. This process should soon be complete, and links within the catalog will be functional for both on-campus and off-campus users. The library will also encourage the use of these links to faculty members and other entities on campus that link directly to specific databases, e-journals, or e-books from their own sites.

LOOKING AHEAD: PLANNED ADDITIONS

Although LORA is a vast improvement over methods used previously by the library to allow users to access electronic resources, LORA will continue to evolve, and plans for improvements have already been made and are on track for implementation.

Advanced Search Methods

With resources being regularly added to LORA, more advanced search methods will soon be necessary to allow more complex queries for precisely locating specific resources. An advanced search screen will soon be available that allows more complex search methods.

- *Search by e-journal provider, aggregator, or vendor:* Users will be able to search for all e-journals provided by a single aggregator, provider, or vendor. This benefits users if they are particularly comfortable with a particular interface.
- *Search by coverage dates:* Users will be able to search for all databases and e-journals that provide full-text coverage for a particular date or date range.
- *Keyword search within subject areas:* Existing search methods will be combined to allow a user to restrict a keyword search to a specific subject area or areas.
- *Boolean searches of resource titles and descriptions:* Currently only resource titles are searchable; users will have the option to also search resource descriptions to find a more comprehensive list of resources.

Catalog Integration

To better integrate resources found in the catalog, LORA search results will soon include a link to the results of a comparable search in the catalog. This will serve to remind users that not all information can be found online and that there are print resources relevant to their topic which may also be available.

Subject Guides

With the volume of material available for each broad subject area within LORA, it can be difficult at times for users to know which resources would be most useful for their particular needs. LORA will soon allow librarians to create subject guides for subsets of their subject areas, either for individual classes or subject specializations. Creating subject guides through LORA will no longer be as much of a time-intensive task as it once was. Librarians will be able to see the resources currently in their areas and select as many, or as few, resources as they wish to be included in a subject guide. Since the subject guides will be merely a small subset of information already contained in LORA, librarians will no longer have to worry about keeping them up to date. When information changes within LORA, those changes will be automatically reflected anywhere the data appears, including within the subject guides.

Usage Guides

Librarians often post usage guides with instructions for using a particular resource. These instructions may include tips for searching the resource, helpful hints for displaying results, or clues on how to find information relevant to the user's topic. In the past, librarians have posted these guides several layers deep on the reference department Web pages where they were often overlooked. LORA provides the capability for making these usage guides accessible at the point of use, and associates the guides with a resource at a granular level by subject area. For instance, a business librarian and an engineering librarian could each write a separate usage guide for the same database. If patrons search within the business subject area, they will see the subject guide written by the business librarian; however, if they look at the engineering subject area, they see the usage guide developed by the engineering librarian. In this way, usage guides may be written and customized for each particular subject's unique needs, and only the information that is the most pertinent to the user's needs is displayed. Subject librarians create usage guides on the intranet interface to LORA. The mechanisms to create usage guides and to provide public access to these guides already exist, but since it is such a new feature, librarians are still in the early stages of writing guides for resources within their areas.

Improved E-Journal Subject Access

Currently the vendor that supplies the list of e-journals with associated subjects uses only sixteen different subjects. These subject areas are used to derive e-journal subject placement within LORA, but with over fifty subject areas listed in LORA, the match between the library's subjects and those provided by the vendor is tenuous and overly broad. However, the vendor will soon be assigning subjects to e-journals based on the subjects provided in *Ulrich's Periodicals Directory*. With more specific subjects associated with each e-journal, subject access to e-journals will become more accurate and comprehensive.

Migration to Oracle

At the time of this writing, LORA still uses a Microsoft Access back end to store all information. With over fifty tables to date and references to information in other library databases, Access is no longer capable of handling LORA's demands. Hardware has already been purchased and is in the process of being configured that will allow the transfer to Oracle. Searching speeds are expected to dramatically increase, and concurrency and locking issues with which the current iteration of LORA occasionally faces, are expected to be eliminated.

Migration of EZProxy

Currently, EZProxy runs on the same Web server that hosts the library Web site. A port number must be assigned for EZProxy to use; that port is then used to proxy Web traffic from off-campus users.

Since the Web site runs on the default WWW port (port 80), EZProxy is configured to use a different port. This often causes problems for users behind firewalls—most commonly affecting users who are in the military and who are attempting to access resources from a military base with strict firewall rules in place. These rules prevent traffic to most nonstandard ports, and therefore inadvertently disallow the use of EZProxy. Within the next few months, EZProxy will be moved to its own server where it can use port 80. This will result in those using protected networks to experience no difficulties with their firewall configurations.

CONCLUSION

With the implementation of LORA, the University of Oklahoma Libraries hoped to find a simple, straightforward way to provide users with access to electronic resource subscriptions, to create a quick and easy method of updating the information without putting undue strain on any one department within the library, and to create a comprehensive staff intranet interface that assists in managing the data associated with electronic subscriptions. In addition to fulfilling these objectives, the library needed a way to ensure that those users attempting to access the resources from off campus could do so, regardless of the point of entry.

LORA provides users with a single point of access to all of the libraries' electronic holdings so they are no longer given the burden of consulting the online catalog, as well as an alphabetical listing of resource titles to see if the library has electronic access to the title they need; LORA allows both on-campus and off-campus access to these resources with little noticeable difference to the end user. Although LORA is continually a work in progress, the underlying infrastructure already in place allows the library to provide better access to its resources and gives librarians the control they desire for adding information to their respective subject areas.

Chapter 13

Developing a Database for E-Journals That Improves Both Access and Management

Kevin Brewer
Betty Rozum
Flora Shrode

INTRODUCTION AND HISTORY

Beginning in the autumn of 1997, the Utah State University (USU) Libraries began to set up Web pages with links to USU's electronic journal (e-journal) collection. USU's first e-journal link was to titles published by the Institute of Physics (IOP) that were offered free with a paid print subscription. The initial link to IOP seemed like a minor departure from the daily duties of the Web master of the Utah State University Library Web site. However, pursuing, creating, and maintaining the library's e-journal collection proved to be too much of a challenge for a single individual as the number of e-journals grew. In December 1997, USU provided access to only one subscription-based e-journals collection, Project MUSE, consisting of approximately forty e-journals, and forty-eight e-journals that were accessible at no additional cost with a paid print subscription. By 2002 the number of titles at USU had increased to over 2,100 individual e-journals.

In hindsight, it is clear that e-journals were one of many technological Pandora's boxes academic libraries faced in the late 1990s. This chapter will examine the growth of e-journals and look at one library's attempt to implement, organize, and maintain access to the emerging and dynamic world of shifting URLs, access methods, license agreements, free online access, and growing numbers of print plus online subscriptions.

The World Wide Web was a nascent technology in 1997, as just two years earlier the now extinct Gopher reigned as the Internet tool of choice, and publishers still promoted the CD-ROM as *the* preferred electronic format. The CD-ROM cover for the July/August 1998 issue of the journal *Human Reproduction* provides a typical example with this statement in a promotional advertisement declaring that it was: "A multimedia and printed journal presenting reviews, training videos and databases in reproductive science and medicine." Similarly, USU subscribed to a handful of online indexes and abstracts that were accessible via CD-ROM or, in the case of LexisNexis, by telnet, where the user could execute searches only by using *function commands* (F8 = New Search) or *dot commands* (.ns = new search). Meanwhile, full-text databases were becoming widely available via the Internet. USU subscribed to the InfoTrac SearchBank, which indexed over 3,000 journals, with many of the citations containing abstracts. Of these, approximately 1,000 could be viewed or downloaded, complete with images, in full-test format. Oh, weren't those the days!

By 1998, USU's e-journals collection had grown to over 300 journals, and the avalanche was just beginning. At the end of 2001, USU maintained an alphabetical list of over 2,100 individual titles, and that list did not include journals made available through aggregators such as EBSCOhost, LexisNexis, and UMI ProQuest. As the number of electronic titles available grew, so did patrons' expectations for easy access to these titles, which was not always feasible. Clearly, e-journals were becoming a management problem that was a source of frustration for reference, cataloging, and serials librarians, as well as for library patrons.

All e-journals, including those that the library had purchased through a paid subscription to the electronic version, those that were available as a by-product of a paid print subscription, and those that were freely available to all, were subject to the following challenges:

- Maintaining an alphabetical Web-based list of e-journals, a labor-intensive task
- Designing a Web graphical user interface (GUI) that enabled users to access the e-journal collection efficiently

- Deciding when a link to free online e-journals should be created
- Deciding what titles to catalog (For instance, should FWP e-journals be cataloged? What about also cataloging free e-journals?)
- Deciding how to catalog an e-journal (Should USU follow standards that called for one record per format, or should electronic holdings simply be added to existing print records?)
- Determining the best methods for handling the elements of the catalog record, such as the ISSN (Should journals be cataloged maintaining separate ISSNs for each version? Many of our indexing resources referred only to the print ISSN.)
- Deciding whether to catalog journals that we accessed through aggregators
- Debating whether to maintain a separate list of e-journals on a Web page outside of the online catalog
- Contending with the lack of persistent URLs
- Grappling with licensing issues, which could result in long delays between selecting a title and making it available to library users
- Sorting through all-or-nothing, lock-in subscriptions, package deals, and consortia pricing

An e-journals discussion group at the American Library Association Mid-Winter 2002 conference demonstrated that little consensus exists on how individual libraries should handle e-journals in order to make optimal use of personnel and fiscal expenditures while also maximizing patron access to these resources. Every aspect of e-journal management continues to be up for grabs, although some trends seem to be emerging, such as the use of ColdFusion or *PHP* to create a Web front end to an e-journals database. Academic libraries appear to be moving toward enlisting assistance from services such as Serials Solutions or TDNet to outsource a portion of the management of their e-journal subscriptions and Web pages.

At USU, the typical progression for establishing access to an e-journal was for the serials department to forward any notifications of FWP subscriptions to the library's Webmaster. These e-journal announcements typically arrived with an invoice or with a journal issue, or they sometimes resulted from a library patron's request to create a link to a journal that was available online. This ad hoc system of building an e-journals collection for an academic library suited the immediate needs of the campus community so long as the library upheld specific principles. One guideline was that the USU Libraries aimed to maintain links to only scholarly resources and to e-journals for which access authorization could be accomplished through campus-wide IP addresses.

This approach worked adequately in the short term. However, while the library scrambled to provide access, publishers were working to develop their networks. This was a difficult time, and both URLs and access methods seemed to change frequently. A typical example of fluctuating access procedures was the case of Cambridge University Press (CUP), which offered FWP e-journals but which also impeded delivery by changing their access avenues at least three times in as many years. At one point, CUP required both IP validation and input of a user name and password. Although the method of defining IP address ranges has become nearly a standard means to govern access to e-journals, ostensibly by majority rule, many publishers still insist on awkward schemes such as single-user licenses, or a model like one that Wiley InterScience recently announced, wherein only a single user may view a single volume of a journal. Wiley adopted the approach of allowing campus-wide access by verifying IP addresses, while restricting access to only one user per specific volume, based on the concept that the volume currently being viewed would be considered to be "checked-out" and thus unavailable to others until it was no longer being viewed (checked back in again). In other words, electronic access to a Wiley journal would be available to the entire campus, but access to each volume would be limited to a single simultaneous user. Some publishers seem intent on following similar print management protocols in an electronic world that does not logically need to be bound by the same constraints. Adding to these issues were expectations expressed by students and faculty who did not and in many cases still do not understand that although society may have entered the Information Age, all information is not simply "free and on the Internet." An ongoing challenge is to educate our patrons about the real cost of quality electronic information.

CATALOGING WOES

As e-journals became a commonplace resource in high demand, USU Libraries formed an Electronic Journals Task Force, which included the Web master and representation from the reference, serials, and cataloging departments, in order to address issues arising from our efforts to provide and improve access to paid e-journals. The Electronic Journals Task Force confronted the difficult tasks of deciding when e-journals should be cataloged and how to catalog them.

The task force first decided to catalog only those e-journals for which USU Libraries specifically paid to have online access. This decision was based on our unwillingness to incur cataloging costs for e-journals whose stability was in question. We knew that access to titles that the USU Libraries purchased would not be discontinued at the publisher's discretion, which could happen where we enjoyed free online access with paid print subscription titles. We also believed these publishers were far less likely to change URLs or any other elements that would require modifications to catalog records. Without hiring additional cataloging staff, it would be unrealistic for us to attempt to catalog, track, and update any other e-journals.

The task force faced a necessary second decision regarding how these electronic resources would be represented in the online catalog. Current cataloging standards dictated that a separate record should be created for each format of a title, but the task force had some serious reservations with this approach. The group examined the benefits and disadvantages of creating a single record or separate records. After much discussion and feedback from the serials, cataloging, and reference departments, the group decided to use the single-record technique, with one record representing both the print and electronic versions of a title. Although separate records would have facilitated the ability to load bibliographic records automatically into our online catalog, the library took the position that patrons would be better served by bringing together all information about each journal in a single record.

With these decisions made, it was clear that only a portion of the available e-journals would ever be cataloged. An obvious conclusion was that the USU Libraries' immediate need was to pursue the development of an e-journals database.

THE E-JOURNALS DATABASE

As USU's list of e-journals grew, the potential advantages of a separate database for e-journal management became more evident. Although it would have been preferable to have the online catalog serve as the sole source of data representing all materials the library provides rather than maintaining separate databases for different types of information, other factors beyond cataloging questions convinced us to follow a different course. It was decided that it would be imperative to build a relational database to manage e-journals so that we could create Web pages to present titles to the public. One driving force was a desire to improve accessibility to journals available in aggregator collections, such as the EBSCOhost suite of databases. An earlier attempt to track aggregators' collections of full-text journals using Excel proved frustrating, as the spreadsheet listing of titles was out of date as soon as it was compiled. The demand for such information pointed to the need to develop a tool that would allow librarians and patrons to verify whether an e-journal was available via an aggregator.

The benefits of an e-journals database are many, since it can provide:

- more accurate and efficient means to track and update links than is possible by maintaining a list manually;
- monitoring and maintenance of license agreements;
- links to aggregators' e-journals;
- multiple access points to e-journals (by title, publisher, subject, and keyword searching);
- a "hook to holdings" for e-journals in cases where the library maintains a print copy;
- the ability to view the extent of coverage by date and content (e.g., cover to cover versus selected indexing) for each title;
- links to multiple sources and holdings of a title, for instance when the electronic edition of *Conservation Biology* is available both in JSTOR and via Blackwell Synergy. An e-journals database can readily supply links to each source and reflect distinctive holdings information.

Working in conjunction with our systems department, librarians who were members of the E-journals Task Force held a series of meetings to determine how we could design a database that met our requirements for e-journal management. These were probably the most difficult task force meetings because of the difficulties in communicating between different departments. We struggled to describe and to explain to the programmer why we needed the database to have certain capabilities, while at the same time the programmer worked to describe and explain to the librarians why some of our requests were impractical or impossible from his perspective. Fortunately, the systems programmer had experience setting up a ColdFusion server, so creating the Web interface was not a significant hurdle, leaving us with only the task of negotiating the divide between library expectations and programming realities.

Basically, there are three key elements to consider in developing the ColdFusion (CF) e-journal database: database construction, the user interface, and data input. Each database record must consist of the following fields:

- Title information
  1. Full title
  2. Short title (for example, *JAMA*)
- ISSN, for both print and electronic editions whenever available
- Publisher
- Provider (e.g., MUSE, JSTOR, HighWire Press, CatchWord)
- URL link: The actual URL to the full text or provider (e.g., LexisNexis)
- URL name: What the patron will see as the hypertext link (e.g., *Newsweek*)
- Holdings information:
  1. Beginning volume/end volume
  2. Beginning issue/end issue
  3. Beginning year/end year
- Additional fields: Subject heading—limit to maximum of three subject headings
- Help or search tips: needed for aggregators such as LexisNexis, ProQuest, Education Full Text, and UMI where it is impossible to link directly to a journal.
- Notes field:
  1. Indicate if articles can be used for interlibrary loan. For example, the IEL database license dictates that IEL content cannot be used for interlibrary loan unless the lender first prints a hard copy and uses that copy for faxing.
  2. Indicate if remote users can access the title by proxy, or if all off-campus use is prohibited.

3. Indicate if there is a maximum number of simultaneous users.
4. Indicate other information, such as limitations stipulated by the license and user name/password restrictions.
5. Print availability: Indicate the title's format availability at USU (e.g., in print, microform, or both). If available, provide a link that runs a search in the online catalog using the ISSN.

After finalizing the database construction, designing the graphical user interface was the next challenge. Fortunately, both Utah State University and the USU Libraries maintain Web development guidelines that the ColdFusion programmer could follow for this project. This simplified the GUI design process so that the focus was on creating a Web interface that had a similar navigational scheme to the previous e-journal Web pages, while maintaining a unique Web presence. This continuity should help users immediately realize that they are navigating a new and, it is hoped, improved set of e-journal Web pages. Users can now access alphabetical lists of titles and publishers, and they have the ability to search by title and keyword for over 14,000 e-journals within the confines of a user-friendly GUI.

Initially we feared that the task of data entry would become too enormous. Fortunately, from the time that USU librarians started developing the ColdFusion e-journals system to the point when staff were ready to enter the data, Serials Solutions (along with TDNet and other companies) began offering their services to compile e-journal data sets for a reasonable fee. With competitive pricing, quarterly updates, and the representation of most aggregators' e-journal data sets in spreadsheet format, this was a timely opportunity that we could not ignore. Having resolved the issue of data entry, the library was able, at last, to offer its community of users a database that would make it easy for them to link to the full text of all available journals, while simplifying the process of maintaining the behind-the-scenes database. In essence, the library progressed from a visible e-journals collection of 2,100 titles to one that offered over 10,000 titles.

Although developing a database for e-journal management solved many problems and improved access to the resources, some challenges remained. One of the biggest continuing difficulties is the task of keeping up with purchases by consortia such as the Utah Academic Library Consortium (UALC), to which USU belongs. Between 1997 and 2000, there was a flurry of purchases made by UALC that presented many challenges to USU Libraries. Since UALC pays for the consortium's purchases through the University of Utah, publishers often overlook the fact that several campuses comprise the customer group, and they do not always understand the need to activate the IP addresses of all member institutions, a problem that still existed as of February 2002. Other problems specific to the purchases that are paid for by the consortium include obtaining copies of license agreements so we understand any limitations on use, tracking and notification of renewal dates, determining the exact amount of money USU must contribute, and obtaining accurate lists of journals included in each deal. These problems are largely logistical, result from working with the relatively new entity of library consortia, and are not unique to our situation. We will continue to focus institutional energies on establishing clear procedures for these purchases, remaining constantly alert to opportunities that benefit our institutional library, and continuing to be wary of restrictive licensing agreements, such as those that limit or prohibit member libraries from canceling print counterparts to the electronic editions of journals.

CONCLUSION

Rather than a completed product, the e-journals management database provides USU librarians with a way to organize the information and tasks associated with the continuing process of making online editions of periodicals available to USU Libraries users. The database improves access to periodicals by providing the university community with a complete and convenient means to determine which titles are available through the World Wide Web. Although the information in the database has always existed, it was formerly dispersed among several locations, and the database now consolidates it into one source. Library users and staff can consult the e-journals database to determine with certainty whether or not USU Libraries has electronic access to a specific article and to find out their options to obtain it. Although the USU Libraries have provided a Web page listing of e-journals since 1997, the collection has grown so large that this approach is no longer realistic, particularly since it is maintained manually using HTML coding. Creating and maintaining an accurate list of the roughly 14,000 URLs associated with various editions of individual periodicals that are accessible via numerous avenues would be impossible. The e-journals database is a good solution since it not only consolidates information but also solves problems associated with maintaining accurate data about sources for full-text periodicals, titles included in aggregators, date and content coverage, current URLs, and the increasingly important licensing agreements.

In addition to presenting access options for online periodicals, the e-journals database has the capability to search the USU Libraries' online catalog and to display details about journal holdings in print or on microform. This is especially useful to our patrons when the online coverage of a journal does not go far enough back in time to include a desired article. A button appears on the database search screen that is labeled, "Is the print available?" giving searchers the option to use this feature to check the online catalog at the same time that they view the database search results. In light of the fact that many unresolved problems limit our ability to create and/or import records for all electronic editions of periodicals into the online catalog, the e-journals database serves to bridge the gaps that occur among multiple sources of information so as to assist the user in locating desired articles.

Librarians and staff in all areas find that the e-journals database is a useful tool. Its value will increase as additional improvements and enhancements are developed that will enable the staff to view elements such as payment records and license agreements. Reference librarians can show users the database in the course of transactions at reference desks, as well as during instruction sessions. When they help patrons to locate specific articles, librarians can consult the database to find those e-journals that require a user name and password.

Interlibrary loan (ILL) staff benefit from the e-journals database because they can use it to determine if articles are available from an electronic source that may not be reflected in the online catalog. In some cases they will be able to direct members of the USU community to electronic sources as an alternative to completing interlibrary borrowing requests. In other situations, ILL staff can use the database to view a license agreement in order to determine if they may use an electronic edition of a journal to supply an article to a requester outside USU. People who work in the USU Libraries' serials, acquisitions, or collection development departments will find that the database makes it easy to get accurate answers to questions that arise about electronic periodicals.

The e-journals management database facilitates tracking usage by title, aggregator, or publisher. Data about the use of electronic resources are important in the process of assessing the USU Libraries' expenditures and in making purchase and cancellation decisions. Usage reports supplied by publishers and aggregators are compiled in disparate formats and arrive on inconsistent schedules, making it difficult to organize them for application to collection management. The e-journals management database records the number of hits each periodical title receives and can generate reports, thus supporting analysis by different criteria. For example, librarians could sort usage reports by aggregator in order to compare the use that each receives and also to look for patterns and significant differences. Any differences or similarities between aggregator usage could then help us make collection development decisions, particularly in times of decreasing serials budgets. However, it must be noted that statistics gathered in this manner are suspect at best, are ripe for misinterpretation, and must be used with full knowledge of their shortcomings.

Asking users for their opinions of services and Web-based resources can provide crucial information to point out problems and to guide improvement in collections and services. USU Libraries will respond to user feedback as we continually make improvements in the e-journals management database. A link appears at the bottom of the database's search page that appeals to users to send comments via e-mail to the USU Libraries' Web master. Shortly after the database is launched for public use, the staff and librarians who are collaborating to build the system will conduct a formal user survey to seek input from students, faculty, and library staff, even though some elements of the system may not yet be fully functional. Users' opinions may even result in adjustments to some of these elements before programming is complete.

Although the process of developing a database to manage e-journals was an often tedious and time-consuming process, we believe it has been extremely beneficial. It does not provide comprehensive information about all journals available in USU Libraries; for this, our users must consult both the database and the online catalog. However, this database certainly improves the ease of access to electronic resources for our patrons and staff. As with most projects, this one will evolve and perhaps in time will be replaced by a newer generation of online catalogs that can accommodate the needs we addressed for the management of our electronic resources.

FURTHER READING

Calhoun, Karen and Bill Kara. "Aggregation or Aggravation? Optimizing Access to Full-Text Journals." *ALCTS Online Newsletter* 11(1) (Spring 2000). <http://www.ala.org/alcts/alcts_news/v11n1/gateway_pap15.html> Accessed March 1, 2002.

Curtis, Donnelyn, Virginia M. Scheschy, and Adolfo R. Tarango. *Developing and Managing Electronic Journal Collections.* How-to-Do-It Manuals for Librarians 102. New York: Neal-Schuman Publishers, Inc., 2000.

Gregory, V. L. *Selecting and Managing Electronic Resources: A How-to-Do-It Manual for Librarians.* How-to-Do-It Manuals for Librarians 101. New York: Neal-Schuman Publishers, Inc., 2000.

Jordan, Mark and David Kisly. How does your library handle electronic serials? A general survey. *Serials: The Journal of the United Kingdom Serials Group* 15(1)(2002):41-46.

Kovacs, Diane. *Building Electronic Library Collections: The Essential Guide to Selection Criteria and Core Subject Collections.* New York: Neal-Schuman Publishers, Inc., 2000.

Program for Cooperative Cataloging Standing Committee on Automation (SCA), Task Group on Journals in Aggregator Databases "Final Report," October 2001. <http://lcweb.loc.gov/catdir/pcc/aggtg2final. html>. Accessed March 1, 2002.

Still, Julie M. (Ed.). *Creating Web-Accessible Databases: Case Studies for Librarians, Museums, and Other Nonprofits.* Medford, NJ: Information Today, 2001.

Index

Page numbers followed by the letter "b" indicate boxed material; those followed by the letter "f" indicate figures; and those followed by the letter "t" indicate tables.

Web site *(continued)*
  ALPSP, 9
  BioMed Central, 199
  e-journal editing software, 199-200
  EPrints, 201-202, 202f, 204-206
  EZProxy, 245
  Geometry & Topology, 199
  HighWire Press, 199
  ICOLC, 3
  IFLA, 7
  JISC, 7
  JMLR,
  John Cox licenses, 7
  Journal of Insect Science, 199
  LANL preprint service, 201
  Living Reviews in Relativity, 199
  LORA, 240
  Loughborough University (UK), 6
  NESLI, 7, 17
  New Journal of Physics, 199
  OAI service providers, 210-211
  PDR, 7
  Psycoloquy, 199
  SPARC, 19
Western Association of Schools and
      Colleges (WASC), e-serial
      standards, 224-225, 232

White Paper On Electronic Journal
      Usage Statistics, CLIR,
      115-116
Wiley
  DDP, 13
  electronic titles, 11
  NESLI model license, 10t
  NESLI pricing initiative, 14t
  UST, 256
Williams, Delmus, 222
Wolff, Ralph, 222, 234
Work flow, Deakin electronic reserve,
      159, 164f, 164-165
Working Group on Online Vendor
      Usage Statistics, PALS, 117
World Wide Web
  e-books, 175-176
  library consortia, 96
Worley, Joan, 222
Writer, e-books article, 186

XML (extensible markup language),
      Deakin digitalization project,
      162

SPECIAL 25%-OFF DISCOUNT!
Order a copy of this book with this form or online at:
http://www.haworthpress.com/store/product.asp?sku=4879

E-SERIALS COLLECTION MANAGEMENT

Transitions, Trends, and Technicalities

_____in hardbound at $44.96 (regularly $59.95) (ISBN: 0-7890-1753-9)

_____in softbound at $29.96 (regularly $39.95) (ISBN: 0-7890-1754-7)

Or order online and use special offer code HEC25 in the shopping cart.

COST OF BOOKS_____

OUTSIDE US/CANADA/
MEXICO: ADD 20%_____

POSTAGE & HANDLING_____
(US: $5.00 for first book & $2.00
for each additional book)
Outside US: $6.00 for first book)
& $2.00 for each additional book)

SUBTOTAL_____

IN CANADA: ADD 7% GST_____

STATE TAX_____
(NY, OH & MN residents, please
add appropriate local sales tax)

FINAL TOTAL_____
(If paying in Canadian funds,
convert using the current
exchange rate, UNESCO
coupons welcome)

☐ **BILL ME LATER:** ($5 service charge will be added)
(Bill-me option is good on US/Canada/Mexico orders only;
not good to jobbers, wholesalers, or subscription agencies.)

☐ Check here if billing address is different from
shipping address and attach purchase order and
billing address information.

Signature_____

☐ **PAYMENT ENCLOSED: $**_____

☐ **PLEASE CHARGE TO MY CREDIT CARD.**

☐ Visa ☐ MasterCard ☐ AmEx ☐ Discover
☐ Diner's Club ☐ Eurocard ☐ JCB

Account #_____

Exp. Date_____

Signature_____

Prices in US dollars and subject to change without notice.

NAME_____

INSTITUTION_____

ADDRESS_____

CITY_____

STATE/ZIP_____

COUNTRY_____ COUNTY (NY residents only)_____

TEL_____ FAX_____

E-MAIL_____

May we use your e-mail address for confirmations and other types of information? ☐ Yes ☐ No
We appreciate receiving your e-mail address and fax number. Haworth would like to e-mail or fax special
discount offers to you, as a preferred customer. **We will never share, rent, or exchange your e-mail address
or fax number.** We regard such actions as an invasion of your privacy.

Order From Your Local Bookstore or Directly From
The Haworth Press, Inc.
10 Alice Street, Binghamton, New York 13904-1580 • USA
TELEPHONE: 1-800-HAWORTH (1-800-429-6784) / Outside US/Canada: (607) 722-5857
FAX: 1-800-895-0582 / Outside US/Canada: (607) 771-0012
E-mailto: orders@haworthpress.com
PLEASE PHOTOCOPY THIS FORM FOR YOUR PERSONAL USE.
http://www.HaworthPress.com

BOF03